Financial Analysis in Pharmacy Practice

Introduction to the Pharmaceutical Business Administration Series

Books in the Pharmacy Business Administration Series have been prepared for use in university level graduate and professional level courses, as well as for continuing education and self-study uses. The series includes books covering the major subject areas taught in Social and Administrative Pharmacy, Pharmacy Administration, and Pharmacy MBA programs.

World-class authors with well-regarded expertise in the various respective areas have been selected and the book outlines as well as the books themselves have been reviewed by a number of other experts in the field. The result of this effort is a new integrated and coordinated series of books that is up to date in methodology, research findings, terminology, and contemporary trends and practices.

This is one book in that series of about 10 subjects in total. It is intended that each of the books will be revised at least every 5 years. Although the books were intended for the North American market, they are just as relevant in other areas.

Titles in the series currently include:
Health Economics
Health Policy and Ethics
Principles of Good Clinical Practice
Research Methods for Pharmaceutical Practice and Policy
Financial Analysis in Pharmacy Practice

The series editor-in-chief is Professor Albert Wertheimer, PhD, MBA, of Temple University School of Pharmacy, Philadelphia, Pennsylvania, USA.

Financial Analysis in Pharmacy Practice

Keith N Herist PharmD CPA
Associate Professor, Clinical and Administrative Pharmacy,
University of Georgia College of Pharmacy, Athens, Georgia, USA

Brent L Rollins RPh, PhD
Assistant Professor, Pharmacy Practice, Philadelphia College of Osteopathic
Medicine – Georgia Campus, School of Pharmacy, Suwanee, Georgia, USA

Matthew Perri III RPh, PhD
Professor, Clinical and Administrative Pharmacy, University of Georgia
College of Pharmacy, Athens, Georgia, USA

London • Chicago **Pharmaceutical Press**

Published by Pharmaceutical Press

1 Lambeth High Street, London SE1 7JN, UK
1559 St. Paul Avenue, Gurnee, IL 60031, USA

© Pharmaceutical Press 2011

(**PP**) is a trade mark of Pharmaceutical Press

Pharmaceutical Press is the publishing division of the
Royal Pharmaceutical Society of Great Britain

First published 2011

Typeset by Thomson Digital, Noida, India
Printed in Great Britain by TJ International, Padstow, Cornwall

ISBN 978 0 85369 897 5

A catalogue record for this book is available from the British Library.

Contents

Preface

It has been said with regard to education that students learn when they perceive a need to learn. For the authors, the experience of many years of teaching business courses in a college of pharmacy has provided a very important insight into how students look at learning the basics of accounting and financial management. From the student's perspective, setting aside the few who are drawn to this subject for one reason or another, there is confusion over why they need to learn about business in pharmacy school.

Over the years, some students have entered the profession of pharmacy with the thought of one day owning or managing a business. These students have recognized the value of understanding the basics of accounting and financial management, and that the application of these principles has value in their practice of pharmacy and personal lives. However, for most others, it is often difficult to dedicate sufficient time and attention to business management courses when study time is monopolized by other, seemingly more important, courses where instructors are often heard uttering phrases like, "this will be on the boards."

However, when students graduate and enter the profession, it is common for us to hear that many wish they had paid more attention to their business instructors. Suddenly, they are running a business and/or answering to high level management, all the while making money of their own, and don't know how to manage it well. Thus, while these new pharmacy professionals are prepared for the day-to-day clinical aspects of their jobs, in many cases they are not prepared for the challenges of operating, or assisting, in the operation of a business. These skill sets are required to maintain a successful pharmacy practice site and to ensure future income and employment.

With this in mind, we have written a text that we believe will provide you with convincing evidence of the relevance of accounting and financial management in many areas of pharmacy practice. We will use case studies, based on real world examples, to make clear not only the relevance of accounting and financial management but also their impact on all pharmacy practice areas. Presenting the material to you in this fashion is intended to make it relevant, provide a learning experience and increase your awareness as to the importance of learning and making sense of accounting and financial management issues. This can then be applied to success at work – and in your personal life.

Keith Herist
Brent Rollins
Matthew Perri
November 11, 2010

About the authors

Dr. Keith Herist received his BS in Accounting in 1978 from Florida State University. After 15 years of diversified practice as a Certified Public Accountant, he earned both his BS in Pharmacy in 1996 and Doctor of Pharmacy in 1997 from the University of Georgia. Dr. Herist is a community pharmacist with a clinical specialty in HIV/AIDS. He is currently a clinical associate professor in the Department of Clinical and Administrative Pharmacy at the University of Georgia. Dr. Herist continues to draw upon his financial experience and currently serves as Treasurer for the American Association of Colleges of Pharmacy and chairs the Audit Committee of the Georgia Pharmacy Association.

Dr. Brent Rollins earned his BS in Pharmacy degree at Ohio Northern University in 2004 and his PhD in Pharmacy Administration from the University of Georgia in 2009. He is currently an Assistant Professor of Pharmacy Practice at the newly formed Philadelphia College of Osteopathic Medicine (PCOM) – Georgia Campus School of Pharmacy. In addition to his research endeavors, Dr. Rollins also has more than six years of community pharmacy practice experience. Dr. Rollins has presented and published on numerous subjects in pharmacy practice, including direct-to-consumer advertising, patient satisfaction, patient drug information, and pharmacy simulation software.

Dr. Matthew Perri obtained his BS in Pharmacy in 1981 from Temple University School of Pharmacy in Philadelphia, Pennsylvania and his PhD in Pharmacy from the University of South Carolina in 1985. He has practiced pharmacy since 1981 in community and long-term care settings and held an academic position at the University of Georgia College of Pharmacy since 1985. At the University of Georgia, Dr. Perri has served as a faculty member, clinical pharmacist, and administrator. He is currently a Professor in the Department of Clinical and Administrative Pharmacy, a member of the University's Graduate Faculty and Adjunct Faculty of Gerontology, University of Georgia, College of Public Health, and an invited member of the University of Georgia Teaching Academy.

1

Introduction

Learning objectives

- Identify the importance of financial analysis and management to pharmacy practice
- Describe the impact of financial analysis and management on customer service
- Discuss the importance of accounting as a background for financial analysis and management
- Describe this text's approach in the upcoming chapters

Importance of financial analysis and management for pharmacists

In today's pharmacy practice environment, through, among other factors, the Doctor of Pharmacy (PharmD) degree and the rise of residency-trained pharmacists, there is an ever-increasing focus on pharmaceutical care/medication therapy management and the clinical services we as a profession can provide. Especially since the introduction of introductory pharmacy practice experiences (IPPEs), students are gaining more hands-on experience earlier in curricula and using the confidence gained to push the profession away from a product-centered practice to a patient-centered model. However, many of these students fail to realize the financial ramifications associated with this professional role expansion.

Regardless of one's role in a pharmacy setting, understanding accounting and financial management is critical, not only to economic success but also to ensure the sustainability of our expanded professional role. Consider for example:

- A staff community pharmacist deciding whether or not to meet a competitor's price. This pharmacist has quite different financial information needs from a pharmacy owner developing an overall pricing strategy for his or her business.
- A hospital pharmacy director who is analyzing inventory and budget levels to ensure adequate inventory compared with a staff pharmacist in

this setting who continually faces inventory shorts or outages caused by overly restricted purchasing.

- A chain pharmacist who sees a "red flag" on his or her computer screen stating that third party prescription reimbursement is below cost and who needs to make a decision about whether or not to dispense a particular product, compared with a home office administrator who negotiates third party prescription contracts or purchasing from pharmaceutical manufacturers.
- A medication therapy management specialist determining the best hourly rate to charge for their services in order to maximize their personal profit as well as being beneficial to the employer/contractor.
- A stockholder who is interested in the financial success of a pharmacy business (regardless of practice setting) and looking for information on how labor costs are being controlled versus the pharmacy manager who must satisfy customer service needs with adequate staff.

These various scenarios demonstrate that while we are concentrating on increasing our clinical place at the healthcare table, we must also not forget the impact financial analysis and management has on the long-term viability of our profession.

Impact of financial analysis and management on customer service

Case-in-point 1.1   New pharmacist in charge

For years, DL had been a loyal customer to her local chain pharmacy, initially because of its convenient location but then primarily because of the personal attention she received from the pharmacists there. However, during her last couple of trips to pick up her monthly refills, she noticed that her favorite pharmacist was not present and another gentleman, barely visible in the back of the pharmacy, seemed to have replaced her. Finally, she asked the technician ringing up her prescriptions if the previous pharmacist was still working. The technician informed her that the previous pharmacist had taken another position within the company and the pharmacist in the back was the new pharmacist in charge and present most of the time. Over the next couple of months when DL picked up her maintenance refills, she noticed that the new pharmacist was usually in the back of the pharmacy; and, on the one occasion that he was in the pharmacy's front and visible, he did not even acknowledge her presence.

One weekend morning DL developed an infection, went to the local walk-in clinic and got a prescription for an antibiotic that the local physician highly preferred and often prescribed. She remembered receiving the same antibiotic the previous year when she had a similar infection. Upon arrival at the pharmacy, she again noticed the new pharmacist barely visible in the back when she dropped off her prescription. After waiting around for approximately 15 minutes, the new pharmacist called DL back to the pharmacy and informed her that he did not have the antibiotic in stock because of its high cost. He said she would have to take the prescription to another pharmacy.

DL reluctantly left the pharmacy and went down the street to the only other pharmacy close to her home. When she arrived, the pharmacist on duty, CJ, greeted DL at the drop-off counter and asked how he could help. DL presented her prescription and, while she was standing at the counter, CJ checked his shelves to see if the medication was in stock. Unfortunately, CJ explained to DL he had just dispensed his last bit of inventory for that particular antibiotic, but he knew the physician and would give him a quick call to recommend an alternative and equivalent antibiotic he did have stocked. After gaining approval to substitute the antibiotic from the physician, CJ quickly filled DL's prescription, counseled her on the new medication's use and side effects, rang her up at the register and thanked DL for her business. The moment she left the store, DL decided she was going to transfer all of her and her family's prescriptions to the new pharmacy.

The hallmark of the pharmacy profession throughout its history has been the excellent service level provided to patients and customers nationwide. Thus, why would the topic of customer service arise in the introduction of a textbook discussing financial management and analysis? When examining the entire contents of this text, every topic either directly or indirectly relates to customer service. Whether budgeting for payroll dollars needed, analyzing the price for a particular pharmaceutical care service or deciding how much inventory to order, a pharmacy manager must take into consideration how these decisions will impact the service level provided to patients and customers, just as it did in Case-in-point 1.1.

In terms of financial statements, the primary issue for pharmacy managers to consider is payroll. Not only is this expected to be tightly controlled in all pharmacy practice environments, but also how it is controlled greatly affects customer service levels. In the community environment, not only must a pharmacy manager keep track of the hours worked and dollars spent on payroll, but he or she must also be fully aware of the times throughout the workday that the payroll is needed most. Varying degrees of prescription volume, store characteristics (e.g., presence of a drive-through window) and community demographics determine when the payroll (i.e., personnel) is needed. For example, a pharmacy in an urban setting without a drive-through window, primarily serving local residents and "nine-to-five" clinics, might increase its technician payroll from 8 a.m. to 6 p.m. to handle the associated volume. Only one technician or clerk, or possibly none, might be needed for the evening hours when prescription volume sharply declines. Conversely, a pharmacy located in an affluent suburb with a largely employed customer base might be much busier during lunchtime (11 a.m. to 1 p.m.) and end of workday hours (4 p.m. to approximately 6 to 7 p.m.). Therefore, this pharmacy may use its payroll to ensure coverage during the late morning to early evening hours.

Secondarily, just as described in Case-in-point 1.1, inventory management is vital to customer service. In the case above, the new pharmacist in charge decided to stop carrying a high-cost antibiotic. However, he failed to understand the local physician market and account for it often being prescribed, and thus a higher inventory turnover for that single medication. This led to him not stocking the antibiotic for DL and her subsequently receiving a much greater level of service at another pharmacy. Day-to-day decisions such as this greatly impact customer relations and service. A perfect example of where this becomes a problem in community pharmacy is the concept of partially filling a medication. In this instance, the pharmacy does not have the full amount of medication to completely fill the prescription. The pharmacy typically dispenses the patient a 3-day supply of the medication (more or less if needed) and the patient must return once the order arrives and the full prescription is ready. One or two instances of this inventory issue and a patient (in the absence of another overriding factor causing the patient to patronise the pharmacy, such as price) may be forgiven. However, continually having to order a regular customer's medications, especially maintenance medications, leads to a decreased service level and moves that individual one step closer to finding another pharmacy to purchase their medication.

Case-in-point 1.2   Customer service with third party insurance

On multiple occasions, the pharmacist, CJ, had counseled the Johnson family on their medications. The issue of third party insurance never came up because CJ knew the family worked at the local factory and the insurance associated with that employment. On the Johnson family's most recent stop in the pharmacy, CJ counseled Mrs. Johnson on the most recent addition to her medication regimen. At the end of the conversation, Mrs. Johnson mentioned the whole prescription process would be so much easier if she didn't have to file the lengthy reimbursement paperwork through her husband's military benefits. At that moment, CJ asked about the exact type of coverage they had for prescriptions and realized he could help Mrs. Johnson. CJ explained the pharmacy had the capability of submitting a coordination of benefits claim, allowing her prescription claims to be billed to both the primary and secondary coverage. CJ informed her she should no longer have to file the reimbursement paperwork and that everything was done at the pharmacy level. Even though the pharmacy was busy at that time, CJ obtained Mrs. Johnson's military benefit information, put it in the computer system and rebilled her claims to both benefit plans. After rebilling, CJ refunded the $75 in co-payments that Mrs. Johnson had just paid, because her secondary benefits fully covered the remaining cost. Mrs. Johnson continually thanked CJ for his time and efforts. She even further explained that she sometimes didn't even submit the reimbursement paperwork because it was "such a hassle."

Instead of ignoring her complaints, CJ saw an opportunity to provide excellent customer service for his patient, and, by taking advantage of the opportunity, gained a lifelong customer.

Another area of concern, regarding inventory, is consistency. Suppose a customer has been coming to your pharmacy for over a decade and has always received the exact same brand of furosemide. That customer is used to their tablet being round and white with a specific number, scoring, and marking. However, when the buying group you are associated with changes the preferred pricing option to a different manufacturer for furosemide, your customer now receives a non-scored, off-yellow tablet. Again, this singular instance may not affect customer relations, but if this were to happen with a large percentage of the customer's medications or if the customer had a negative reaction to a different generic, customer relations and service levels would decline. In this case, the customer might demand for her previous generic manufacturers to be the ones stocked. You could certainly honor the request, but an inventory management decision must then be made, especially if the carrying costs of this customer's generic manufacturer are much greater than the buying group's preferred option. If you choose not to stock the previous generic and inform the customer what they are currently receiving is what will be stocked in the future, this customer might seek out a pharmacy stocking her preferred generic option and transfer out all of her prescriptions.

A not-so-obvious area tying into customer service is pricing. One might ask how pricing decisions affect customer service levels. As a pharmacist, you could provide the best counseling sessions and know your patients' full family and medical history, but still lose business because your competitor across the street charges half the price. In what is, in some cases, viewed as a commodity market (in that my Lipitor® at pharmacy A is no different than Lipitor® at pharmacy B), the distinguishing controllable characteristic is the level of service provided (location would be another characteristic but is more often than not uncontrollable). In a saturated and primarily insurance-based pharmacy market, price is often the same no matter where the customer goes and, in this case, location and service level are often the customers' primary deciding factors. However, when discussing the pricing of pharmaceutical care or ancillary services, the level of customer service provided must be discussed. This comes into play not so much related to the actual price but more because of the expectations associated with the defined price. By setting a higher price for your pharmaceutical care/cognitive service, the customer expectation of the service level provided is also higher. You must therefore be ready to meet the customer's expectations. If done well, you could ensure continual demand for the service while also increasing profitability. In the end, it is vital to remember how the prices set also set the customer expectation level throughout your entire pharmacy.

Case-in-point 1.3 General customer service

Even though good financial management decisions for issues related to customer service can positively affect business, nothing goes as far as genuine customer service and caring. The pharmacist, CJ, had gone to the local university to do some research for a couple of his patients. On his way back across campus to his vehicle, he passed one of his customers, Mrs. B. He casually nodded his head and greeted his customer, calling her by name. She stopped and asked CJ where he knew her from; CJ explained that he was her pharmacist and they had talked previously on a couple of occasions. Mrs. B said that she didn't recognize him without his smock and the two went on to have a quick, but very good, conversation. Less than a month later, Mrs. B came into the pharmacy distraught and asked specifically for CJ. She explained that her physician had just informed her she had type 1 diabetes, even though her age was past the usual age for this diagnosis. She was overwhelmed with the information thrown at her, especially the fact that she would have to now inject herself with insulin. The physician had written her a prescription for a blood glucose meter, test strips, lancets, insulin syringes, and insulin. CJ calmly explained to Mrs. B everything she was receiving and slowly went over with her how to test her blood sugar and administer the insulin. She was amazed at the time and effort that CJ put into explaining the important details associated with her diagnosis. Mrs. B felt much better about what lay ahead of her, and was immensely thankful to CJ for his time. CJ then told her that, if she had any questions once she got home, she should just give him a call. Once again, through knowing a customer's name and then calming a patient's concerns about her diagnosis and treatment, CJ gained a lifelong customer.

As Case-in-point 1.3 demonstrates, not only does financial management greatly affect your "bottom line," it also affects the service level provided to the customers who help maintain that profit. It is important to remember the impact of "word of mouth" marketing. In the cases presented, those patients/customers not only discuss these events among themselves but also with family, friends and maybe even colleagues. Therefore, though the initial impact of good or bad customer service may be a single customer, that person can help determine where their circle of contacts does their pharmacy business. In the end, whether it is inventory, payroll or pricing, the managerial decision's impact on customer service levels must not be forgotten, because extra customer service effort goes a long way towards gaining and maintaining profitability.

Importance of accounting to all businesses and pharmacies

Regardless of the organization or business, accounting is one common denominator among all. It provides the basis for recording and summarizing each individual transaction. The details supporting this record keeping, such as reports, financial statements, journals and ledgers, etc. are not complex, but there are many transaction types which must be summarized to get the information needed. Just as the initial pages of this text described, pharmacists must realize they will always be managing change, risk, personnel, operations, and money.

Every day, pharmacists make treatment decisions based upon all available objective and subjective data. Accounting is no different. With an understanding of accounting and financial statements in place, pharmacist managers can best decide which medications to put on formulary, whether or not to purchase the new bar coding administration system or how to manage their personnel properly, just to name a few. The beauty is the terminology and understanding of accounting and financial statements can be applied to any pharmacy practice setting.

Overview of this book

The understanding gained through reading this book should allow pharmacy managers and students to maximize operating performance and, it is hoped, financial/business success, while continuing to provide exceptional patient care and customer service.

The book begins with three chapters devoted to understanding the guiding principles of accounting and how individual business transactions are summarized in financial statements and reports. This basic understanding should allow pharmacy managers to determine the source and flow of financial information within their pharmacy and form a knowledge base of how their financial information should be categorized, recorded, and then reviewed. In Chapter 4, the importance of financial statements in analyzing a company's economic activity is discussed as well as a review of the various users and types of financial statements used to determine the success or failure of a pharmacy business over a specified time period. Pharmacy managers must be familiar with the basic principles of financial statements and how their analysis affects the current and future business direction.

Chapter 5 reviews the basics of financial analysis, including the time value of money, simple and compound interest, using comparative financial statements, trend analysis, and ratio analysis. Through comparative financial statement analysis, it describes how the pharmacy manager can apply financial information to create usable metrics to assess the internal business performance. These analyses can then be used to determine the necessary resource allocation for staffing, inventory, and investment, as well as the overall current and future business direction.

Subsequently, Chapter 6 shows how pharmacy managers can use the financial information from their businesses, along with knowledge of the marketplace and customer needs, to appropriately control the inventory of a pharmacy operation. Proper inventory control can result in optimal levels that keep inventory costs to a minimum while at the same time ensuring customer satisfaction.

In Chapters 7 and 8, the concepts of budgeting and pricing goods and services are explored, including the idea that budgets, as a planning and control tool, are only as good as the information put into them. If forecasts and cost projections are inaccurate, the resulting budgets are less useful and lead to poor management decisions. Budgets are also useful in planning to deliver and price new services. Thus, in Chapter 8, the development of pricing strategies for prescriptions, cognitive services and over-the-counter (OTC) products is examined. In addition to the accounting information, an understanding of the competitive nature of the marketplace is required to develop sound pricing strategies and the implications of the pricing strategy used.

In Chapter 9, personal financial goals and strategies are examined, which is especially important from the student's perspective, because a large income boost is in their near future.

Each chapter also contains discussion and review questions reinforcing the subject matter's application in pharmacy, and a glossary.

Finally, you have already seen, and will continue to see, "cases-in-point", such as Case-in-point 1.4, demonstrating how each accounting or financial management topic is applied in various pharmacy practice settings. Continually re-examine them as a demonstration of financial management's impact on all aspects of a pharmacy business.

Case-in-point 1.4 Big D Pharmacy

In about 1980, Big D Pharmacy was started by an entrepreneur who believed that some customers were interested in price more than any other pharmacy patronage motive. To this end, Big D sold all prescriptions on a cash basis and did not take credit cards or accept any third party insurance programs. As for front-end merchandise, Big D purchased merchandise in large lots, often buying manufacturer's, and even other retailer's, surplus inventories. The benefit of this kind of purchasing was that the savings attained could be passed on to customers. Big D's customers liked the low prices and the store was instantly successful. However, a downside to this large-lot-surplus style of purchasing was that no consistency of product mix could be assured. In other words, Big D sold what it could get when it could get it. At least initially, Big D monopolized on this strategy and turned it into a comparative benefit: customers soon came to value the excitement associated with not knowing what would be available for sale on any given day. In fact, this strategy brought customers back to the store frequently in the hope of not missing anything exceptional that Big D might be offering.

Over several years, the Big D operation proved so successful that the owner decided to expand and open additional outlets. With only two or three stores, the owner was able to manage the business. However, when this number of outlets was exceeded, he quickly realized he would need to bring in purchasing, finance and management professionals to take Big D to the next level. When Big D exceeded a dozen stores in number, the owner began thinking about expanding even further. Ultimately, the decision was made to franchise the operation. This meant there would be both company-owned and franchised stores. Big D still handled all purchasing corporately and the franchise owners agreed to participate in the group purchasing, to keep buying power high. This enabled Big D to obtain even lower prices in the marketplace and stabilize, to a certain extent, its product offerings, as major manufacturers could sell directly to the chain at very attractive prices.

Big D's business strategy changed over time in response to marketplace trends. This was especially true with respect to third party prescription programs. In about 1990, as the percentage of customers with third party insurance grew to over 50%, Big D began to selectively accept third party prescription insurance that provided an acceptable level of reimbursement. This was determined by calculating an average cost to dispense plus profit and only accepting programs that met or exceeded this level of reimbursement. While it was cumbersome for Big D and its customers to keep up with which third party programs were being accepted and which were not, this process did work to maintain profits. To assist customers, Big D kept a list at each pharmacy outlet showing exactly which third party plans were being accepted. Again, customer acceptance of this practice was high and prescription business increased as more plans were offered.

Big D eventually also began to accept credit cards as a payment form at its corporate and franchise stores. This move proved quite positive, as both customer satisfaction and the average sale per customer increased. The cost of accepting credit cards was at least in part passed along to customers in the form of slightly higher prices. Because the price increases were spread over a large volume of sales, this went largely unnoticed by customers. Big D's business strategy proved so successful that its competition began to adopt some of Big D's practices; especially trying to create excitement associated with the shopping experience (such as bringing in unusual merchandise that could be sold at very attractive prices and added fun to the shopping experience).

By about 1992, Big D noticed that prescription volumes, store sales and average sales per visit were not growing as rapidly as in the past. In fact, they had begun to decline. Customer research revealed the increasing trend toward third party prescription insurance and Big D's very selective acceptance of these plans was forcing customers to the competition – which routinely accepted most or all third party plans. Relying on the convenience factor, customers who left Big D in search of prescription program acceptance also made ancillary front-end purchases at these competitive outlets. In response to these lost sales, and without any financial analysis of the impact of this decision, Big D decided to accept all third party prescription programs.

At first, this decision stabilized the prescription volumes at the Big D stores. Many new customers were brought in and they found the prices of the front-end merchandise attractive. However, these customers were also more accustomed to a higher level of service and more consistent product supply. In short, Big D was beginning to act more like the competition rather than bringing something new to the marketplace – which was what had made Big D successful in the first place. Big D was built on low prices, not customer service, and lagged behind the retail industry in customer service.

Over the next few years, Big D's margins began to decline. Initially operating at a 26% gross margin, which allowed ample profits given Big D's efficiency of operation, Big D's margins were declining annually and, by 1998, had decreased to approximately 20%. Big D's response, as in the past, was to continue to control costs. For example, staffing levels were reduced (e.g., cashiers, stockers, janitorial, and pharmacy technicians) and routinely allocated based on sales volumes. Once gross margins reached the level of 20% or less, management knew that drastic action was necessary to ensure the success of the operation.

Corporate management called together the franchisees and discussed the decline in profitability. At this meeting, several strategies were developed to try to bring Big D back to profitability, specifically:

- freeze salaries of current employees
- reduce staffing levels immediately to match existing store sales levels
- reduce average inventory (prescription and over the counter) to increase cash
- pay all invoices at net, rather than taking a 2% cash discount for prompt payment
- have regional meetings to communicate directly with store level personnel and inform them of the trend toward decreased profits – and the impact this was having on the company.

At the regional meetings, which included all store personnel including the pharmacy staff, Big D employees were told to look to their right and to their left and to note that within 6 months one of those people would be gone. The result of this was a loss of morale and many critical employees sought and found other employment. This initially resulted in some improvement in the financial analyses, but as service levels continued to decline, so did the number of customers and the average sale per customer.

Big D had effectively ensured its own failure by responding to sales declines with staffing and service cuts – rather than strategies aimed at bringing in more customers. Thus, in response to changes in the marketplace, Big D made decisions as if it were still the low-cost industry leader – when, in fact, its business model had changed to be more in line with the competition. While some actions did change, customer service did not. This trend continued to spiral down for another 2 years until profitability was so low that all corporate stores were closed. Only a few of the franchisees were successful enough to remain open.

Assessment and analysis

By monitoring its comparative income statements and balance sheets, Big D was able to identify significant trends in its business operations. However, this financial information, without a good understanding of marketplace trends and customer needs, was useless in helping Big D make changes that were responsive to the marketplace. In sum, Big D had good and sound information, but did not know how to make the appropriate changes to the business to remedy the trends noted in the accounts. The use of financial information to monitor only the company's individual success, without prudent customer-oriented decision making and market analysis, led to the ultimate failure of Big D pharmacies.

This case illustrates the importance of proper financial analysis by management. One of the most important operating ratios is the gross margin percentage, which is calculated as gross profit divided by net sales. This ratio is often cited by market analysts when there is any change, even of 0.5–1%, either positive or negative. Understanding the factors that can affect this ratio will aid pharmacy managers in understanding their business and making better decisions. Gross profit is determined as total net sales less the cost of goods sold (COGS). When changes in the gross margin percentage occur, the major contributors are either decreased sales prices owing to increased market competition or increased inventory costs.

Clearly, Big D's gross margin percentage reduction from 26% to 20% consisted of both. However, the major portion appears to have been from reduced prescription selling prices, as evidenced by the increased proportion of prescription sales from third party insurers. While competition may have been a perfectly acceptable reason to make this move, Big D managers should have anticipated this effect on overall profitability that these decisions would ultimately make. If accepting all insurance plans was an absolute necessity to stay competitive in the marketplace and attract customers, there should have been a major shift to reducing inventory costs. The purchasing department should have been given clear goals for obtaining more favorable purchasing contracts. At the individual store level, pharmacy managers should have been informed of the need to reduce inventory carrying costs and that increasing inventory turnover within each store was critical. Concentrating efforts in these areas may have produced results equaling the negative effects of accepting new insurance plans.

Decreases in gross margin percentage can also be attributed to the COGS. While the purchasing price of additional prescription inventory is addressed above, the front-store inventory, which originally proved quite successful, may have also been an area where management could have acted more aggressively. When analyzing decreases in gross margin percentage, the product mix is important, as different lines of products often provide a higher gross margin percentage than others. Detailed analysis of the front-store inventory provides important information. Developing individual inventory turnover calculations by product line is important, since a low gross profit percentage on a particular line can be mitigated if there is a very high turnover, such as 50 or so, indicating inventory lines sellout on a weekly basis. More aggressive marketing may have determined customer preferences, which might have been profitable to Big D if purchased in the proper proportion. With a more aggressive front-store line of products, the original Big D excitement might have returned and customer loyalty reinstilled, which could have restored profitability to the company as a whole.

2

Understanding the guiding principles of accounting

Learning objectives

- Describe the different roles accounting has within organizations
- Describe the history and evolution of accounting and its importance and usefulness to pharmacy managers
- List the four basic financial statements and their purpose
- Identify the role of internal control within an organization's accounting system
- Understand the underlying principles that guide the development of financial statements through transaction analysis
- List and describe the various forms of legal ownership and structure for companies

Introduction

Each and every day, pharmacists evaluate and make clinical decisions on a patient's health based upon their own knowledge base and all available information, with each additional piece leading to a more informed decision and, more often than not, better patient care. Even though not as dynamic or life saving, pharmacists also make financial decisions in various practice settings that affect the overall economic health of their organization. Good financial decision making ultimately leads to the existence, and subsequent prosperity, of an organization, allowing for provision of more effective patient care services by the entire healthcare team.

In today's healthcare environment, not only must pharmacists be medication experts and highly knowledgeable clinicians, they should also understand that healthcare, and especially pharmacy, is a business which necessitates the need for effective managers. To fully comprehend the impact of each of the numerous transactions involved in the day-to-day operations, pharmacists and pharmacy students should gain an understanding and appreciation of the assumptions and guiding principles of accounting. This chapter provides the background principles governing the consistent application of recording and reporting of individual transactions. Consistency is the key concept, as it should instill a confidence in the recording, reporting and analysis of each individual financial transaction, which then hopefully leads to more effective management and increased patient care and customer service levels.

History of accounting

Throughout the history of accounting, economic progress and development have always been closely linked with accounting and financial reporting and will continue to do so in the future. Based on his 1494 publication of *Summa de arithmetica, geometria, proportioni et proportionalita*, many historians often refer to Luca Pacioli as the "father of accounting," given that his work provided the official codification of accounting practices at the time. However, this is not the complete story.

Certainly, economic progress played a significant part in the development of the science of accounting. But, just as the age-old question of which came first, the chicken or the egg, did the development of more advanced accounting techniques fuel economic expansion throughout time or did the inevitable growth of commerce and the need for accurate financial information necessitate accounting's development? Regardless of the true answer, the two have been intimately connected over the ages.

Why is Italy credited with the development of modern-day accounting techniques, given that ancient Greece or Rome certainly provided enough economic activity, power and impetus with which to claim credit? Accounting scholar AC Littleton references seven "key ingredients" that ultimately led to the development of accounting as it is known today[1]:

- the advent of private property, rather than that of the state, requiring appropriate record keeping for documentation of an individual's ownership
- the increase in capital and its use in the development of wealth and commerce
- increased commerce, from local trading and rudimentary systems to far-reaching international exchange requiring more complex and uniform systems
- credit, or the use of future goods and services in the present, requiring documentation, whereas completed transactions did not
- the development of writing, allowing for both economic expansion and the resulting bookkeeping required
- establishment of a common denominator for money and the resultant money measurement concept

- arithmetic, which provided the means of calculating the complexities of transactions in a monetary form.

Although many of the ingredients noted above existed in various forms in ancient history, it was not until the Middle Ages that the quantity and strength of world commerce required a major push in the development of accounting systems that could meet local, regional, national, and international needs.

Today's glossy financial statements contain many photos, perfectly tabulated columns of data, and can be generated relatively easily through the use of powerful computers and accounting programs. Seen as a far cry from clay tablets, papyrus paper and other ancient forms for source documents, the essence of accounting remains the same, to provide essential information on a timely basis, and which can meet the needs of various financial information users.

Introduction to financial statements

Accounting's fundamental unit, the accounting equation (Chapter 3), provides the basis for the development of current financial statements, and, much like a patient's health is documented in their medical chart, the financial health of a company is quantified in these various written reports. There are four basic financial statements, including:

- the *balance sheet,* which provides a picture of all of a company's assets (property owned), liabilities (amount owed on property), and shareholder's (owner's) equity (net worth) at a particular date, or point in time
- the *income statement,* which reflects a company's revenues and expenses over a specific time period
- the *statement of shareholder's (owner's) equity* (also called statement of retained earnings), which are activities that relate to the company's ownership and results of operations during various operating periods
- the *statement of cash flows,* which are the sources (inflows) and uses (outflows) of cash, classified in three general categories (operating, investing, and financing).

(See Chapter 4 for further discussion of the individual characteristics of each of these statements.)

Guidance for the proper preparation of financial statements in the United States is provided within the *Generally Accepted Accounting Principles* (GAAP), a recognized set of accounting procedures, standards, and principles. GAAP serves to provide relevant and reliable information within financial statements regardless of who prepared them, in addition to enabling them to be comparable between different companies. The Financial Accounting Standards Board (FASB; http://www.fasb.org/) sets authoritative standards (rules and regulations; http://asc.fasb.org/) for American companies, which helps ascertain the consistency among various financial statements within and between business sectors and industries. However, given the globalization of business in recent times, there is an initiative to transition from GAAP to the International Financial Reporting Standards (IFRS; http://www.ifrs.org/). This convergence will require the adoption of IFRS by both the FASB and International Accounting Standards Board (IASB), which is anticipated for full implementation by December 31, 2011. The consistency of global standards increases the financial statements users' assurance of comparability between all companies regardless of their country of origin or operations.

The question then becomes, who are the users of financial statements? Financial statement users can consist of a multitude of individuals; however, they are broadly classified as either internal or external users. This could include individuals such as:

- owners who monitor company profitability (internal)
- managers who make frontline decisions affecting the operations of the various departments and divisions (internal)
- lenders, current shareholders and potential investors who evaluate the business's financial strength to make appropriate decisions with regards to loaning or investing money with the company (external).

Managerial reporting

Upper-level administrators often oversee the operations and accounting systems of multiple departments responsible for generating reports to evaluate performance. These individuals are responsible for planning, organizing, and controlling resources to ensure that an organization's goals are met. Managerial accounting is used to refer to the various reports and supplemental information supplied to internal users of the accounting system's information. Departments operate with the intent of producing a profit or not (i.e., cost centers), depending on the department's purpose and its place in the overall organizational structure. *Profit centers* are those sections of a company that are responsible for producing profits (e.g., the pharmacy department or photography center). *Cost centers*, on the other hand, are non-revenue-generating sections of a company considered critical to the optimal performance of the company's overall operations (e.g., home delivery of prescriptions or human resources department). Table 2.1 reflects the various reporting responsibilities within a given organization.

Balance sheet (real) and income statement (nominal accounts)

To analyze business activity over a period of time or at specific points in time, individual transactions must be grouped into various accounts. Accounts, the

Table 2.1 Accounting functions

Department	Functional reporting
Management – executive (i.e. corporate chains and hospitals), pharmacy directors at hospitals, pharmacists in charge at individual retail locations	Performance (managerial) reporting, financial reporting (financial statements), budgets Note: Level of detail of each type of report is different depending upon the user
Human resources	Payroll reports (current and historical)
Inventory management	Inventory purchasing reports, sales reports (by class, i.e. prescription, over the counter, individual item, merchandising classifications; warehousing and distribution reporting
Finance department	Cash flow reports (payroll, inventory, store operations expenses, capital expansion)

most basic element of an accounting system, are used to collect all data transactions of the same type; therefore, while there are many accounts common to all companies, such as *cash* and *accounts payable*, the creation of additional accounts is based upon an individual company's need, and is simply named for the type of economic transaction that the company wishes to track (i.e., front store sales and prescription sales). To facilitate grouping these accounts, two distinct classes are used, balance sheet (real) and income statement (nominal) accounts.

Nominal (or temporary) accounts are used within the income statement, and will be referred to as *income statement accounts*. These accounts are created with a zero beginning balance, used to reflect revenue and expense data for a specific period and then closed or, again, reduced back to zero. This process allows the business to determine its profitability (or lack thereof) during a specific time period.

On the other hand, since a company exists for the long term (the going-concern principle, discussed in more detail later in the chapter), the effects of many periods of operations activity need to be reflected in accounts showing cumulative balances from one or more periods. These are known as real (or permanent) accounts and located on the balance sheet. The real accounts' (hereafter referred to as *balance sheet accounts*) ending balance represent the cumulative effect of all account transactions recorded since the company began operations, often including many periods. Balance sheet accounts, found on the balance sheet and statement of shareholder's (owner's) equity, include accounts such as cash, accounts receivable, accounts payable, and retained earnings.

Cash and accrual basis of accounting

To be consistent with how individual transactions are grouped into the above accounts, the transactions must follow one of two methods in how they are recorded, either cash or accrual basis of accounting. *Cash basis accounting* is defined as recording revenue and expenses in the period in which they are actually received or expended in cash. While this method may seem easy, it is not very effective when a company's operations are analyzed, especially when the matching principle is considered (again, fully discussed later in the chapter). Under this principle, all expenses incurred in the generation of revenue are matched in the same period. For example, when building a house, many expenses must be paid prior to the actual sale of the completed house. During the construction period, the income statement would have no revenue and many expenses (since the home has not sold), showing a significant loss for the company and indicating poor performance. During the year the completed house is sold, the opposite effect is seen with large revenues and few expenses, creating a large amount of income for the period. This distortion is seen in two periods under the cash basis of accounting, which, again, only reflects the movement of actual cash, either in receipts or payments.

Conversely, *accrual basis accounting* would alleviate this distortion and show a more accurate financial position reflecting the activity of building the house. With this type of accounting, revenue and expenses are recorded in the period in which they are essentially earned or incurred, regardless of whether cash is received or disbursed. Continuing with the previous example, during a home's construction phase there would be absolutely no expense shown on the income statement. Although there are many payments being made for supplies and contract labor, etc., these amounts would be recorded as a prepaid expense on the balance sheet, reflecting the exchange of cash for the accumulating value of the house, although it is still in progress. In the next period, when the house is completed and sold, the revenue from the sale is recorded on the income statement. Additionally, the prepaid expenses on the balance sheet will be transferred to the income statement. Therefore, the expenses incurred in generating revenues will be matched to the receipt of the revenue in the same period, which hopefully results in a profit. Given this, GAAP requires the use of the accrual basis of accounting in all but a few limited special circumstances, such as a very small company or with income tax reporting.

> *Case-in-point 2.1   Cash versus accrual basis accounting in a community pharmacy*
>
> In a typical community pharmacy, where prescriptions are reimbursed by a third party insurance carrier, the expected payment is recorded

immediately as revenue in the current period, even though the actual cash reimbursement may not be received for several weeks, which might be another period. The costs, or expenses, of the medications are also recorded in the current period, whether or not cash payment to the medication supplier (such as wholesaler or direct purchase from a pharmaceutical manufacturer) has been made. Using cash basis accounting would show no revenue for the dispensed prescriptions until the actual reimbursement from the third party payer was received. This could be several weeks later or even in another accounting period. The cost of the prescription inventory used to fill those prescriptions would have been recorded when the actual payment to the vendor was made, which also could have been in another period. In this example, there is no matching of revenue with expenses. Use of cash basis accounting generally is not considered to be in conformity with GAAP as it does not appropriately reflect the matching principle. Given the simplicity of cash basis accounting compared with accrual basis accounting, cash basis accounting is only used in selected situations, such as very small companies and, when permitted, for income tax reporting.[2]

Definition of accounting

Accounting encompasses all of the processes necessary to record, report, and analyze the financial activities of a company. The recording process, known as bookkeeping, captures operating information at the very lowest levels and often consists of huge volumes of transactions. Consider a community pharmacy which dispenses 400 prescriptions each day; every prescription dispensed must be recorded, summarized, and reported in the appropriate financial statement. Fortunately, pharmacy automation and computer advancement has allowed for the majority of bookkeeping to be completed relatively easily. The reporting function of accounting occurs with the financial statements, which represent the summarized financial activities of a company and conform to standardized formats. By adhering to standard reporting formats, the various users of financial statements can analyze its data. The analysis and interpretation of financial data (see Chapter 5) is the final step in accounting, and allows for pharmacy managers to evaluate the effectiveness of their company's performance and take appropriate action.

Transaction analysis

Today, a person decides to go out for lunch instead of bringing their usual peanut butter and jelly sandwich. He/she happens to stop at a local café and purchase a hot, ham-and-cheese sub. With this simple act, the person has just created a transaction, the basic exchange of economic considerations between two entities, by exchanging cash for food. Even though, as an individual, you might not record this, for a company's purposes, every transaction must be recorded. Another example is when a paycheck is written to an employee, this transaction is recorded as a payroll expense on the income statement and reduction of cash on the balance sheet. Specific to pharmacy, the purchasing of OTC naproxen could be a transaction in which one asset (cash) is swapped for another (product).

While most transactions occur between a company and its customers, there are many transactions between different departments within a company, which should also be accurately measured and recorded. To facilitate this, the "money measurement concept" states all individual transactions must be expressed in monetary terms or it cannot be recorded.

Case-in-point 2.2   Money measurement concept

The money measurement concept essentially ties the value of tangible assets being sold or acquired into a common measurement of dollars and cents. Additionally, the value of resources expended on a particular operational activity is also quantified in terms of dollars. For example, when a large chain pharmacy's home office creates a new advertising campaign, certain personnel work to create the advertisements using supplies and computers to develop layouts and media spots. The payroll costs for the time spent by various employees on this campaign are recorded as part of this process (rather than just recorded as a payroll expense of the sales department), as well as the assets' value (specific invoices for photos, outside printing, media, etc.). With this method, the entire campaign is reduced to monetary terms, reflecting the cost of all human efforts as well as actual costs of physical materials and other outside services.

Accounting entity principle

Accountants are guided by several principles when they record individual transactions. These broad principles have been established in practice for many years and are the essence of financial statements. More specific principles arise out of needs for individual companies within specific industries, and are often established through authoritative bodies. The focus of the following sections will be on explaining the rationale and application of the following 10 broad accounting principles in the development of financial statements:

- the accounting entity principle
- the going concern principle
- the accounting period principle
- the historical cost principle
- the objectivity principle
- the conservatism principle
- the consistency principle
- the matching principle
- the materiality principle
- the revenue recognition principle.

Whether you are a business owner, an executive, store-level manager, or frontline employee, you are working for a business or company considered to be an accounting entity, also known as a legal entity. Given this status, the information derived from the accounting entity's (i.e., the company) operations belongs to the accounting entity itself and is created to serve the needs of owners, employees, and others. Therefore, the accounting entity can be sued, make a profit, pay taxes, or even support a local cause.

Each accounting entity, or company, is a group of people organized for a specific activity or service. In pharmacy practice, delivering quality patient care is the main purpose, although it can take on many forms based upon the practice setting. Whatever the activity, there are two broad company classifications, either for-profit or not-for-profit (non-profit). Most pharmacies are operated as *for-profit*, with the intent to generate a profit based upon the basic economic activity provided. In turn, the profits of the company are eventually returned to the owners, or shareholders, in the form of dividends, to provide a return on their investment. In addition, the company's profits are taxed, usually on several levels, such as federal, state, and local corporate income taxes.

The term *non-profit* can be misleading. Even though it implies a company does not make a profit, it is actually a legal term stipulating that any profits generated are not returned to the owners (as return on investment, dividends, or cash withdrawals). The profits remain as assets to the company in order for it continue with its primary economic activity. Many charities and service organizations use this as their corporate structure; however, major hospitals and other institutions may have this structure. Additionally, non-profit companies are often exempt from income taxes.

Going concern principle

Now that a company's basic legal structure has been established, it is important to recognize the overall purpose of all companies, to exist and succeed for as long as possible. This is the essence of the *going concern principle*, which states that all businesses/companies exist to provide goods and/or services and operate for the long term (i.e., thrive and survive). Using this principle as a basis for operation, business decisions must always consider different time frames, both short and long term. Often, the ultimate decision made is impacted by the time horizon. Therefore, companies create and maintain accounting records from the beginning of its operations and management in order to make decisions in the company's long-term interest, perspective and viability. However, in today's corporate structure, many managers are evaluated on decision making aimed at maximizing short-term profits, which over time can sacrifice the company's long run economic viability.

Case-in-point 2.3   Going concern principle – community pharmacy

The going concern principle explains how individual decisions need to be examined in light of the "big picture". In a community pharmacy, a pharmacist may opt to dispense a prescription which is reimbursed at an amount less than the product's actual acquisition cost, thereby dispensing that particular prescription at a loss. On an individual basis, this is a negative transaction which possibly should not be done. However, under this principle, the decision is viewed in a longer time frame (i.e. does not forget the big picture) – where the individual decision is an attempt to gain sales elsewhere or build customer loyalty, with the expectation that the loss will be regained elsewhere in the company over time.

Accounting period principle

Even though pharmacies must consider the long-term implications of decisions, from an accounting perspective, the time period must be defined and is usually defined as a one-year period, sometimes called the fiscal year. The United States Department of the Treasury, Internal Revenue Service (IRS) recognizes, by convention, the calendar year (January 1 to December 31) as the standard accounting period; however, an accounting period may be of any duration and begin and end on any date (e.g., July 1 to June 30). The natural start and end of the revenue process cycle, or operating cycle, of a company is a common determinant of a fiscal year or an accounting period.

It is important to note that internal management needs current financial information from which to operate, and a year is a very long time in many businesses to operate without updated information. Therefore, many companies use the *accounting period principle* and prepare interim financial statements in order to compact the information needing to be gathered and analyzed. Often the periods are each calendar month;

however, some companies use 4-week periods and have a total of 13 periods in their fiscal year.

> ### Case-in-point 2.4   Accounting periods
>
> Let us analyze a company producing sunscreens. Even though these products are used year round, they experience significantly higher utilization in the summer months. Therefore, inventory levels need to increase during the winter months in order to be sufficient during the summer demand. Thus, a more representative business cycle for a company such as this could begin on September 1 and end on August 31 of the following year rather than using the calendar year accounting period.

Historical cost principle

As the name implies, companies must record their economic activities based upon the costs initially incurred. Over time, prices tend to rise and, therefore, the amounts shown in financial statements for assets may be undervalued from current values. However, accountants must not change these values until some economic event involving these assets occurs. Otherwise, financial statements become more subjective in their determination and ultimately of little value. The *historical cost principle* provides a point of reference for all financial statement users and appropriate market values may be used in financial analysis when deemed necessary. From the pharmacy perspective, the most common example would be the long-term assets on an independent pharmacy owner's balance sheet. The physical building (real estate) would be recorded at the original cost, which is usually not reflective of the current market value (usually much higher).

Objectivity principle

Next, the *objectivity principle* simply states that some form of independent evidence, or reference, is used when accounting transactions are recorded, excluding personal feelings or opinions from interfering when forming the basis of an accounting entry. Cash is referred to as the most objective amount, and the majority of transactions are recorded in the amount of the exchange of cash as the value of the goods or services. However, sometimes it is necessary to use subjective estimates to determine the exchange value of a certain transaction. In such cases, this principle relies upon what a reasonable person would determine, or the consensus of a group would be, thereby eliminating the bias of using only the statement preparer's opinion.

Conservatism principle

While less often used, the *conservatism principle* is necessary primarily in the absence of objective, verifiable evidence (i.e., objectivity principle). Under these circumstances, when accounting estimates, evaluations, or opinions need to be made, the option with the least optimistic economic (or most conservative) outcome should be chosen in order to fairly characterize the effect in the financial statements. One of the most common uses is with the valuation of a company's inventory. In certain instances, the historical cost may be considered to be of a higher value than what the current market will bear, such as with a medication which has been recalled by the Food and Drug Administration. In this case, the medication certainly has an uncertain current market value lower than the purchase price recorded by a company, because of the product's removal. In this instance, adjusting the historical inventory cost to equal that of the current market estimated value is the less optimistic option and allowed as a result of this principle.

Consistency principle

Just as a pharmacist would continually recommend a specific OTC product for a specific condition/issue, the *consistency principle* requires that similar accounting procedures, including the use of estimation techniques, are used during the entire and future accounting periods. Again, this allows the users of financial statements to have a level of comfort in the reported information, especially when comparing results between different time periods. Essential to the consistency principle is the clear notation and explanation of any changes of accounting procedures used in the preparation of financial statements when a deviation is made from the prior period, which allows users to make a more informed decision after consideration of the impact of the accounting changes.

Matching principle

One of the most important and fundamental principles of accounting is the *matching principle*. This principle plays a significant role in the income statement, which records all of a company's revenues and expenses. All expenses directly associated with the production of the reported revenues must be reported within the same period on the income statement. Revenue is then realized when it is earned and the sale has been completed or a service has been fully provided. Accordingly, all of the expenses necessary to get the product into sale condition, or for the service to be completely provided, must be matched to this realized revenue in order to obtain the correct profit from the transaction.

Case-in-point 2.5   Matching principle

As discussed with the development of an advertising campaign in Case-in-point 2.2, transactions are expensed in the current period if the value of these expenses is received in the current accounting period. However, a large campaign (intangible asset) is usually expected to last for more than one accounting period and the total cost of the campaign must be shown over all future accounting periods in which the advertisement will run. A prorated portion of the original total cost, or amortization expense, of this asset is recorded on the income statement in each future period in which the advertisement is run. As a result, there is a matching of the benefit of the additional revenues from the campaign with the original costs in each of these future accounting periods.

Important in both revenue and expense recognition is that cash from the sale does not have to be received, as well as payment of the expenses does not have to be made. The effect of the receipt of cash in respect to revenues and expenses is also known as *timing differences*. In the same manner that pharmacists ensure drugs and dosages match diseases and patients, the matching process is used to account for differences in timing between, for example, the sale of a prescription and payment by a third party insurance; or ordering inventory from the wholesaler but not paying for these medications and supplies until the end of the month. In this instance, the inventory account (an asset) would be increased for the item actually received by the end of the accounting period, and a corresponding liability (accounts payable) is recorded until such time as the check is actually written.

When using financial information, it is essential to know what accounting period the information covers. For example, a pharmacist planning to administer influenza immunizations during the fall might purchase and pay for the vaccines months earlier, causing an increase in the cost of inventory and a decrease in cash. It is important to note that these two transactions only represent an exchange of assets and, therefore, will only impact the balance sheet. There is no impact on the income statement, which reflects the company's revenues and expenses, until the vaccines are administered and the resulting revenues collected. In this example, the increase in the balance sheet for the period of the vaccine purchase should "make sense" to the financial statement reader, who knows there will be future revenues and expenses on the income statement in future periods when they are actually administered to patients; hopefully at a price higher than that of the cost of the vaccine and the pharmacist's time.

Case-in-point 2.6   Matching principle and accounting periods

How much expense is recorded in the June income statement when $300,000 of influenza vaccine inventory is purchased for cash and immunizations will not begin until September? Answer – zero. Since the company paid cash when the vaccine was purchased there was an exchange of only assets, between cash and inventory. This transaction is recorded only on the June balance sheet. Specifically, inventory would increase and cash would decrease by the same amount. Thus, the net effect on the balance sheet is zero. When the vaccines are administered and sold, the expense of the vaccines is matched with revenues received and is recorded on the September income statement. Additionally, the September balance sheet will now reflect a receipt of cash and a decrease in vaccine inventory, matching the inventory activity of September in the September balance sheet. Note that had the inventory been financed on credit, only the June balance sheet would still have been affected. In this case, the inventory account would increase in the same amount as the accounts payable account, with an increase in an asset in exchange for a liability.

Materiality principle

Next, the *materiality principle* acknowledges the significance of various financial transactions being recorded in the accounting records and ultimately being reflected in the financial statements. The importance of this principle stems from the fact that financial statements are meant to present fairly, and not exactly, the results of a company's operations. While companies have many small transactions which make up their final results, the omission of recording only one of these transactions would not impact the reported results overall.

For example, assume a national community pharmacy chain has 6,000 stores reporting daily sales averaging $20,000. On the annual income statement, annual sales would be $43,800,000,000. If a power outage caused one store to miss reporting one day's sales of $20,000, this would be immaterial to the overall revenues as shown on the annual income statement. In general, if the omission of any financial transaction or information would impair the financial statement user's judgment, then that item would be deemed material and should be properly recorded and reported. In this case, having the accounting department expend time and resources recreating the missed day's activity would not be necessary.

Revenue recognition principle

Revenue is the income-generating portion of business activity basic to all companies. It is therefore critical to record the appropriate amount of revenues within each accounting period in order to properly reflect the operations of the business. There are two principles that help guide accountants in the revenue recognition process. First, the revenue must be earned. Businesses operate to provide goods or services and this process can vary widely between different companies. However, revenue is earned when the process of providing the goods or services is completed from the business's viewpoint, and the right to receive payment from the customer is also complete, or earned. When both the business and customer have agreed to complete the transaction, the revenue earning process is complete and therefore may be recognized, or recorded, into the accounting records. Secondly, the payment for the earned revenue, or completed transaction, does not have to be in the form of cash. Although the majority of revenue transactions are ultimately received in cash or cash equivalents, the *revenue recognition principle* states the earning process is the most important and actual cash collection is not required when recording earned revenues. Accounts receivable reflects the value of earned revenues which have not been received. If future collection of an account receivable is deemed to be uncertain, the conservatism principle would dictate that a reserve for uncollectible accounts receivable be established at that time, while the matching principle dictates that this transaction be recorded in the current income statement period.

Case-in-point 2.7   Summary of accounting principles

Since the main purpose of financial statements is to provide information to various users, reliability and overall accuracy are critical needs which must be met in the preparation of financial statements. By adhering to the accounting principles noted in this chapter, the users can gain assurance these needs are indeed being met. The financial results of the company's operations will not be overvalued, or "pie in the sky," because of the conservatism, objectivity, and materiality principles. One can make important comparisons between different operating periods, knowing that the consistency, matching, and revenue recognition principles have been appropriately applied in the development of the accounting system, which ultimately generates the financial information contained in the financial statements. The accounting entity, along with the going concern, accounting period, and historical cost principles provide a foundation to capture a company's physical operations in a financial format.

Accounting systems and internal control

Every company has the need for information regarding the performance of their economic activities, as it provides the basis for proper future decision making. In order to meet that need, an accounting system must be designed to capture the relevant information from all events and transactions produced in the course of pursuing their economic activity. In order to achieve this goal, a set of procedures, both manual and computerized, must be implemented. The beginning of any accounting system lies with the paper trail, or the documents created during the course of a company's business activities. In a busy community pharmacy, prescription dispensing creates a set of high volume, recurring transactions that must be recorded. While the prescription label created is placed on the prescription vial and given to the patient, the prescription itself is the paper trail filed at the pharmacy. The accounting system is responsible for recording and summarizing these transactions on a daily basis, and this information is recorded in a prescription log for the day. While the actual prescriptions may constitute a large amount of physical paper, the prescription log reduces this to only one sheet and is also electronically stored for future use by the computerized portion of the accounting system.

Additionally, the company incurs many other transactions, such as monthly payment of utilities, which occur on a much more infrequent basis. Again, these transactions must also be recorded by the accounting system, and the source document to begin the recording process is the actual invoice received from the utility company. After all relevant information within a company is recorded for a certain time period; it is summarized and reported, mainly in the form of operating reports and financial statements.

A company's management is usually provided with operating reports including a great level of detail, which is necessary for internal management decision making. The basic tenant of an accounting system is it cannot become too burdensome in recording transactions that it actually begins to prevent, or delay, the very activities for which the company exists; however, reliable information must still be provided from the final design of the accounting system.

The "checks and balances" within an accounting system are known as the *system of internal control*. The policies and procedures, or internal controls, contained within the system have three main functions. They must:

- provide for the accurate recording of transactions appropriately authorized
- properly maintain recorded data
- safeguard the company's overall assets.

A segregation of duties is implicit in any internal control system, which strives to prevent any one person from having the recording, reporting, and safeguarding of any one transaction process, which can lead to theft and embezzlement. Given recent problems in the financial reporting of large public corporations, effective systems of internal control are the express responsibility of a company's executive management. It is important to note that the cost of an effective system of internal control should not exceed the derived benefit. In other words, while accurate and reliable accounting information is essential, the actual operations of the company must not be overburdened by that process.

Basic legal structures

All of the aforementioned accounting organization elements work under the umbrella of the company's legal structure. Legally, companies are classified and operate as one of three basic legal structures:

- sole proprietorship – owned exclusively by one person
- partnership – two or more owners (partners)
- corporation – owned by the shareholders who share in profits and losses generated through the firm's operations.

A summary comparison of the various forms of legal company ownership is presented in Table 2.2.

For both sole proprietorships and partnerships, liability for the business's operations accrues to the business owners or principals according to their share of ownership. This means all assets, as well as liabilities, are owned by the sole proprietor or partners. In the event of a company's failure, personal assets of the sole proprietor or partners can be used in order to satisfy the company's debts. The legal theory (reasoning) to support this stems from the flow of money over time; i.e., in the good times, the owners took money out of the company and bought personal items and "made their living", hence in the bad times when creditors are owed money, the personal assets from previous financial successes are deemed "fair game" to satisfy current liabilities.

To limit the potential liability against personal assets, the corporation was formed. Corporations, by virtue of their legal status, protect the principals, or owners, from liability arising from operations, beyond the amount of their personal investment, which is usually the purchase price of the shares owned by any one individual. Personal assets of the corporation's individual owners cannot be used to satisfy corporation debts. In extreme cases of a company's failure, all physical assets of a company would be sold, and payments to creditors are made with the proceeds. Often times, many creditors do not get full values for the amounts owed to them. If this occurs, the value of the company is essentially zero and the corporation is dissolved. The shares of

Table 2.2 Comparison of various forms of legal ownership of companies

Description	Sole proprietorship	Partnership	Corporation
Who are the individual business owners?	Owner/operator	Partners/operators	Shareholders
Are the owners active in the management of the business?	Yes	Yes	Usually not
How many owners does the business have?	One	Two or more	Depends on the number of shares authorized and the various percentages of ownership of these shares, e.g. 10,000 shares outstanding, may have up to 10,000 owners
Are stock certificates issued and sold for ownership?	No	No (partnership agreement)	Yes
Are the business owners liable for business debts?	Yes	Yes (may be expressly limited between various partners by agreement)	No
Who pays the business's taxes on earnings?	Owner/operator	Partners/operators	Corporation (however, individual shareholders pay taxes on any dividends received from the business)

stock owned by shareholders become worthless, and the shareholders receive no additional payments to return their original investment. Because of this protection from liability, the corporation is the most common form of a business enterprise. On the other hand, shareholders can earn dividends, which are paid out of the company's earnings. This represents a return to the shareholders for their investment in the shares of stock which they have purchased. Additionally, the value of each share increases as the company gains in financial strength, and this increase is noted as the market value. The market value of a share of stock can increase quite substantially over time, and, if shareholders sell their stock, they can realize great amounts of profits over their original investment.

When a corporation is formed, ownership is divided into equal parts, called shares or stock. The shares are awarded, or sold, to shareholders who become the actual owners, or stockholders, of the corporation. Dividends represent the return of profits of the company to the individual shareholders. Exact dividend payment amounts and dates are determined by the company's board of directors, based upon financial performance. Some companies strive to pay a set amount of dividend per share of stock on a consistent basis (i.e., quarterly every year), whereas other companies declare dividend payments based solely on the company's financial performance over time.

Major decisions affecting company management are voted upon by stockholders, and each share of stock is assigned voting and other rights. Generally, there are two classes of stock: common and preferred. Common stock is the most frequently issued and usually has voting rights. Preferred stock is usually non-voting, but has specified dividend payments. Individual shareholder preferences can influence which type of stock they enjoy owning. For those seeking a fixed income stream from dividends, preferred stock is the best option. Common stock, while having no fixed dividend guarantee, does have the potential of increased market value over time. The major benefit of the incorporation of a company versus a sole proprietorship or partnership is that shareholders are not financially liable for more than the invested dollar amount in the purchase of shares, and creditors, by law, cannot file a claim against a shareholder's personal assets. Limiting creditors from attacking personal assets, referred to as "piercing the corporate veil," is crucial to potential investors.

Aside from the liability issue surrounding various legal structures, taxation of profits also differs. The income from a sole proprietorship and partnership "passes" through to the owner, and is taxed at individual taxation rates, which currently vary from 10% to 35%, depending upon the amount earned (0 to $373,650). Corporate income tax rates currently range from 15% to 35%, depending upon the amount earned (0 to $18,333,333). Wages paid to employees are income to each employee, and the corporation subtracts these amounts in determining the income of the corporation, which is then subject further to the corporate income tax. The specific legal and tax implications for the various forms of entities are complex and often changing, and are beyond the scope of this text. Interested readers should seek expert advice within this area.

Case-in-point 2.8   How does the book value of a share of stock compare with its market value?

Each share of stock issued by a corporation has a stated value, called its par value. After the corporation sells an original share of stock, the par value has little relevance to either the book value or market value. Book value of a single share of stock of a particular corporation is an accounting term, which is simply the result of the net worth of the company divided by the current number of shares outstanding. This provides a value reflecting the historical results of operations in terms of the total shares of stock outstanding and is used by financial analysts in a company's evaluation. The market value is a much more complex value, and is a market term, often referred to as a market price per share. This value is determined by the stock market in general, which consists of all potential buyers and sellers. The value the market places on a particular stock reflects a variety of factors. The stock market, as a whole, allows various buyers and sellers a forum with which to determine an individual's stock value, or market price. Investors in the stock market analyze various factors, such as the past, current, and estimated future earnings of a company in determining a fair market value. Historical and current dividend payments, which represent a return on investment, also contribute to the fair market value. Finally, the emotional component of whether or not people simply want to own a piece of a particular company can significantly alter the market value of a stock.

Summary

In this chapter, the importance of financial information in the pharmacy manager's performance of their duties has been described. To effectively understand financial information and its origin, a brief history of accounting as it has evolved over time was presented, along with descriptions of the basic methods of accounting, transactions, and accounts as an introduction to financial statements. The 10 broadest accounting principles were reviewed in order for pharmacy managers to obtain a better understanding of the creation of financial statements and apply these principles to determine the source and flow of financial information within their operation.

References

1 Littleton AC. Accounting evolution to 1900. In: Alexander JR, ed. *History of Accounting*. New York: American Institute Publishing Co., 1933. Reissued 2002 by the Association of Chartered Accountants in the United States.
2 Chisholm-Burns MA, Vaillancourt AM, Shepherd M. *Pharmacy Management, Leadership, Marketing, and Finance*. Sudbury, MA: Jones & Bartlett Publishers, 2011.

Suggested reading

Carroll NV. *Financial Management for Pharmacists: A Decision-Making Approach*. Baltimore, MD: Lippincott Williams & Wilkins, 3rd edn, 2007.
Friedlob GT, Plewa FJ. *Financial and Business Statements*. Hauppauge, NY: Barron's Educational Series, Inc., 3rd edn, 2006.
Warren CS, Reeve JM, Duchac JE. *Accounting*. New York, NY: Random House, 23rd edn, 2008.
Walther L. *Principles of Accounting*. Logan, UT: Utah State University. www.principlesofac-counting.com

Review questions

1 As a clinical profession, pharmacists learn to evaluate patient symptoms objectively, such as through the development of SOAP notes (subjective, objective, assessment and plan). Describe how this same objectivity used in clinical decisions should also apply to accounting decisions.

2 When preparing their financial statements, all companies adhere to Generally Accepted Accounting Principles. Describe the importance of adhering to GAAP from the viewpoint of the users of financial statements.

3 Discuss the implications on net income of choosing to use the accrual basis of accounting over the cash basis on interim statements versus annual operating reports.

4 Where do the contents of income statement accounts go when the accumulated balance for the period are closed (zeroed out) at the end of a specific accounting period?

5 What accounting principle prevents the cost of seasonal influenza vaccine being raised when there is a national shortage and the market value of these vaccines is certainly much higher?

6 Describe the reasons an investor might choose preferred stock over common stock.

7 Which of the following accounting principles states that some form of evidence, or reference, is used when accounting transactions are recorded?
A Conservatism principle
B Objectivity principle
C Materiality principle
D Going concern principle

8 By classifying itself as a non-profit business, a company is explicitly stating it will not generate a profit. True or false?

9 According to which of the following must all business transactions be expressed in monetary terms?
A Historical cost principle
B Cash basis of accounting
C Accrual basis of accounting
D Money measurement concept

10 Discuss the main advantage of owning stock of a corporation rather than being the sole proprietor of a company.

Answers

1 Objectivity is critical to provide appropriate patient care, especially when determining the most effective course of treatment and an appropriate drug regimen. Accordingly, when recording the financial transactions of a company, objectivity also plays an important role. While the money measurement concept reduces a company's financial transactions into monetary terms, estimates must often be made regarding the timing or number of events that will occur in the future. Since profitability is the ultimate measure of a company's success or failure, more subjective, or overly optimistic measurements will tend to distort the true financial health of the company and ultimately result in financial failure.

2 The importance of adhering to GAAP lies in the continuity of the financial information reported in the financial statements. By having a uniform set of guidelines, the users of financial statements can gain some assurance in the fact that the statements from one company are comparable in format and classification of the operating activities in monetary terms, even though the actual operations of companies may be quite diverse. This concept is similar to that of having national guidelines for various disease states. Through the existence of treatment guidelines, patients can expect that their care will be consistent and appropriate regardless of the actual location where they receive treatment.

3 The income statement is often most affected by using the cash basis of accounting instead of the accrual basis of accounting due to what is known as timing differences. These timing differences result from the actual movement of cash from one company's accounts to that of other companies, and recording the corresponding revenues and expenses. The accrual basis of accounting eliminates timing difference by focusing on the recognition of revenue (i.e., the earning process is completed) or the incurring of an expense (i.e., the legal obligation to pay an amount to a creditor) rather than when the cash (or check) is received or paid. If interim reports are used using the cash basis of accounting, monthly net income fluctuations may be quite significant.

4 Since the income statement accounts are maintained to reflect periodic revenues and expenses, the net effect of all the

accumulated balances (i.e., a profit or loss) must be recorded in a permanent or real account on the balance sheet. In this case, the account is called retained earnings, to signify the result of all period's earnings since the inception of the company and its continuous operations.

5   Several accounting principles would prevent the cost of the influenza inventory from being recorded at a higher level when a shortage existed. The historical cost principle primarily applies and does not allow for this asset being recorded at a higher value, as well as the consistency and objectivity principles. The matching principle will effectively account for the increase in the market value of the influenza vaccine through the recording of higher sales revenues that may certainly result from the national vaccine shortage. In turn, the income statement for the period in which the vaccines were administered will show an abnormally high net income, which can be attributed to the seasonal shortage. The conservatism principle will also be in effect, which does not allow for reflecting "anticipated profits" from the national shortage until they actually occur.

6   Preferred stock provides the stockholder with a more predictable dividend payment, which can help them in managing their personal finances. Common stock does not offer this feature; however, the market value can vary significantly over time. When significant increase in the market value of common stock occurs, the stockholder may or may not take advantage of the increased value, based upon their own personal financial goals and knowledge.

7   B is correct: the objectivity principle.

8   The statement is false.

9   D is correct: Money measurement concept.

10 The important concept in the different types of ownership is financial liability. Although the accounting entity assumption provides for a distinct owner of the financial information, liability to those users relying on the integrity of financial statements can differ greatly. In the event of financial loss to users of financial statements, a sole proprietor is often liable for claims that extend beyond the assets of the company and into his or her personal

wealth. Through the incorporation of a company, this liability is limited. The concept of "piercing the corporate veil" comes into play, which in essence legally allows for the corporation to assume all of the liability, as well as rights, that individuals such as the sole proprietor are legally entitled to. What this effectively does is limit the liability of a shareholder in a corporation to the amount invested through the stock purchase. In the event of financial loss to users of the corporation's financial statements, only the corporate assets may be used to satisfy these losses. Personal assets of the individual shareholders may not be used to satisfy any claims of the corporation. This advantage is the main reason for the corporation being the largest form of ownership of companies.

Glossary

Accounting period principle	The time period for which operating information is gathered and accounts are prepared. This is usually defined as a 1-year period, sometimes called the fiscal year.
Accounts payable	Represents amounts owed by a company for the purchase of goods and services used in the business operations.
Accrual basis accounting	Revenue and expenses are recorded in the period in which they are earned or incurred, regardless of whether cash is received or disbursed.
Balance sheet	Also known as the statement of financial position, this financial statement lists the assets, liabilities, and net worth of a company at a specific point in time.
Balance sheet (real) account	Account that reflects cumulative balances and the effect of all account transactions recorded since the company began operations, often including many periods.
Cash basis accounting	Recording revenue and expenses in the period that they are actually received or expended in cash.

Common stock	The most frequently issued stock, which usually has voting rights, but is not awarded automatic dividends.
Conservatism principle	Accounting estimates, evaluations, and opinions should be made in the fairest manner possible. Aggressive estimates, based upon current business activity levels, should be adjusted, as well as too conservative estimates.
Consistency principle	Accounting procedures, including the use of similar estimation techniques, are used during the entire accounting period as well as for future periods. This allows the users of financial statements to have a level of comfort in the reported information, especially when comparing different time periods.
Corporation	Company that protects the principals, or owners, from liability arising from operations, beyond the amount of their personal investment, which is usually the purchase price of the shares owned by any one individual. Personal assets of the corporation's individual owners cannot be used to satisfy corporation debts.
Cost center	Non-revenue-generating sections of a company considered critical to the optimal performance of the company's overall operations (e.g., home delivery of prescriptions or human resources department).
Financial statement	The financial health of a company is quantified in various written reports, called financial statements. There are four basic financial statements, including the balance sheet, income statement, statement of retained earnings, and statement of cash flows.
For-profit	A company with the intent to generate a profit based upon the basic economic activity provided. The profits of this company type are eventually returned to the shareholders, in the form of dividends, to provide a return on their investment.

Generally Accepted Accounting Principles (GAAP)	Recognized set of accounting procedures, standards, and principles. GAAP serves to provide relevant and reliable information within financial statements regardless of who prepared them, in addition to enabling them to be comparable between different companies.
Going concern principle	All businesses/companies exist to provide goods and/or services and operate for the long term. Business decisions must always assume different time frames, near and long term.
Historical cost principle	Companies must record their economic activities based upon the costs incurred. Provides a point of reference for all financial statement users and appropriate market values may be used in financial analysis when deemed necessary.
Income statement	Also known as the profit and loss statement, this financial statement reflects the results of operating revenues and expenses for a given period of time.
Income statement (nominal) account	Temporary account created, used and then closed to record revenue and expense transactions within a certain period, thereby allowing for an evaluation of the profitability of each period.
Legal entity	A business or company considered an accounting entity. Given this, the information derived from the company's operations belongs to the legal entity itself and is created to serve the needs of owners, employees, and others. The legal entity can be sued, make a profit, pay taxes, or even support a local cause.
Matching principle	Provides for expenses used to generate revenues to be recorded in the same accounting period as revenues are generated.
Materiality principle	If the omission of any financial transaction or information would impair the financial statement user's judgment, then that item would be deemed material and should be properly recorded and reported.

Money measurement concept	All business transactions must be expressed in monetary terms. If an event or transaction cannot be measured in these terms, it will not be included in accounting records.
Non-profit (not-for-profit)	A company whose profits generated are not returned to the owners (as return on investment, dividends, or cash withdrawals). The profits remain as assets to the company in order for it continue with its primary economic activity. Many charities and service organizations have this as their corporate structure; major hospitals and other institutions may also use it. Additionally, non-profit companies are often exempt from income taxes.
Objectivity principle	Some form of evidence, or reference, is used when accounting transactions are recorded. Personal feelings or opinions should not interfere when forming the basis of an accounting entry.
Partnership	A company that has two or more owners. Liability for the business's operations accrues to the business owners or principals according to their share of ownership.
Preferred stock	Usually a non-voting stock, but has specified dividend payments.
Profit center	Those sections of a company that are responsible for producing profits (e.g., the pharmacy department or photo center).
Revenue recognition principle	Revenue must be earned and is earned when the process of providing the goods or services is completed from the business's viewpoint, and the right to receive payment from the customer is also complete, or earned.
Sole proprietorship	A company owned exclusively by one person. Liability for the business's operations accrues to the business owner.
Source document	A physical representation of an economic transaction of a company.

Statement of cash flows

The sources (inflows) and uses (outflows) of cash, classified in three general categories (operating, investing, and financing).

Statement of shareholder's (owner's) equity

Activities that relate to the company's ownership and results of operations during various operating periods.

System of internal control

The "checks and balances" within an accounting system. Must provide for the accurate recording of transactions appropriately authorized, properly maintained recorded data, and the overall assets of the company safeguarded.

3

From detailed transactions to summary reports

Learning objectives

- Define and understand the two different transaction types
- Identify and understand the accounting and expanded accounting equation, where its data originates and how it is reflected in the appropriate financial statements
- Define goodwill and understand its application in pharmacy valuation
- Illustrate the principles of double-entry accounting and, in particular, distinguish a debit and credit

Introduction

Just as the use of medication therapy requires adherence to basic principles and guidelines, e.g., Joint National Committee (JNC) guidelines for hypertension treatment, the accounting profession follows principles (discussed in Chapter 2) which must be implemented in a business in order to provide any meaningful or useful information. However, these principles only provide the foundation for the treatment of individual transactions. This chapter, then, examines the step-wise process of organizing and understanding financial information, from the aforementioned individual transactions up to general summary reports.

Transactions

When examining individual transactions, one must first classify the transaction type into one of two alternatives, either external or internal. *External transactions* are those arising from the company's economic activities with their customers, suppliers, and creditors, and they account for the vast majority of transactions, the bulk typically being sales transactions. Those economic transactions occurring solely within the company are called *internal transactions*. For example, recording the payment of payroll is unique to the company and does not require input from anyone outside the company.

Regardless of whether a transaction is external or internal, each transaction will affect one of five major account classifications. The balance sheet contains three of these classifications, including assets, liabilities, and shareholder's (owner's) equity. *Assets* include everything that the business owns, while *liabilities* represent what the business owes to others, such as creditors. The third classification, *shareholder's (owner's) equity*, represents the net difference between assets and liabilities and is also known as the company's net worth. These three classifications share a relationship represented by the basic accounting equation. These three classifications on the balance sheet, which are referred to as the balance sheet accounts (Figure 3.1), also represent the "real" accounts described in Chapter 2. The income statement accounts, or "nominal" accounts, consist of two classifications, revenues and expenses, and are discussed later in this chapter. Figure 3.2 summarizes these relationships.

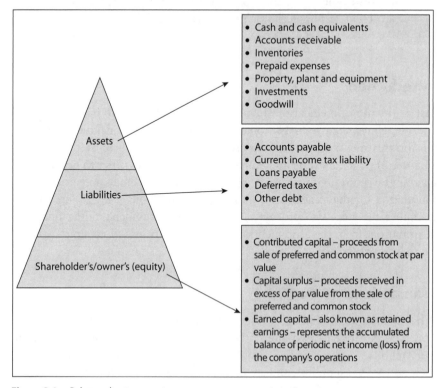

Figure 3.1   Balance sheet accounts.

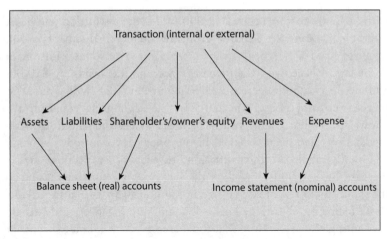

Figure 3.2 Flow of transactions from income statement to balance sheet.

Accounting equation

Fundamental to the organization of all accounting entities, the basic accounting equation is expressed as:

Assets = Liabilities + Owner's equity (sole proprietorship)

Assets = Liabilities + Shareholder's equity (corporation)

The accounting equation is both a conceptual and mathematical representation describing the company's basic financial position at a single time point. In essence, it shows the net effect of the summarized detailed economic transactions in the accounting records which have occurred over time and how these transactions impacted the company's financial position. It is important to note when only balance sheet ("real") accounts are involved, the changes in the various account balances which occur over the course of an operating period simply are a result of a "swap" between classifications. An example of this "swap" would be a reduction in the accounts payable (a liability) when a payment is made to a vendor, as well as the corresponding cash decrease in the bank account (an asset) when the payment is made. This transaction is simply a change of the same magnitude in both the company's assets and liabilities and maintains the equality of the accounting equation. There is no profit recorded as a result of these exchanges in assets.

Case-in-point 3.1   Accounting equation example – institutional pharmacy

In an average medical center, the pharmacy may have five boxes of tenecteplase on hand for proper patient care of myocardial infarctions, with each box costing around $2,000. When the institution purchased these medications for $10,000 cash, the financial statements would have reflected a "vertical swap" *within* the assets classification on the balance sheet, with the inventory account increasing by $10,000 and the cash account decreasing by the same amount, with a net effect of zero on total assets. Alternatively, the accounting equation also allows for a "horizontal swap" *between* assets and liabilities if the medications had been received in the pharmacy on credit, which is commonly done. In this situation, the inventory account would increase by $10,000 as well as the liabilities account increasing by the same amount. Notice that in a horizontal swap, the entire balance sheet increases in total while still maintaining the equality of the accounting equation. Note that the increase in the balance sheet total is not a result of any *service* provided to a patient; it arises simply from a *swap* of assets and liabilities.

The accounting equation forms the basis of the most common financial statement used in business, the balance sheet (see Chapter 4 for a full discussion of the balance sheet). The balance sheet relates assets to liabilities and shareholder's (owner's) equity and provides a snapshot of the company's financial position. The information contained in the balance sheet is used by managers, creditors, and investors alike to establish a picture of the company's financial position. However, depending on the perspective of the balance sheet user, the information deemed most pertinent may be different. Specifically within a pharmacy, managers/pharmacy directors may be more concerned with inventory levels (an asset) or payment terms (a liability) in the day-to-day pharmacy management, while investors are primarily focused on changes over time in shareholder's (owner's) equity, which reflects the net profit or loss from operations. Lenders, on the other hand, usually focus on the liability levels carried by a company in relation to the total assets and the company's ultimate ability to repay its debts.

In addition to the balance sheet accounts, it is important to remember the income statement accounts, as these accounts provide the details of a company's operations from their individual economic activity. Therein lays the importance of the shareholder's (owner's) equity account, which reflects activities of ownership as well as the net profit or loss from operations at the end of each operating period. The official classification for the periodic earnings is retained earnings, since essentially they are "retained" in this account as the company continues operations over future periods. Retained earnings contains the cumulative effect of all prior periods' earnings from the income statement, as well as contributions from shareholders to start the company, keep it running or fund expansion. However, for simplicity, retained earnings will be referred to as earned capital.

Furthermore, a different type of capital, contributed capital, is another component of the shareholder's (owner's) equity account. Contributed capital represents the proceeds from the owners (or shareholders within a corporation) investing in the company. When a company issues and sells preferred and common stock, the proceeds are recorded in these two accounts based upon the par value of the individual stock certificates. Any amounts received in excess of par value are recorded in the capital surplus account. It is important to note that only the original sale of stock by the company to investors is recorded. Future sales, or trading in the stock market, represent transactions between current and potential owners of the shares of a company's stock, and these transactions are not recorded in the company's accounting records.

Expanded accounting equation

Since the balance sheet reflects the activities and resulting amounts of those specific accounts, another financial statement is needed to reflect the revenue and expense activities. The income statement accounts are used to record the business activity of only a specific period of time (discussed in Chapter 2) and included on the income statement. The income statement is based on the equation:

Revenues – Expenses = Net income (loss)

Since businesses want to make a profit, the difference between revenues and expenses is expected to be positive. However, if this difference is negative, it represents a loss to the company and is shown in brackets.

Case-in-point 3.2 Income statement equation – continuation of institutional example

Continuing with our medical center tenecteplase example, the income statement equation provides the solution for showing the profit earned when the tenecteplase is used in conjunction with treating a patient. Assume that the patient's medical insurance company is billed for $3,500, generating the institution $3,500 of revenue. Remember, the associated cost of the medication is $2,000. The income statement equation results in a net income of $1,500 (ignoring all other expenses such as staffing, overheads, etc.). Note that there is no revenue or expense as a result of simply purchasing the inventory (the swap of assets and liabilities); rather they occur as a result of providing a service to the patient.

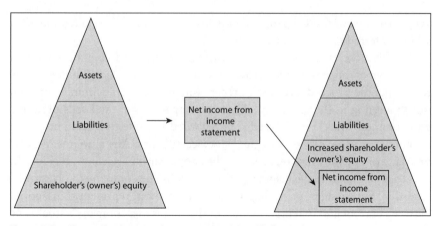

Figure 3.3 Connection between income statement and balance sheet.

Thus, the initial accounting equation (earlier in this chapter) in its simplest format consists of only the balance sheet accounts at a specific point in time, while in the real world companies continue to operate on an ongoing basis. The income statement accounts recognize this difference and reflect summarized activity over a period of time. The "connection" between these two equations (Figure 3.3) is reflected in the shareholder's (owner's) equity section on the balance sheet itself, with the net effect of income statement accounts being transferred to the earned equity account on the balance sheet at the end of each operating period.

In essence, the income statement is the report linking the balance sheet from the beginning of a specific accounting period to the end of that accounting period. To bridge the gaps between these two financial statements, the expanded accounting equation may be used to help understand the complete realm of activity for company's operations over an accounting period. The expanded accounting equation is:

$$\text{Assets} = \text{Liabilities} + \text{Equity} + \text{Revenues} - \text{Expenses}$$

When the economic activities or transactions involve a change to both the balance sheet and income statement accounts, the expanded accounting equation is needed to follow the effect. For example, a sale on credit (i.e., cash payment to be received at a later date) is recorded as both sales revenue (an income statement account) and an accounts receivable (a balance sheet account). A corresponding entry is also needed to properly match the reduction in the inventory account (a balance sheet account) for the goods sold and to record the corresponding cost of goods sold (an income statement account) and fully reflect all the accounts affected by this one sale transaction. Figure 3.4 shows the process.

Example:
Assume the sale of a prescription for $100 with third party insurance. (1)
The inventory cost of this prescription sale is $80. (2)

Assets = Liabilities   +   Shareholders /   + Revenues   –   Expense
                                Owner Equity

(1) Accounts Receivables (Asset↑) $100 ⟷ Revenue (↑) $100
(2) Inventory (Asset↓)   -$80   ⟷ Drug Cost (COGS – Expense↑)-$80

Shareholder / Owner Equity $20   Net Income $20

Note: the net effect on the balance sheet accounts is an increase of $20
and the income statement account increased by this same amount.

Figure 3.4   Effect of transactions between the income statement and the balance sheet.

When using the expanded accounting equation to reflect these entries, the difference in the income statement account amounts will show the profit (or loss) on the sale immediately. Alternatively, if the original accounting equation was used, it would be necessary to wait for the accounting period to end and allow the income statement accounts to "close," whereby the net effect of all income statement accounts activity would be reflected in earned capital account, which is a subset of the shareholder's equity account.

There are two additional adjustments necessary to obtain an expanded accounting equation that fully reflects all transactions of a company, not just those derived from the basic economic activities of operations. First, the transactions that reflect changes in ownership of the company are also recorded within the shareholder's (owner's) equity section under the contributed capital account. These types of transactions occur infrequently and include sale of additional shares of stock or the repurchase of existing shares that are currently being traded in the stock market. Secondly, the return of net income (profits) to the shareholders in form of dividends is also an infrequent, but necessary transaction to include in a fully expanded accounting equation. Declaring dividends, along with their subsequent payment to stockholders are income statement transactions. The fully expanded accounting equation is:

Assets = Liabilities + Equity + Revenues – Expenses
             – Dividends + Contributed capital from sale or
             repurchase of company stock

By more closely examining this equation, starting with the balance sheet accounts, one can see the equality of accounts was maintained, even when the effect of the income statement accounts was included. Transactions affecting contributed capital and return of capital also must be included.

Table 3.1 Example of goodwill computation

	Pharmacy A	Pharmacy B
Net assets	$5,000,000	$5,000,000
Generally accepted rate of return for this industry	15%	15%
Expected rate of return on assets	$750,000	$750,000
Expected net income	$750,000	$800,000
Expected net income above average	$0	$50,000

Goodwill

Of particular interest to pharmacy professionals interested in buying or selling a pharmacy business is the concept of *goodwill*, which is generally included on the balance sheet as an intangible asset. Figure 3.1 presented examples of some of the more common accounts that are usually present on a balance sheet. Goodwill reflects the portion of a company's value not related to the historical cost of its assets or liabilities, and attempts to quantify the subjective amount representing the company's ability to make future profits in excess of established industry norms. It is important to note that the determination of goodwill is done only when an entire company is being purchased. Goodwill is represented by the formula:

Goodwill = Purchase price – Fair market value of net identifiable assets

In Table 3.1, companies A and B are shown with selected financial estimates. Company B currently has redesigned their store and included a drive-through window, which is expected to add additional sales and profits. Other factors affecting the estimated value of goodwill in a pharmacy business may include a particularly favorable location, pharmacy staff quality, the business's reputation in the community or even a unique product/service offering.

Pharmacy professionals seeking to sell or purchase a pharmacy business examine goodwill from the perspective that it estimates any inherent value of the business when compared with the identifiable assets and liabilities. In this example, pharmacy B may expect to have above-average earnings of $50,000 for the next 4 years; therefore, a reasonable goodwill estimate would be $200,000. Conversely, the current owner of pharmacy B expects the above-average earnings to continue indefinitely; therefore, dividing the $50,000 by the current industry rate of return of 15% would yield an estimated goodwill of $333,333 ($50,000/15%). Regardless of the method of computation, final determination of goodwill is established between the owner and the buyer when the final purchase price is ultimately determined.

Double-entry accounting

A transaction has been previously defined as an exchange of economic considerations between two entities, or an exchange between different departments within a single entity. Since all transactions have two components, the *double-entry accounting* concept helps us understand this duality and enables the proper recording of all transactions into the accounting records. As the name implies, there are always two entries made for each transaction, known as a debit and credit. Within these two entries, two accounts will be affected (i.e., increased or decreased), either balance sheet accounts, income statement accounts, or a combination of both. Consequently, using the double-entry accounting system ensures the equality of the accounting equation at all times.

For example, when paying a vendor account, the amount of decrease in the liability account, called *accounts payable*, is equal to the decrease in the *cash in bank account*. The accounting equation therefore remains balanced, as the asset side decreases in the exact amount as the liability account on the equation's other side. The term *journal entry* is used to represent the actual recording of a transaction (or a summary of the many of the same type of transactions) as both a debit and a credit in the appropriate account. All transactions within a business entity for an accounting period are recorded with journal entries. The operations of a company usually serve as the basis of the transactions needing to be recorded through the production of source documents.

In a community pharmacy, dispensing a prescription provides a transaction that needs recorded. Assuming the patient pays cash for a prescription, the journal entry necessary is as follows:

Left side (debit)   *increases*   Cash in bank $XXX

Right side (credit)   *increases*   Prescription sales $XXX

Notice that this entry contained one balance sheet account and one income statement account. Since the income statement reflects the revenue and expense activities of a company, another entry is needed to show the expense portion of the transaction of selling a prescription, shown below:

Left side (debit)   *increase*   Cost of goods sold $XXX

Right side (credit)   *decrease*   Inventory $XXX

Note that with the two entries completed, the income statement accounts represent both revenues received and corresponding expenses being incurred.

Within the balance sheet accounts, there was an exchange of one asset (inventory) for another (cash).

There are a variety of different source documents, such as invoices, cash or credit payment receipts, purchase orders, etc., which reflect the actual economic events that occurred and serve as the source of various journal entries. These documents provide a permanent record of the transaction details needed in the accounting records. Again, the money measurement concept allows all transactions to be assigned a monetary value, which is then recorded into the accounting records. Given the detailed transactions are quite voluminous, computers aid in the summarization of all activity reflected in the financial statements.

Debits and credits

As just discussed, double-entry accounting requires two entries for each transaction. Therefore, accounts are designed with two sides, or columns, that will reflect either an increase or a decrease in the account balance for each transaction recorded within a specific account. There is also a designation for the account name, final balance, and an explanation of the transaction being recorded. By definition, an entry on the left column of an account is called a *debit* (abbreviated dr), and an entry on the right column of an account is called a *credit* (abbreviated cr). The double-entry accounting concept, in conjunction with the expanded accounting equation, demands that a credit perform the opposite function of a debit within each individual account. Each account has its own "base" reference, meaning there is an expected balance on either the left or the right side, which is then referred to as a debit or credit balance for that account. To begin to understand the effects entries have on either increasing or decreasing an account balance, let us rearrange the expanded accounting equation:

$$\text{Assets} + \text{Expenses} = \text{Liabilities} + \text{Shareholder's equity} + \text{Revenues}$$

Since a debit is a transaction recorded on the left side of an account, by definition debits will reflect an addition to any asset or expense account, as they appear on the left hand side of the accounting equation. Therefore, increases in balance sheet accounts and income statement accounts are a result of debits to assets and expenses. Conversely, given that the accounting equation must remain balanced at all times, it is implicit that decreases to assets or expense accounts will occur with transactions recorded on the right side of an account, which are known as credits. Carrying the simplicity of the accounting equation further, by definition, a left side entry to an account (debit) must decrease a liability, shareholder's (owner's) equity, or revenue account. Again, the converse it also true. A right side entry to an account (credit) will, by definition, reflect an addition to any liability, shareholder's (owner's)

Table 3.2 Effects of debits and credits on accounts					
Entry	**Assets**	**Liabilities**	**Shareholder's (owner's) equity**	**Revenues**	**Expenses**
Debits	Increased	Decreased	Decreased	Decreased	Increased
Credits	Decreased	Increased	Increased	Increased	Decreased

Assets = Liabilities + Shareholder's (owner's) equity + Revenues − Expenses.

equity, or revenue account. To maintain the equality of the expanded accounting equation, the opposite for each example noted above is required. A credit reflects a reduction from an asset or expense account, since they are on the left of the equal sign in the accounting equation. Table 3.2 provides a summary of the effect of debits and credits on balance sheet and income statement accounts – noting that for assets and expenses, debit and credit effects are mirrored. The same can also be said for liabilities, shareholder's equity, and revenues.

Case-in-point 3.3   Journal entries

Does a journal have to have an entry on both sides of the equal sign of the accounting equation? Absolutely not! Remember our example of purchasing flu vaccine for immunizations in the future months? That entry required an increase entry (or debit) to the inventory account (an asset) noting the receipt of vaccine, as well as a decrease (or credit) entry to the cash account (also an asset) noting the decrease of cash for payment of the flu vaccine. This entry is a swap of two types of assets, but still followed the rules of the double-entry concept. This was previously referred to as a "swap" of assets, with one asset account increasing by the same magnitude as the decrease in another asset account. Remember, since both of the affected accounts were asset accounts, the accounting equation maintained equality with the equal amount of increase in one asset account with the left side entry and the equal amount of decrease in another asset account with the right side of the double entry.

Posting of accounts and journals

Businesses generate many transactions on a daily basis, and eventually all of these transactions need to be recorded. *Posting* is the term used to describe the process of recording transactions with debits and credits through the use of journal entries. A journal entry must always include a minimum of two accounts, one for the debit and one for the credit, to maintain the equality of the accounting equation (i.e., net effect of zero).

Case-in-point 3.4   Journal entries

What is an example of a journal entry that records only one transaction yet requires three accounts? A common occurrence would be a prescription sale in a community pharmacy where the patient has insurance, which includes a co-payment at the time of dispensing the prescription and the remaining payment is received from the insurance company at a later date. The journal entry would be as follows:

Left side	(debit)	*increases*	Cash in bank	$20
Left side	(debit)	*increases*	Accounts receivable	$100
Right side	(credit)	*increases*	Prescription sales	$120

Many accounting systems are automated, and employees are not required or expected to prepare or maintain accounting records. The purpose of this section is to provide information on the processes that must follow the activities of a community pharmacist dispensing prescriptions and ordering inventory.

General journal and ledger

Just as physicians, nurses, and pharmacists record all patient data in a chart, all transactions are recorded in what is known as the *general journal*, or book of original entry. The general journal is kept on a daily basis and records entries to various accounts during the accounting period. At the end of an accounting period, the general journal entries are summarized and the information is posted to the general ledger in summary format. A *general ledger* is a listing of all the company's accounts organized by account; beginning with all assets, then liabilities, shareholder's (owner's) equity, revenues, and expenses. The difference between the general journal and the general ledger is simple. The general ledger only has the summary total for an accounting period, whereas the general journal has the entire, voluminous data from the accounting period. This allows for changes to all accounts to be reviewed easily. If the change in a particular account seems peculiar for a certain accounting period, additional detail may be seen in the general journal for that same accounting period. In some instances, the volume of a certain transaction type may be quite voluminous, such as cash receipts or prescription sales, and specialized journals, specific to the transaction type, are often used. Specialized journals are summarized at the end of a shorter accounting period (usually daily) and recorded in the general journal. For transactions to be classified properly according to their economic activity, a chart of accounts is used. The chart of accounts lists all of the different account names contained in the general ledger.

Case-in-point 3.5   Community pharmacy journal entries

What is the benefit of posting information in accounts via a double-entry accounting system? Owing to the volume of information generated through the business activities, this accounting system allows for minimization of large datasets. For example, a daily prescription sales journal can have an average of 300 entries for each day of a particular month. The general journal would then only contain 30 entries, representing the total of each individual day's activities. Finally, the general ledger would have only one entry, representing the summary total of all daily transactions for the 30-day month period.

The format of a general journal, or a specialized journal, is columnar, with a separate column for the date, accounts used, reference number, left side (debit) amount and right side (credit) amount. A sample general journal is illustrated in Figure 3.5. Recording an entry begins with the date and then the name of the account along with the left side amount shown in the "debit" column. Next, the account name containing the right side amount is listed, with the amount shown in the "credit" column. Beneath the account name is a brief description of the transaction details which supports the journal entry. The reference column is left blank until these journal entries are actually recorded or posted in the general ledger. At that time, the account numbers of the individual accounts used are referenced.

Trial balance and general ledger

Although the double-entry accounting process may seem simple, mistakes may, and often, do happen. One of the ways errors may be detected prior to preparing financial statements is through the use of a trial balance. The *trial balance* is simply the final left side (debit) or right side (credit) balance of all the general ledger accounts. The total of all debits must equal the total of all credits, or one or more of the journal entries must have been posted incorrectly.

The trial balance is not foolproof. Although the total of all debit balances equals the total of all credit balances, individual account classifications may

Any Pharmacy, Inc. General journal			
Date	Account title and explanation	Debit $	Credit $
03/01/XX	Rent expense	2,500.00	
	Cash		2,500.00
	To record payment of monthly		
	rent		
03/10/XX	Accounts receivable	12,345.67	
	Prescription department sales		12,345.67
	To record third party		
	prescription sales		
03/15/XX	Inventory	5,432,10	
	Accounts payable		5,432.10
	To record drug order received		
	on credit from wholesaler		
03/15/XX	Salaries expenses	18,656.32	
	Cash		18,656.32
	To record bi-monthly payroll		
03/24/XX	Accounts payable	5,432.10	
	Cash		5,432.10
	To record payment to wholesaler		
	for purchases on account		

Figure 3.5 Sample general journal.

be incorrect. For example, the debit entry for cash received from the sale of OTC products may have been recorded to another asset account, such as accounts receivable, while the credit portion was correctly recorded to OTC sales. Even though the trial balance would reflect equality, the cash in bank account and accounts receivable account balances are respectively understated and overstated by the same amount.

Once the trial balance is prepared, the general ledger is closed for the period and financial statements are prepared. To begin the closing process, adjusting and closing entries are prepared. For simplicity's sake, the adjusting entries are made by the accounting department to properly reflect account balances on an accrual basis and correct any obvious errors noted up to this point. Closing entries are needed to reflect all the activity of the income statement accounts for the period and transfer the net result to the balance sheet account earned capital (retained earnings), which is part of the shareholder's (owner's) equity section of the balance sheet.

T accounts

Knowing pharmacy managers are not accountants, there is a way for them to be effective in the financial management of their workplace. Armed with basic knowledge of accounting principles and the accounting equation already discussed, the tool known as a T account can help a pharmacy manager predict the financial impact of projected scenarios in a relatively simple and quick manner.

A T account, such as in Figure 3.6, consists of three basic elements: an account title, a left side (for debits), and a right side (for credits). For each anticipated transaction, the transaction amount is recorded on the appropriate side of the "T". When all transactions of a particular scenario have been recorded in the necessary T accounts, the final balance is determined by drawing a line across the bottom. The left (debit) and right (credit) sides are totaled, including any beginning balances, with the final balance shown on the appropriate side. It is important to note that any account may have a balance on either side. For example, although the asset account cash in bank should have a debit balance (indicating there is a positive cash balance actually in the bank), the T account analysis might show a credit balance. This would mean the account will be overdrawn at the bank when every check already written clears the bank. Fortunately, this analysis enables the pharmacy manager to take corrective action, possibly before there is chaos at the bank because of "bounced" employee paychecks. Remember, there are five basic types of accounts and each has an expected debit or credit balance: assets (debit),

Account name	
Left side (debits)	Right side (credits)
Beginning balance	May exist on either side
Transaction activity	Transaction activity
Ending balance	May exist on either side

Figure 3.6 Elements of a T account.

liabilities (credit), and owner's equity (credit), comprising the balance sheet accounts, and revenues (credit), and expenses (debit), which are the income statement accounts. Fortunately, many software programs are used to create and maintain accounting records and produce informative reports without extensive input from the pharmacy managers.

Summary

In this chapter, the accounting process associated with going from a specific transaction to various summary reports has been explained. Specifically, the external and internal transactions work to make up the various balance sheet ("real") accounts or the income statement ("nominal") accounts. These all feed into the general accounting equation and form the basis of the key documents reviewed by managers, that is, financial statements. Pharmacy managers should use this accounting background information to form a knowledge base of how their financial information should be categorized (transaction or account type), recorded (debit or credit), and then reviewed.

Suggested reading

Chisholm-Burns MA, Vaillancourt AM, Shepherd M. *Pharmacy Management, Leadership, Marketing, and Finance*. Sudbury, MA: Jones & Bartlett Publishers, 2011.

Carroll NV. *Financial Management for Pharmacists: a Decision-Making Approach*, 3rd edn. Baltimore, MD: Lippincott Williams & Wilkins, 2007.

Friedlob GT, Plewa FJ. *Financial and Business Statements*, 3rd edn. Hauppauge, NY: Barron's Educational Series Inc., 2006.

Warren CS, Reeve JM, Duchac JE. *Accounting*, 23rd edn. New York, NY: Random House, 2008.

Walther L. *Principles of Accounting*. Logan, UT: Utah State University. www.principlesofaccounting.com.

Review questions

1 Explain the difference between balance sheet (real) and income statement (nominal) accounts as they relate to the income statement and balance sheet.

2 Describe how the information presented in the income statement differs from information provided on the balance sheet.

3 Explain why credits increase certain account types and decrease others.

4 Cook's Pharmacy has done exceeding well over the past 5 years since its owner opened the pharmacy. Located near one of the busiest downtown intersections, yet, having ample parking, Mr. Cook has

managed to grow the business to over $1.5 million in total sales in this short period of time. Net income has also been favorable at about $75,000 this year. Customers flock to Cook's because it is the only pharmacy in the area where the employees seem to be concerned with solving your problems, which is a direct result of Mr. Cook's strong leadership. With a decline in health, Mr. Cook now finds himself in a position where he needs to sell the pharmacy. Describe how you would arrive at a figure for "goodwill" and explain the positive and negative pressures impacting your figure.

5   Contrast the general journal and general ledger.

6   In all T accounts, credits are on the left and debits are on the right. True or false?

7   Goodwill is a very objective figure and easily identified in pharmacy valuation. True or false?

8   In the basic accounting equation, assets are equal to liabilities plus owner's equity. True or false?

9   The trial balance is a foolproof method of ensuring all debits and credits are recorded properly. True or false?

10   A good example of an internal transaction is the payment of company payroll. True or false?

Answers

1   The real, or balance sheet accounts, represent permanent accounts and reflect the current financial position of a company at any specific point in time. On the other hand, the income statement (nominal) accounts are temporary accounts, used to accumulate the results of transactions over a specific period of time. At the end of each accounting period, the income statement (nominal) account balances are transferred (closed or zeroed out) to the balance sheet (real) accounts. The balance sheet is a permanent record, whereas the income statement reflects periodic activity only.

2   The income statement reflects transactions over a period of time and provides information on the various categories of economic activity of a company. The balance sheet represents a snapshot of the assets, liabilities, and shareholder's (owner's) equity at a specific point in time.

3   Double-entry accounting requires that all transactions affect at least two accounts. Therefore, to maintain the equality of the accounting equation, when there is an increase on one side of the equation, there must be a corresponding increase on the opposite side of the equation. Convention dictates that debits increase the left side of any account and credits increase the right side of any account. Maintaining equality of the accounting equation results in the fact that debits and credits affect specific accounts differently.

4   Goodwill is defined as the purchase price less the fair market value of net identifiable assets. Clearly, in a sole proprietorship, there is an unusually large component of personal bias in the overall evaluation of the business. Values of the buildings, inventory, and condition of the store can be obtained with some degree of objectivity from outside consultants. However, when it comes to the value of customer service in generating the revenues, and resulting profitability of the pharmacy, there may be personal bias, depending on the evaluator. Mr. Cook, as an active member of the pharmacy leadership team, may feel his value is extremely high and "the business could not run without him." Practically, this is not true especially if the staff is well trained. Continued customer loyalty can be called into question with the absence of Mr. Cook. In the final analysis, goodwill will only be recognized by the new owner if the purchase price exceeds the value of the physical assets of the business as reflected on the balance sheet.

5   The general journal, or book of original entry, is where all detailed transactions are recorded. It is kept on a daily basis and records entries to various accounts during the accounting period. Whereas the general ledger is a listing of all the company's accounts organized by account; beginning with all assets, then liabilities, shareholder's (owner's) equity, revenues, and expenses. This has the summary information for an accounting period and cumulative balances as of a particular date for balance sheet (real) accounts.

6   The statement is false.

7   The statement is false.

8   The statement is true.

9   The statement is false.

10   The statement is true.

Glossary

Assets	Includes everything that the business owns.
Double-entry accounting	Helps us understand the duality of all transactions and enables proper recording into the accounting records. As the name implies, there will always be two entries made for each transaction, a debit and a credit.
External transaction	Transactions that arise from the economic activities of the company with their customers, suppliers, and creditors and account for the vast majority of transactions. Sales transactions usually account for the bulk of any company's external transactions.
General journal	Where all transactions are recorded; also called the book of original entry. It is kept on a daily basis and records entries to various accounts during the accounting period.
General ledger	A listing of all the company's accounts organized by account; beginning with all assets, then liabilities, owner's equity, revenues, and expenses. This has the summary total for an accounting period and cumulative balances as of a particular date for balance sheet (real) accounts.
Goodwill	Reflects the portion of a business's value not related to the historical cost of its assets or liabilities. Rather, it attempts to quantify the subjective amount, which represents the company's ability to make future profits in excess of established industry norms.
Internal transaction	Economic transactions occurring solely within the company. For example, recording the payment of payroll is unique to the company and does not require any input from anyone outside the company.
Journal entry	Represents the actual recording of a transaction (or a summary of the same type of transactions) as both a debit and credit in the appropriate account. All transactions within a business entity for an accounting period are recorded with journal entries.

Liabilities   Represents what the business owes to others, such as creditors.

Posting   The process of recording transactions with debits and credits though the use of journal entries.

Shareholder (owner's) equity   Represents the net difference between assets and liabilities and is also known as the company's net worth. May also be referred to as retained earnings, net worth, owner's equity, or just simply equity, depending on the company's structure and needs.

Trial balance   The final debit or credit balance of all the general ledger accounts. The total of all of the debits must equal the total of all of the credits, or one or more of the journal entries must have been posted incorrectly.

4

Financial statements

Learning objectives

- Describe the two different sets of financial statements users and their analytical focus
- Identify and describe the four basic financial statements
- Describe and understand the primary components of the four basic financial statements and their implication on the business's success or failure
- Apply the principles and knowledge from the four financial statements to a community pharmacy case

Introduction

The preceding chapters provided a basic understanding of how all of a business's economic activities are reduced to monetary value, recorded in a consistent and logical process, and then summarized. From the summarized information, various reports are created and designed to reflect the results of a company's various transactions in a useful and meaningful format. These reports are known as financial statements and are common to all companies, even pharmacies and other healthcare institutions. Remember that the accounting principles previously discussed are applied by all companies and are there to provide continuity between the basic statements themselves, as well as with companies in similar business sectors.

Before the different financial statements are explored, it is important to recognize the distinct sets of business operations information users. Of primary importance are the *external users*, who, as defined in Chapter 2, are those who are not a part of the daily business operations, including creditors, shareholders, and prospective buyers of existing pharmacy businesses, from one independent community pharmacy to the acquisition of an entire regional chain pharmacy. Conversely, *internal users* are those individuals who are intimately involved with the daily business operations and consist of employees, managers or owners.

Internal users

The role of accounting in providing information to internal users is often referred to as *managerial accounting*. Management reports serve all levels of an organization and, as such, these types of reports and financial statements are unique to each company. Managerial reporting is designed to enable an understanding of the company's intricate operations and allow informed decision making by management. Review of the company's operations from this perspective is vital, as managers can take corrective action to quickly prevent further problems; or they may rest comfortably with the knowledge operations are proceeding as planned. Summary internal operating performance reports, budgets, and financial statements are critical for executive level managers to assess performance and help guide the company's future direction.

Detailed information on sales and inventory cost reports are supplied to sales managers on a regular basis so as to understand the company's current market share and market conditions as a whole. Timely information and analysis can result in rapid turnaround of poor performance areas. The finance department relies upon accounting reports to help analyze company cash flow, while payroll information regarding the amount of work performed by all of the company's employees is needed by the human resources department. Within a specific company, the reporting information design and frequency is tailored to meet the managers' needs and should be changed when deficiencies are noted or warranted improvements are suggested.

Case-in-point 4.1   Internal users – institutional setting

An institutional pharmacy manager may routinely receive on a monthly basis the pharmacy departmental income statement and inventory activity. However, most computer systems allow for this pharmacy manager to receive information on an "as needed" basis. With this capability, the pharmacy manager can track trends in prescription order entry by the hour, day, week, or the entire month to determine the most cost-efficient staffing of his pharmacists in order to provide the best patient care.

External users

External users are those who have interests outside the daily company operations, and where economic viability and overall operating performance of the company is the primary concern. Therefore, the specific financial reports necessary for external users, identified as investors, creditors, and others, is known as *financial reporting*. For shareholders, profitability is the main focus, given that it increases the probability of dividends being paid and generation of an immediate investment return. Additionally, better financial performance each period also increases the company's market value and, usually, the stock value. As companies often need to borrow funds to maintain efficient operations, creditors evaluate the credit risk through financial statement analysis. Finally, potential investors make the same evaluations before they decide to buy a particular company's stock, or even purchase the entire business. Not only is a particular company evaluated through a review of their financial statements, but the performance of a particular company is often compared to others within the same business sector. Just as there are "norms" when evaluating a patient's blood pressure, so too are commonalities between different business within the same market sector. Therefore, it is crucial that the financial statements discussed in the next section are prepared in a comparable manner. This is achieved through the standardization of each statement's formats, guided by frameworks such as GAAP and authoritative boards such as FASB, as well as the application of the 10 basic accounting principles.

Four basic financial statements

The following sections discuss the purpose and basic format for each of the four basic financial statements used by companies, which include the balance sheet, income statement, statement of owner's equity, and statement of cash flows. Each of these statements is prepared at the end of a reporting period and is usually shown with the previous period's results for comparison purposes. Knowing the results of operations in previous periods can provide valuable information into understanding the current period's results. Although it is not necessary to be an expert in the actual development of each statement, a fundamental understanding of each statement can enable better decision making.

Balance sheet

The *balance sheet*, as defined by the basic accounting equation, is simply a listing of all of a company's assets, liabilities, and owner's equity accounts at a specific point in time. Also known as the statement of financial position, the main function is to portray the company's net worth (difference between assets and liabilities) at any moment in time and, therefore, is always dated "as of" a specific date. This "snapshot" is useful in analyzing a company's current position. By following both the historical cost and conservatism principles, the balance sheet amounts reflect the historic cost of items, or the amount actually paid, in the assets section or the agreed amount to be paid in the liabilities section. Even though the current market values for various items on the balance sheet may significantly change over time, nothing is reflected on the balance sheet until an actual economic transaction occurs. The balance sheet may be a single column, or consist of two columns, with the assets shown on the left side and liabilities and shareholder's equity on the right side. According to the accounting equation, the totals of each column should be equal. A *liability* represents a claim against a business and arises through the ordinary course of business. The importance of the balance sheet can be seen from a potential creditor's viewpoint, where the company's overall credit risk is assessed. The lower the total liabilities are, especially in relation to total assets, the lower the credit risk. Another way of thinking is the company has a larger "cushion" between what is owned and what is owed. The final component of the balance sheet is the *equity*, defined as the residual amount in company assets after all liabilities have been deducted, and also sometimes referred to as net worth. The following paragraphs describe the design and purpose of the balance sheet.

Assets

As Figure 4.1 shows, assets represent future economic potential for a company and may be owned outright or have an associated loan or mortgage. While many think assets are simply all the tangible items a company legally owns, intangible assets, or assets the company has a legal right to, are also listed (e.g., patents for medications). Company value is great, but often difficult to quantify; therefore, while a value is included on the balance sheet, only the costs incurred in the patent acquisition are recorded, providing the proper application of the conservatism, objectivity and historical cost principles.

To provide comparability for users of financial statements, the balance sheet follows a classification system based upon certain common characteristics. The first of these characteristics is *liquidity*, or ease of conversion to cash without a loss in value of the assets. Therefore, cash will be listed first. Within each asset category, it is important to note the expected life of the asset to the company also comes into play and the terms "current" and "long term" are used. *Current assets* are usually those assets that are expected to be consumed or converted to cash in less than a year, which also often corresponds to one operating cycle. Referring to the cash account, sometimes cash is invested into vehicles, such as certificates of deposit or notes receivable, which either have a maturity of greater than a year or it is the intent of management to hold these investments for an indefinite period of time. Therefore, those with a maturity date of less than a year would be included in the cash section, sometime expanded to cash and cash equivalents, with the

Sample Pharmacy Balance sheet As of December 31,	2011	2010
Assets		
Current assets		
Cash and cash equivalents	$525,321	$487,321
Short term investments	357,159	214,635
Accounts receivable, net	1,451,987	1,632,541
Inventory	858,654	963,258
Prepaid insurance	198,456	156,753
Other current assets	321,754	298,521
Property, plant, and equipment		
Land and buildings	385,000	385,000
Machinery and equipment	652,412	485,325
Office furniture	98,521	65,123
Total	1,135,933	935,448
Accumulated depreciation	(852,741)	(798,654)
Net PPE	283,192	136,794
Total assets	$3,996,523	$3,889,823
Liabilities and shareholder's (owner's) equity		
Current liabilities		
Accounts payable	1,321,478	1,198,231
Notes payable	852,555	965,147
Other current liabilities	275,354	306,252
Total current liabilities	$2,449,387	$2,469,630
Long term debt	695,647	433,307
Shareholder's (owner's) equity		
Common stock (contributed capital), no par value, 100,000 shares issued and outstanding	200,000	200,000
Retained earnings (earned capital)	651,486	786,886
Total liabilities and shareholder's (owner's) equity	$3,996,520	$3,889,823

Figure 4.1 Sample balance sheet.

remaining items classified further down the line in long-term assets under investments.

Accounts receivable, which represents the future receipt of cash from a customer as a result of a completed sale, is a classification common to many companies and listed next. For pharmacies expecting insurance reimbursements for medications or services previously provided, the expected payment is usually 30 days or less. The term "net" is often used in conjunction with accounts receivable. When dealing with thousands of customers, a company will encounter several who temporarily do not have the ability to pay on time, and may actually never pay on some amounts owed to the company. The credit manager reviews the various operating reports showing amounts sold and the corresponding due dates. Based upon historical performance, an amount is usually deemed to be uncollectible in the future, and is expressed as a percentage of current sales. The matching and conservatism principles help guide this decision, with the bad debt expense shown on the income statement for the current operating period, and a reserve for bad debts account, known as a *contra account*, established in the same amount. A contra account provides the users with more information than if the amounts from the two accounts are simply netted together. However, for the balance sheet presentation, the reserve for bad debts is netted against the total accounts receivable balance and the notes to the financial statements provide additional details to readers.

The next asset listed is inventory, which can represent a significant portion of total assets and is also listed in the current assets section. The inventory balance consists of the value of those items available for sale. While inventory management is discussed further in Chapter 6, it is important to note that companies usually strive to sell and then replace the entire stock of inventory several times within a year, which qualifies placement in the current assets section. However, as there is no express promise to buy any of the inventory, this account is deemed less liquid than accounts receivable and is therefore listed after accounts receivable.

Other current assets consist of a variety of other resources that a company owns. One common amount in this account is prepaid insurance. Most insurance policies are paid in advance for the following year, and, under the matching principle, provide a benefit to more than one operating period. The entire premium is shown in the prepaid insurance account and reduced by the expired amount representing the actual operating period expense. Other current assets include office and store supplies when volumes exceed the usual amounts to be consumed in the current operating period.

The next major asset classification is long-term assets, which include investments, property and equipment, intangibles, and other assets having an expectation to benefit the company over several operating cycles. Property and equipment consists of all buildings, furniture, computers, and the like used to run the company's operations.

Within the property and equipment classification, an important concept associated with the matching principle must be noted. Since the economic benefit to the company arises from the "usage" of these assets during future periods, an attempt must be made to match that economic benefit to those future periods. *Depreciation expense* is used to allocate these asset acquisition costs to future periods. There are several allocation methods available, the most common being the straight-line method of depreciation.

When a particular asset is purchased, the economic life must be estimated, such as 5 years for a new computer system. The cost of the computer system would be divided by five, and the result is known as the depreciation expense for each future 1-year period. Depreciation expense is a nominal account and, therefore, recorded on the income statement. However, a real (balance sheet) account, accumulated depreciation, is also required to complete the double entry of this transaction. Since directly reducing the original computer system asset account by the amount of depreciation expense each year would distort the historical cost shown on the balance sheet, the accumulated depreciation account is listed directly under property and equipment and contains the total depreciation expense incurred since the acquisition of the computer system.

To accurately depict the computer system's worth, a *net book value*, or the net difference between the original acquisition costs of the computer system less the accumulated depreciation balance, is determined, for example:

- A $10,000 computer system would have an annual depreciation expense of $2,000 ($10,000 ÷ 5 years of economic life)
- Year 2: accumulated depreciation account = $4,000
  Computer's net book value = $6,000
- Year 3: accumulated depreciation account = $6,000
  Computer's net book value = $4,000
- Year 4: accumulated depreciation account = $8,000
  Computer's net book value = $2,000
- Year 5: accumulated depreciation account = $10,000
  Computer's net book value = $0

For intangible assets, the term *amortization expense* is used in the same manner as depreciation expense. As noted in the accounts receivable account, the term "net" may also be used to reflect the ending depreciated balance on the balance sheet; however, the details of the depreciation expense calculation and the accumulated depreciation is provided in the notes section of financial statements.

Case-in-point 4.2   Depreciation in the hospital setting

Your hospital has just acquired a robot to help manage patient medications. It was purchased and installed at a cost of $1,000,000. As pharmacy manager, you have decided that, based upon the manufacturer's literature for the robot, it is expected to be running for 10 years. Using the straight-line method of depreciation, what would the net book value of the robot be after 3 years of service? Answer: $700,000. The original cost of $1,000,000, divided by 10, results in $100,000 depreciation expense per year. After 3 years, the accumulated depreciation account balance would be $300,000 which, subtracted from the original $1,000,000 acquisition cost, results in $700,000.

While the straight-line method of depreciation is often used, sometimes the asset depreciation is not justifiable as being even each year over its useful life. Therefore, accelerated methods attempt to match the useful life of the asset in a more meaningful way. First, the declining balance method uses a depreciation rate each year which is applied to the book value of an asset and determines the annual depreciation. Since the book value of the asset will decline each year by the amount of the prior year's depreciation, the depreciation expense also decreases in each additional year of use of the asset. The depreciation rate used in the declining balance method may not exceed twice the amount as normally would be taken under the straight-line method. In addition, the units of production method assigns productivity, expressed in hours of operation or miles driven, to the estimated useful life of the asset. The amount consumed in any one operating period is taken as a percentage of the total estimate. Beyond the scope of this text, there are often mandated systems from governmental taxing agencies, which attempt to restrict companies which inappropriately accelerate depreciation expense in order to reduce net income and incur lower taxes.

Case-in-point 4.3   Declining balance method

Referring back to the dispensing robot within a hospital setting, the declining balance method may be set at 20% annually, given the extensive rate of new technology in this area. Therefore, during the first year of operation, the depreciation expense would be $200,000 ($1,000,000 × 0.20), and the net book value would be $800,000. During the second and third years of operations, the depreciation expense would be $160,000 ($800,000 × 0.20) and $128,000 ($640,000 × 0.20), respectively. After the 3-year period, the net book value is $512,000, which is significantly less than the $700,000 net book value determined using the straight-line depreciation method. While both methods may be allowed under GAAP, the one that yields a net book value closer to the current market value for used robots should ultimately be the method used to reflect a more accurate balance sheet.

Liabilities and shareholder's equity

Having completed the listing of all asset accounts, the balance sheet continues with the right side of the accounting equation, where the liabilities and shareholder's equity classifications are shown.

Liabilities are those amounts that are owed by the company to others as a result of the various transactions which have occurred over time. Just as the asset side of the balance sheet made a distinction between current and long-term items, so must the equity side. The expectation of having to make payment within the next operating cycle forms the basis for each liability's classification. The most common liability classification is called *accounts payable*, and consists of payments not yet made for inventory, utilities, and other operating expenses. Most items included in accounts payable have due dates of 30 days or less. Within long-term liabilities, items such as notes payable, bonds payable, and other long-term contingencies may be listed. Since most notes and bonds payable have a portion due within the next operating cycle, that amount is usually shown as a current portion of long-term debt in the current liabilities section. Notes payable are created when a company expressly promises to pay another company and executes a promissory note, which includes a payment schedule usually requiring a current and long-term portion be recorded on the balance sheet. Bonds payable are also used as debt instruments by companies. However, whereas a promissory note is usually with one bank or creditor, a bond payable is issued in $1,000 increments and sold to many different lenders. Again, the bond issue payment schedule usually requires a current and long-term portion be recorded on the balance sheet.

Finally, the shareholder's equity section is presented. There are two distinct sections within the shareholder's equity section: *preferred and common stock* (contributed capital) and *retained earnings* (earned capital).

Preferred and common stock

A company sells its stock to raise capital and operate the company while giving partial ownership of the company in exchange. The shareholder's equity section of the balance sheet accounts for these stock transactions, while the cash received is in the current assets section. The company's capitalization (i.e., the amounts contributed by shareholders) is represented by the balance in this section and is distinctly separated from retained earnings.

Retained earnings

Retained earnings are defined as the company's cumulative net earnings over time that have not been paid out to shareholders in the form of dividends as of the balance sheet date. These earnings have been "retained" by the company. Although retained earnings is a balance sheet (real) account, the balance does represent the cumulative effect of all income statement accounts. Remember, the income statement contains all nominal accounts and at the end of each accounting period, these accounts are all closed, or zeroed out, and the net difference, known as income (or loss), is reflected in retained earnings.

Case-in-point 4.4   Retained earnings (earned capital)

Even though it may seem so, the retained earnings account balance does not reflect a pool of money. Cumulative profits and losses are reflected in this account; however, net income (or loss) does not consist of cash. Why? The accrual basis of accounting mandates revenues and the corresponding expenses incurred to generate them be recorded in the same period in which they are recognized as providing economic benefit to the company. This matching process produces a net income amount that is not the actual amount of cash a company received or paid out during the period. The accounts receivable and accounts payable accounts are used to reflect the timing of the actual receipt and/or payment of cash.

Income statement

The fiscal year, or natural operating cycle, of each company is reflected in the income statement; also known as the profit and loss (P&L) or operating statement. The income statement records the company's revenues and expenses for a specific period of time, and, therefore, is dated "for the period ended" (Figure 4.2). *Revenues* are defined as the inflows of net assets in exchange for the company's goods or services, and may also occur as a decrease in existing liabilities. Conversely, *expenses* are defined as the outflow of net assets associated with the company's economic activity of the same period, and may also occur as a reduction in an existing asset or an increase in liabilities. The basic income statement equation is as follows:

Revenues – Expenses = Net income

The net income reflects the profitability of a company, or the ability to provide an economic activity at a profit, by having excess revenues after expenses.

As with the balance sheet, the design of the income statement is quite uniform. The statement begins with the revenue classification first, with levels of detail determined by each individual company. Next, the various expense account classifications are shown, usually ranked in the order of magnitude. Cost of goods sold is then subtracted from total revenues to provide gross profit. Gross profit is an important item, as it shows the

Sample Pharmacy Income statement for the years ended December 31,	2011	2010
Net sales	$7,834,656	$8,565,765
Costs and expenses		
Cost of goods sold	5,155,202	6,933,224
Gross profit	2,679,454	1,632,541
Selling, general, and administrative	1,952,552	963,258
Depreciation	535,967	412,753
Operating profit	190,935	256,530
Interest and other income (net)	45,876	38,765
Income before income taxes	236,811	295,295
Income taxes	101,411	89,561
Net income	$135,400	$205,734

Figure 4.2 Sample income statement.

amount available for all other expenses. Other operating expenses are also listed, including selling, general, and administrative categories. Subtracting these expenses yields an intermediate balance, usually called profit operating profit (loss). Any remaining items are those expenses incurred during the period not directly related to core business activities, such as interest income or income tax expense. A final addition or subtraction of these line items and operating profit gives net income, which is the remaining amount of excess revenues after all expenses for the operating period have been listed. The level of detail shown in the income statement should be sufficient to provide important information for the various users of the income statement.

Revenues

Revenues, also known as sales or sales revenue, are presented as the first line of the income statement. The amount shown is actually net sales, which reflects any returns or discounts associated with the sales for the period, instead of these expenses being shown as a separate line item. The net sales resulting from the company's primary economic activity are listed first, with any secondary activities listed next. Remember, only those revenues that have been completely earned are recorded during the period.

Case-in-point 4.5   Long-term care contracts

Some community pharmacies contract with long-term care facilities to provide medications to patients. While the contract covers an entire year, a single payment may be made to the community pharmacy for the entire period, rather than in monthly installments. It is important to note that only one-twelfth (1/12) of this amount is shown as contracted pharmacy sales each month on the community pharmacy's income statement since the duty to continue to service the patients exists for many more months. The balance sheet would show a liability for the remaining months of contracted service.

Expenses

The basic format of the income statement is a subtraction of different expenses in a certain order, with subtotals shown at various points. The largest expenses are usually shown first, with others shown in order of decreasing magnitude. For most companies, the first expense account classification shown is the *cost of goods sold*, abbreviated as COGS. As the name implies, COGS represents the cost of the items sold during the period. In all pharmacies, since the delivery of medications to customers/patients represents the major economic activity, COGS is usually the largest expense amount on the income statement and is shown first.

The first subtotal is calculated by subtracting COGS from net sales, with the resulting amount defined as gross profit. Gross profit is an important number in the financial analysis of all companies as it represents the excess amount received in the established selling price/reimbursement for the medications (set by the company, Medicare, insurance companies, etc.) and the total costs paid by the company to purchase the medications dispensed, or sold. The importance of gross profit is seen quickly, as it represents the amount of initial "gross profit" remaining (after COGS) that is available to pay for all other expenses involved with running the company. Obviously, higher gross profit is more advantageous than a lower gross profit, since making a profit is the primary business objective. Higher sales prices and lower inventory purchase prices maximize gross profit; however, given mandates by third party payers, including recent reimbursement cuts by state Medicaids and other payers, maximizing the selling price is not always within the control of company management.

As expenses are continually deducted proceeding down the income statement, the next general classification of expenses listed are the operating expenses, sometimes referred to as general, administrative, and selling expenses. While these broad classifications are common to all companies, within a single company's income statement, the various categories shown are unique and provide important information regarding the company's economic activity. Usually, the classifications are listed in descending order of the relative amounts, with payroll expenses being a major component of overall operating expenses. The total of all operating expenses is sometimes provided, depending on the level of detail needed.

After the operating expenses have been subtracted from the gross profit, the next subtotal obtained is called operating profit or income. Net operating profit reflects the residual profit (or loss). However, there are two important classifications – interest and income tax expense – that remain, and are shown as separate line items. Since many companies may require external financing in order to meeting cash flow needs during their operating cycle, convention dictates that interest income or expense be shown separately for users to see the extent of this need. Finally, income tax expense must also be included to arrive at the final amount, net income or net profit. Net income reflects the net economic benefit for the period determined after recording all of the period's transactions. In the event that total sales minus expenses are a negative amount, the result is expressed as net loss.

Statement of shareholder's (owner's) equity

To understand the statement of shareholder's (owner's) equity, it is important to remember that the income statement shows the results of the company's economic activity over a period of time and consists of all income statement (nominal) account activity, with the result being net income. Each period, the net income is "transferred" to the balance sheet (real) account called retained earnings. Since the statement of shareholder's (owner's) equity, shown in Figure 4.3, is adjusted to reflect a company's cumulative net income over each time period, this statement is dated "for the period ended" of each accounting cycle. The basic function of this statement is to provide a reconciliation of the retained earnings balance at the beginning of the period with the retained earnings balance at the end of the period. Dividends represent a return of earnings to the shareholders; therefore, the major transactions recorded on this statement are net income (or loss) and the payment of dividends. The sale of stock is also recorded on this statement during the period in which it was sold. Stock transactions tend to occur more frequently during the earlier years of existence and become less frequent as the company's operations mature.

Sample Pharmacy Statement of shareholder's (owner's) equity for the year ended December 31, 2011		
Beginning of year balance		
Common stock (contributed capital)	$200,000	
Retained earnings (earned capital)	786,886	
Total shareholder's (owner's) equity		$986,886
Net income for the year 2011	135,400	
End of year balance		
Common stock (contributed capital)	200,000	
Retained earnings (earned capital)	922,286	
Total shareholder's (owner's) equity		$1,122,286

Figure 4.3 Sample statement of shareholder's (owner's) equity.

Statement of cash flows

At one time, the income statement was the only statement that provided detailed information on the operations of a company during each reporting period. Over time, the necessity for users to have a better understanding of a company's cash flow and use of cash during each period was determined and is provided by the statement of cash flows. During the accounting period, all major inflows (cash receipts) and outflows (cash payments) are classified into one of three activities; operating, investing, or financing. The conversion of accrual-based net income to cash-based net income derives the amount of cash from operating activities. All cash collections from the sale of goods or services, along with the corresponding cash payments made for operating expenses are included. Both the receipt of dividends and interest, as well as the payment of interest and taxes, is included in operating activities. Investing activities refers cash movement related to the company's management of long-term assets. Therefore, disposals of existing assets are sources of cash in the category, while the cash purchase of equipment and related items is a use. Note that if an asset is acquired by obtaining a loan, it is not shown as a cash activity within investing activities for the period. Finally, financing activities uses include those cash payments which reduced long-term liabilities (reduction of notes payable) or shareholder's equity (the payment of dividends). Sources of cash shown in the financing activities section would be the negotiation of additional long-term debt or proceeds from additional sales of company stock.

For a specific period, the beginning cash balance is reconciled to the ending cash balance on the balance sheet within the statement of cash flows. Only sources and uses of cash are included in the statement of cash flows; non-cash items are excluded. Since both balance sheet and income statement accounts affect cash over an operating cycle, the statement of cash flows is dated "for the period ended" of a specific date. The statement of cash flows can then be used as an analytical tool to assess a company's short-term viability. Potential external financial statement users, such as lenders, investors, and even employees, all have different interests when reading this statement.

There are two methods of preparing the operating activities section of the statement of cash flows: *direct* and *indirect*.

The direct method reports gross cash receipts and payments, and then reconciles the beginning and ending cash balances from the balance sheet.

In contrast, the indirect method begins with net income, makes adjustments for all non-cash items, then adjusts for all cash items and ends with the current cash position shown on the balance sheet. Under either method, the statement of cash flows adjusts net income, as determined by the accrual basis of accounting, to a cash basis of accounting and presents the results of a company's operations in terms of how cash was used during an accounting period.

The sample statement of cash flows displayed above shows the reconciliation of the prior year's cash balance to that of the current year, and attempts to provide answers to questions such as:

- How does the company obtain its cash?
- Where does a company spend its cash?
- What explains the change in the cash balance?

Cash inflows and outflows are determined in the three major categories shown in Figure 4.4.

- Operating activities include those transactions and events that determine net income, revenue generation, and associated expenses.
- Investing activities represent those transactions and events that affect long-term assets, most notably the purchase of long-term assets.
- Financing activities identify those transactions and events that influence long-term liabilities and owner's equity. Transactions that involve the company's owners and creditors, such as cash received from issuing debt or repayment of amounts borrowed, are also shown in the financing activities section.

New PharmD Pharmacy		
Statement of cash flows		
for the month ended July 31, 20XX		
Cash provided from operating activities		
Cash from customers	6,250.00	
Cash from third party payers	21,521.00	
Cash for medication purchases	(13,984.00)	
Cash paid for rent	(2,500.00)	
Cash paid contract labor	(2,000.00)	
Cash paid to RG for salary	(7,720.00)	
Net cash from operating activities		$1,567
Cash provided from investing activities		
Purchase of laser printer	(3,000)	
Net cash used by investing activities		($3,000)
Cash provided from financing activities		
Investment from parents	5,000	
Net cash used by financing activities		$5,000
Net increase in cash		3,567
Cash balance June 30, 200XX		700
Cash balance July 31, 20XX		4,267

Figure 4.4   Sample statement of cash flows – direct method.

Case-in-point 4.6   New PharmD Pharmacy

RG, a recent pharmacy graduate, has decided the pioneer spirit is strong within her and has decided to open her own community pharmacy. The following case reflects the first 2 months of her experience.

To begin her process, RG sought the advice of her uncle, a lawyer, who helped her incorporate her new business for a fee of only $300.00. Calling the new corporation New PharmD Pharmacy, there were 10,000 shares authorized with a par value of $1 each. RG was able to contribute $1,000 to purchase 1,000 shares. In addition, the regional wholesaler is promoting the start-up of independent community pharmacies through a special program providing an initial inventory of $75,000.00, computer equipment of $15,000.00 and furniture and fixtures in the amount of $12,000.00. This start-up package, totaling $102,000, is provided as a 3-year note payable, interest free, with a balloon payment due at the end of the agreement; however, more frequent payments are encouraged. As the pharmacy began to take shape during June for the July 1st grand opening, RG negotiated to obtain, on account, $3,000.00 worth of supplies from a local pharmacy supply store. These supplies consisted of pharmacy prescription labels, vials, and bags.

Figure 4.5 reflects the following general journal entries necessary to record the result of all these transactions, while Figure 4.6 shows the balance sheet as of June 30, 20XX. Note the retained earnings for June 30, 20XX only reflects the expense of $300.00 which was paid to RG's uncle for his work with the incorporation. This amount could have been included in the capitalization of New PharmD Pharmacy, but was expensed to show a loss for the initial period and the resulting effect on retained earnings.

	New PharmD Pharmacy, Inc. General journal for the month of June, 20XX		
Date	Account title and explanation	Debit $	Credit $
06/15/XX	Cash	1,000.00	
	Capital stock (contributed capital)		1,000.00
	To record initial sale of stock of new PharmD pharmacy corporation		
06/22/XX	Inventory	75,000.00	
	Computer equipment	15,000.00	
	Furniture and fixtures	12,000.00	
	Note payable - wholesaler		102,000.00
	To record start-up package and note payable from wholesaler		
06/29/XX	Legal expenses	300.00	
	Cash		300.00
	To record legal expenses with incorporation of any pharmacy		
06/29/XX	Supplies	3,000.00	
	Accounts payable		3,000.00
	To record supplies obtained on credit with local vendor		

Figure 4.5 New PharmD pharmacy June general journal.

New PharmD Pharmacy, Inc. Balance sheet as of June 30, 20XX		
Assets		
Cash in bank	700.00	
Inventory	75,000.00	
Supplies	3,000.00	
Computer equipment	15,000.00	
Furniture and fixtures	12,000.00	
Total assets		$105,700.00
Liabilities and shareholder's (owner's) equity		
Accounts payable	3,000.00	
Note payable to wholesaler	102,000.00	
Capital stock (contributed capital)	1,000.00	
Retained earnings (earned capital)	(300.00)	
Total liabilities and shareholder's (owner's) equity		$105,700.00

Figure 4.6   New PharmD pharmacy balance sheet.

Although it was stressful, RG was quite successful during the first month of operations. RG had to begin the month with a rent payment of $2,500 due by the 5th of July. Since her cash balance was only $700, RG recognized that starting a business with such little cash was probably not the smartest thing to do. Thus, RG obtained additional capital contributions from her parents, who had made a previous offer to do so. In return for a capital contribution of $5,000, RG's parents purchased 5,000 shares of the remaining 9,000 shares authorized in the initial incorporation. By the end of the first week, RG needed another printer to help print prescription labels, given her already steady business. This new laser printer was $3,000, purchased in cash. RG also had hired a part-time technician whom she paid $500 per week for the month.

At the end of the month, business was great. RG determined additional inventory was needed and placed a cash order with the wholesaler for $13,984.00. Cash prescription sales for July totaled $6,250.00 and third party prescription sales were even better at $34,567.89. Thankfully, the third party insurance payers send her checks quickly, and RG received $21,521.00 by the end of the month. Using the perpetual inventory software provided in her start-up package from the wholesaler, RG recorded COGS for July in the amount of $32,654.13, which represented a gross margin percentage of 20%.

RG then closed her accounting records for July by paying her technician the previously contracted amount of $2,000 and herself $7,720 (ignore any payroll tax effects). RG estimated that 20% of the supplies inventory had been used. Her company's depreciation expense, calculated at straight line for 3 years resulted in a monthly amount of $833.33 (total equipment, including the new laser printer, of $30,000 divided by 36 months). The general journal for July, shown in Figure 4.7, provides the results of these monthly activities. Figure 4.8 shows the income statement for July for New PharmD Pharmacy, Inc. (all income taxes and interest expenses were ignored).

Student practice assignment

Record the July month general journal entries (shown in Figure 4.7) in T accounts. Include all the balance sheet accounts together on one page (remember to use the June 30, 20XX balances as your July 1, 20XX beginning balance) and then group all the income statement accounts on another (all these accounts have a beginning balance of zero). Compare your results to Figure 4.8. For simplicity, ignore the effects of all income taxes and interest expenses.

A balance sheet for July 31, 20XX has been prepared for the July operations after preparing a T account analysis, the ending balances from both the balance sheet accounts as well as the income statement accounts are simply shown on the monthly balance sheet (see Figure 4.9) and income statement (see Figure 4.10).

Once these financial statements are prepared, RG is much better equipped to analyze the results of operations for July than by only reviewing the general journal entries. As can be seen on the balance sheet, although RG's bank balance has improved and her gross margin percentage appears relatively adequate at 20%, the loss of $5,489.57 does not appear sustainable. However, given this is only the first month of operations, it is not unreasonable to assume that sales at some rate will enable New PharmD Pharmacy, Inc. to begin showing profits. If RG can continue to provide good customer service without significant increases in payroll expenses, both contract and for her, RG should have a great beginning for her business. Attention needs to be given to cash flow in order to be able to service the note payable to the wholesaler over the next few years.

Student practice case

Prepare a statement of cash flows – direct method on the July operations for New PharmD Pharmacy. (Hint: It will look exactly like Figure 4.4.)

	New PharmD Pharmacy, Inc. General journal for the month of July, 20XX		
Date	Account title and explanation	Debit $	Credit $
07/01/XX	Cash	5,000.00	
	Capital stock (contributed capital)		5,000.00
	(A) To record sale of stock of new pharmd pharmacy corporation		
07/3/XX	Rent expense	2,500.00	
	Cash		2,500.00
	(B) To record month rent expense for the month		
07/06/XX	Computer equipment	3,000.00	
	Cash		3,000.00
	(C) To record purchase of new laser printer		
07/31/XX	Inventory	13,984.00	
	Cash		13,984.00
	(D) To record drug order received and paid in cash		
07/31/XX	Cash	6,250.00	
	Prescription sales - cash		6,250.00
	(E) To record cash prescription sales for the month		
07/31/XX	Accounts receivable	34,567.89	
	Prescription sales - third party		34,567.89
	(F) To record prescription sales - 3rd party for the month		
07/31/XX	Cash	21,521.00	
	Accounts receivable - third party		21,521.00
	(G) To record cash payment from third party for the month		
07/31/XX	Cost of goods sold	32,654.13	
	Inventory		32,654.13
	(H) To record COGS for the month		
07/31/XX	Salaries - contract	2,000.00	
	Salaries - employee	7,720.00	
	Cash		9,720.00
	(I) To record payroll expenses for the month		
07/31/XX	Supplies expense	600.00	
	Supplies		600.00
	(J) To record 20% of supplies inventory used for the month		
07/31/XX	Depreciation expense	833.33	
	Accumulated depreciation		833.33
	(K) To record depreciation expense for the month		

Figure 4.7   New PharmD pharmacy general journal July 20XX.

```
                                New PharmD Pharmacy
                                 T account analysis
                           for the month ended July 31, 20XX
                        Balance  sheet and income statement accounts
```

	Cash			Accounts receivable			Inventory	
	700.00						75,000,00	
A	5,000.00		F	34,567.89		D	13,984.00	
B		2,500.00	G		21,521.00	H		32,654.13
C		3,000.00						
D		13,984.00						
E	6,250.00							
G	21,521,00							
I		9,720.00						
	4,267.00			13,046.89			56,329.87	

	Computer equipment			Furniture and fixtures			Supplies	
	15,000,00			12,000.00			3,000.00	
C	3,000.00					J		600.00
	18,000.00			12,000.00			2,400.00	

	Accumulated depreciation			Accounts payable			Note payable	
					3,000.00			102,000.00
K		833.33						
		833.33						

	Capital stock (contributed capital)			Retained earnings (earned capital)	
		1,000.00		300.00	
A		5,000.00		5,489.57	
		6,000.00		5,789.57	

	Prescription sales - cash			Prescription sales - third party			Cost of goods sold	
E		6,250.00	F		34,567.89	H	32,654.13	
		6,250.00			34,567.89		32,654.13	

	Rent			Depreciation			Supplies	
B	2,500.00		K	833.33		J	600.00	

	Payroll - employee			Payroll - contract	
I	7,720.00		I	2,000.00	

Figure 4.8 New PharmD T account analysis July 20XX.

New PharmD Pharmacy, Inc. Balance sheet as of July 31, 20XX		
Assets		
Cash in bank	4,267.00	
Accounts receivable	13,046.89	
Inventory	56,329.87	
Supplies	2,400.00	
Computer equipment	18,000.00	
Furniture and fixtures	12,000.00	
Accumulated depreciation	(833.33)	
Total assets		$105,210.43
Liabilities and shareholder's equity		
Accounts payable	3,000.00	
Note payable to wholesaler	102,000.00	
Capital stock (contributed capital)	6,000.00	
Retained earnings (earned capital)	(5,789.57)	
Total liabilities and shareholder's (owner's) equity		$105,210.43

Figure 4.9   New PharmD pharmacy July 20XX balance sheet.

New PharmD Pharmacy, Inc. Income statement for the period ended July 31, 20XX		
Sales		
Prescription sales - third party	$34,567.89	
Prescription sales - cash	6,250.00	
Net sales		$40,817.89
Cost of goods sold		32,654.13
Gross profit		8,163.76
Operating expenses		
Salaries - employees	7,720.00	
Salaries - contract	2,000.00	
Rent	2,500.00	
Supplies	600.00	
Depreciation	833.33	
Total operating expenses		13,653.33
Net income		($5,489.57)

Figure 4.10   New PharmD pharmacy July 20XX income statement.

Summary

The importance of financial statements to compile and analyze a company's economic activity cannot be understated. This chapter has shown the various users (both internal and external) and types of financial statements (balance sheet, income statement, statement of shareholders'/owner's equity and statement of cash flows) used to determine the success, or failure, of a pharmacy business over a specified time period. Specifically through the New PharmD Pharmacy case, one can see the knowledge, time, and effort required to turn your clinical skills and entrepreneurial spirit into business success. Pharmacy managers must be familiar with the basic principles of financial statements and how their analysis affects the current and future business direction.

Suggested reading

Chisholm-Burns MA, Vaillancourt AM, Shepherd M. *Pharmacy Management, Leadership, Marketing, and Finance*. Sudbury, MA: Jones & Bartlett Publishers, 2011.

Carroll NV. *Financial Management for Pharmacists: a Decision-Making Approach*, 3rd edn. Baltimore, MD: Lippincott Williams & Wilkins, 2007.

Friedlob GT, Plewa FJ. *Financial and Business Statements*, 3rd edn. Hauppauge, NY: Barron's Educational Series Inc., 2006.

Warren CS, Reeve JM, Duchac JE. *Accounting*, 23rd edn. New York, NY: Random House, 2008.

Walther L. *Principles of Accounting*. Logan, UT: Utah State University. www.principlesofaccounting.com

Review questions

1 Why is the value of employees not listed as an asset on the balance sheet?

2 What are the effects of buying inventory for $10,000 on the balance sheet?

3 Describe the different focus of external versus internal financial statement users.

4 Which of the following is listed on the balance sheet?
   A Cash paid for rent
   B Cost of goods sold
   C Inventory
   D Sales commissions

5 Which of the following is listed on the income statement?
  A Cash paid for rent
  B Cost of goods sold
  C Inventory
  D Common stock

6 Which of the following is listed on the statement of owner's equity?
  A Cash paid for rent
  B Cost of goods sold
  C Inventory
  D Common stock

7 Which of the following is listed on the statement of cash flow?
  A Cash paid for rent
  B Cost of goods sold
  C Inventory
  D Common stock

8 Which of the following is usually the highest expense on the income statement?
  A Rent
  B Payroll
  C Advertising
  D Cost of goods sold

9 In general, depreciation of certain assets is used to reduce net income and incur lower income taxes. True or false?

10 In general, cash is the least liquid of all assets. True or false?

Answers

1 At first glance, this question seems quite reasonable. After all, many of us have heard that employees are the company's most valuable asset. However, after a little thought and review of some of the basic accounting assumptions, the answer will become very clear as to why employees are not recorded on a company's balance sheet. First, assets are recorded at their historical purchase price based upon the objectively determined price. In this instance, the company does not actually "own" their employees. While there is usually an ongoing relationship that is beneficial to both the employer (who can plan company operations knowing there is a trained and dedicated workforce) and the employee (who can expect to continue to receive a paycheck and benefits based upon good performance). The conservatism principle would also make recording employees as assets on the balance sheet a very difficult process. How would a reasonable value for each employee be developed given the uniqueness of individual employees and the variability in their motivation, drive, and abilities? However, this concept is not totally ignored and the matching principle helps solve this problem. Remember that the matching concept requires transactions to be recorded in the same period where the recognition of revenue is matched to the expenses from which the revenue is derived. Since employees work each week on a continual basis, their wages paid each period are shown as an operating payroll expense, unless an employee's work effort will directly benefit another period. For example, in the manufacturing process of large inventory items, the direct labor associated with the production process is included in the final inventory cost. When the inventory is sold, often in another period, the cost of the inventory shown in COGS includes employee labor costs from prior periods. Application of the matching principle in this manner provides a better approximation of the "matched" labor effort and the resulting sale.

2 There are several ways in which to think about the effects of purchasing inventory for $10,000, especially since the details of the purchase were not provided. Let's assume the easiest method of simply paying cash. From the accounting equation, this transaction would be affecting only the "assets" side of the equation, with the $10,000 decrease in the cash account being offset with a $10,000 increase in the inventory account, a simple swap between two current asset classifications. However, remember liquidity is an important concept when discussing different assets and liabilities. In this transaction, liquidity has been significantly reduced, given that inventory requires a buyer in order to return it to the most liquid state again, i.e., cash. Without knowing the entire details of this company's balance sheet, the significance of the effect on liquidity cannot be seen. If the company was currently experiencing a cash squeeze, perhaps rent or payroll could not be met, which would have negative impacts on the operations of the company. If the inventory purchase had been purchased on credit, the accounts payable account would have increased in direct proportion to the inventory account, again keeping the equality of the accounting equation. In addition, most items included in accounts payable are due in 30 days, which will increase the company's liquidity. In this case, the effect upon liquidity can be very beneficial as the

company continues to have the use of the $10,000 cash for about a month. During this month, payroll, rent, and other critical items may need to be paid. While the due date of the $10,000 approaches, the operations of the company may have enabled the entire amount of inventory purchased to be sold, perhaps on a cash basis. In this case, the effect would have increased the profitability of the company through the sale of the inventory and the corresponding gross profit. The balance sheet effect would be unchanged until the end of the period, when the net income for the period is included in retained earnings on the balance sheet.

3   Internal users of financial statements are often focused on the daily operations of the company and how to improve efficiencies. The type of reports that they use are often referred to as management reports, since they enable managers to make better decisions. Management reports are not as complete as the four basic financial statements, and are tailored specifically to individuals throughout a company. For example, the production department personnel, who are responsible for the smooth and efficient completion of budgeted production levels, must be kept informed about current performance and be immediately notified about any problems that would prevent inventory levels meeting budgeted quotas. The importance of this information extends beyond the production department itself. The sales department must also be informed about current production levels, as this department has the responsibility of selling the materials that the company produces and has its own quotas to meet. However, it is also critical to inform the sales department about any production shortfalls, as this would hamper the sales department's ability to provide good customer service if promised deliveries to the company's customers cannot be met. The finance department, which is managing the company's cash flow based upon the master budget, would also need to know of production problems if they were of the magnitude to impact sales. Obviously, if sales goals are not going to be met, there will be reductions in cash inflows available for the operations of the company, and the finance department must take some form of corrective action. External users mainly consist of lenders, owners, and potential members of both of these groups, and are not involved in the actual operations and management of the company. Their concerns are more focused on the company's ability to generate profits, meet debt obligations, and provide dividends and other forms of returns to investors. As such, they rely on the four basic financial statements and their own ratio

analysis. The objectives of ratio analysis and examination of financial statements are to determine levels of profitability, solvency, and financial leverage.

4   C is correct: Inventory.

5   B is correct: Cost of goods sold.

6   D is correct: Common stock.

7   A is correct: Cash paid for rent.

8   D is correct: Cost of goods sold.

9   The statement is true.

10   The statement is false.

Glossary

Accounts payable	Consists of payments not yet made for inventory, utilities, and other operating expenses. Most items included have due dates with 30 days or less.
Accounts receivable	Represents the future receipt of cash from a customer as a result of a completed sale.
Balance sheet	Simply a listing of all of a company's assets, liabilities, and owner's equity accounts at a specific point in time.
Cost of goods sold (COGS)	Represents the cost of the items sold during a period. In all pharmacies, the delivery of medications represents the major economic activity and, therefore, COGS is usually the largest expense amount on the income statement.
Current assets	Those assets that are expected to be consumed or converted to cash in less than a year.

Depreciation	Used to allocate asset acquisition costs to future periods. With the straight-line method of depreciation, a particular asset is purchased and then the economic life estimated, typically over a period of years.
Equity	The residual amount in company assets after all liabilities have been deducted.
Expenses	The outflow of net assets associated with the company's economic activity of the same period.
External users	Those who are not part of the daily business operations, including creditors and shareholders.
Financial reporting	Specific financial reports necessary for external users, identified as investors, creditors, and others.
Internal users	Those individuals who are intimately involved with the daily business operations, which consist of employees and managers of the company, or the owners, if the company is a sole proprietorship.
Liability	The amount owed by the company to others as a result of the various transactions that have occurred over time.
Liquidity	Ease of conversion to cash without a loss in value of the assets.
Managerial accounting	Role of accounting in providing information to internal users.
Retained earnings	The cumulative net earnings of the company over time that has not been paid out to the shareholders in the form of dividends as of the balance sheet date.
Revenues	The inflows of net assets in exchange for the company's goods or services.
Statement of owner's equity	Financial statement used to provide a reconciliation of the equity balance at the beginning of the period with the equity balance at the end of the period.

5

Basics of finance and financial analysis

Learning objectives

- Identify the concept of time value of money and its importance in the financial operations of a business
- Identify and explain the difference between simple and compound interest
- Discern the importance of future and present value in various investment alternatives
- Describe the basic components of ratio analysis, the utility of financial ratios and the importance of their analysis
- Characterize the uses and meaning of various financial ratios

Introduction

Pharmacy managers know that understanding the external operating environment is critical to a business's success. Managers routinely examine the operating environment to assess a business's strengths, weaknesses, opportunities and threats (SWOT). However, both the internal and external SWOT information is not sufficient to fully understand a business. To develop an overall assessment of the business, in addition to looking at the competitive, internal and external operating environment, a thorough financial statements analysis is necessary and can provide valuable information about internal business performance. When examining past and present information, trends can be identified that assist the pharmacy manager in decision making regarding the appropriate allocation of resources and overall business direction. For example, studying changes in sales over a period of a few years can assist the pharmacy manager in making staffing, inventory or long-term capital investment decisions. When sales are growing steadily over time, the manager will have more confidence in hiring additional staff to meet customer service needs.

As with any business planning or analysis tool, the starting point is to develop analysis objectives. For example, is an analysis of the financial statements being done to plan for the future, get a loan to invest in a new facility, assess current staffing levels or determine a business's selling price? Once an objective (or objectives) has been established, the pharmacy manager is ready to undertake an examination of company financial statements.

Accountants have developed numerous tools to use in financial statement analysis. In this chapter, the focus is on comparative financial data, e.g., comparing current data with standards or comparison of financial data spanning multiple periods to assess trends. To perform these analyses, an understanding of the basics of finance, including concepts related to the *time value of money*, must first be discussed.

Time value of money

In financial terms, a dollar today is worth more than a dollar at some date in the future because the dollar today can earn interest (or be invested) and the value of the dollar can grow as the future date is approached. Phrased differently, money available at the present time is worth more than the same amount in the future due to its potential earning capacity. This core principle of finance dictates that money can earn interest and any amount of money is worth more the sooner it is received.

For example, if given a choice between $1,000 today and $1,000 in one year, individuals should choose to take the money now. Taking the $1,000 now would enable the individual to earn interest and have a greater sum at the end of a year. At an interest rate of 5%, $1,000 today is worth $1,050 in a year, known as the future value of a sum. Another way of saying this is the receipt of $1,000 in a year is only worth $952.40 today, known as the present value of a sum. The effect of the difference between the value of the money in a year and the value of taking the money now (in this case $50) is known as the time value of money. In essence, the future earning potential of money and its capacity to grow, if invested in other vehicles, forms the basis of the time value of money concept.

Interest

Interest is a fee paid on a borrowed asset, most commonly money, and can be thought of as the "rent" for a principal sum of money. Interest is the most common way to quantify the time value of money and is usually expressed in terms of an annual percentage rate. The annual percentage rate is applied to the principal to calculate the interest amount to be paid. When money is deposited in a bank, interest is typically paid to the depositor (or investor) as a percentage of the amount deposited. When a business borrows money, interest is typically paid to the lender as a percentage of the amount owed. For the investor, interest is the motivating factor for allowing the bank to hold or use your money in exchange for the interest earned.

Simple interest is defined as the interest computed on the principal amount for one year's period of time and is calculated as:

$$FV = P \times (1+r)$$

where *FV* is the future value of the original principal, *P* is the principal amount invested, and *r* is the annual interest rate.

Thus, $1,000 for 1 year at an interest rate of 7% would earn interest of $70 and have a future value of $1,070. If a multiple year calculation were needed to project future balances, the formula would change to:

$$FV = P \times (1+rt)$$

where *t* is the number of years.

For example, if the above calculation were needed to project a 5-year period of earning interest:

$$
\begin{aligned}
FV &= P \times (1+rt) \\
FV &= 1,000 \times (1+(0.07 \times 5)) \\
FV &= 1,000 \times (1.35) \\
FV &= \$1,350
\end{aligned}
$$

The *compound interest* principle applies to interest over more than one period. To calculate compound interest, we begin just as with simple interest; however, during the second and all future periods the interest rate is applied to both the original principal plus the interest earned in the first period and each subsequent period. Compound interest is calculated with the following formula:

$$FV = P \times (1+(r \div n))^{nt}$$

where *FV* is the future value of the original principal, *P* is the principal amount invested, *r* is the annual interest rate, *n* is the number of times per year that interest is compounded, and *t* is the number of periods expressed in years.

If, in the previous 1-year simple interest example, we invested the $1,000 for 2 years, the interest earned for the second year would be $74.90, or 7% applied to the total value of $1,070 at the end of the first year. Based on the compound interest formula, the future value of the investment for the second year including interest and principal is:

$$
\begin{aligned}
FV &= \$1,000 \times (1+(0.07 \div 1))^{1 \times 2} \\
FV &= \$1,144.90
\end{aligned}
$$

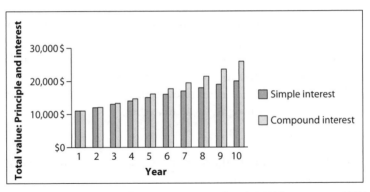

Figure 5.1 Simple and compound interest comparison for a $10,000 investment at 10% interest over 10 years.

Over time, the effect of compound interest is significant because the amount of interest earned in the previous period, or the accrued interest, is included in the principal balance for the next period's interest calculation. However, one point of notice is how the compound interest formula mirrors the simple interest formula if interest is only compounded once yearly.

Figure 5.1 shows the effects of simple interest and compound interest (compounded annually) on the FV of a $10,000 investment for several 1-year periods. However, the full effect of compounded interest is seen when smaller time periods, such as daily or quarterly, are used because, generally, the more frequent (i.e., shorter) the period of compounding, the greater the impact of compounding on the principal balance. As can be seen in Table 5.1, simple interest is significantly less than compounded interest over 30 years. While annual compounding yields $289,599 in interest over the 30-year investment period, even greater benefit is seen when the amount is compounded quarterly over the same 30-year period and interest rate.

While the effects of compounding on an original invested balance of $10,000 is quite significant, to fully appreciate the impact of compound

Table 5.1 Power of compounding

Type of interest earned	Number of periods	Interest rate (%)	Beginning principal ($)	Total interest earned ($)	Final balance ($)
Simple	30	12	10,000	36,000	46,000
Annual compounding	30	12	10,000	289,599	299,599
Quarterly compounding	30	12	10,000	337,110	347,110

Adapted from: http://www.getobjects.com/Components/Finance/TVM/iy.html 5/2/2010

Table 5.2 Compound interest rate comparison

Years invested	Amount invested ($)	Interest rate (%)	Interest earned ($)	Ending balance ($)	Interest rate (%)	Interest earned ($)	Ending balance
10	110,000	5	38,357	148,357	7.5	62,691	172,692
20	210,000	5	163,726	373,726	7.5	298,004	508,004
30	310,000	5	430,827	740,827	7.5	889,093	1,199,093

http://www.moneychimp.com/calculator/compound_interest_calculator.htm 5/2/2010

interest, let's examine the results of making regular annual contributions of $10,000 to the original $10,000 investment. Over a period of 30 years at both 5% and 7.5% interest rates, Table 5.2 shows the ending balances with interest. The principal balance with interest is over 100% greater than the amount invested over the years at 5%, while an interest rate of 7.5% results in almost a quadrupling of the original invested amount. Furthermore, by securing a slightly higher interest rate of 7.5%, the ending principal balance with interest translates into an amount approximately $458,000 greater than the total with a 5% interest rate.

From the pharmacy manager's perspective, the effects of interest and compounding are also seen when, for example, seeking to borrow money for the purchase of a new delivery vehicle for a pharmacy selling durable medical equipment. In Table 5.3, we see the details of borrowing to purchase a $40,000 delivery vehicle at 7.5% interest for either a 3- or 6-year loan period. Since most loans for vans are calculated at a simple interest rate, from a total cost perspective, the 3-year loan is a more cost-effective choice with a just over 50% reduction in total interest payments. Therefore, the shortest loan period should be chosen while still being able to meet the monthly payment amount.

When examining both borrowing and saving scenarios, it is important to understand how interest rates are determined. Risk, or the possibility of loss from either a borrower's failure to repay a loan or the expected loss in market value of other investments or assets, is an essential element in

Table 5.3 Total cost of borrowing: new delivery van

Assumptions: $40,000 loan at 7.5%		
Length of loan	3 Years	6 Years
Monthly payment amount	$1,244.25	$691.60
Total interest paid	$4,792.95	$9,795.52

http://www.bankrate.com/calculators/auto/auto-loan-calculator.aspx (accessed May 2, 2010).

determining the borrower's credit worthiness and the interest rate charged. Additionally, the current market interest rates also play a major role. In general, though, the higher the credit risk is deemed to be, the higher the interest rate charged.

Comparative financial statement analysis

The development and overall purpose of the four basic financial statements is reviewed and described in Chapter 4. It is important to remember that a business's financial statements summarize the detailed transactions underlying operations over each period, as well as a certain point in time. This information is extremely useful in understanding the current position of a business. However, when comparing financial statement data for two or more periods, pharmacy managers can begin to develop management information describing business trends.

Before beginning the discussion of comparative financial statement analysis, it is important to understand the two general formats of financial analysis that are often employed, known as vertical and horizontal financial analysis. *Vertical financial analysis* refers to the process of comparing the financial performance and current condition of a company in relation to a base amount. For example, individual asset account balances on the company's balance sheet can be expressed as a percentage of total assets, or various revenue and expense accounts from the income statement are shown as a percentage of total sales. Taken one step further, vertical analysis can be useful in comparing different companies within the same industry, without regard to the absolute dollar values of each company. In this way, a pharmacy manager at a rural hospital could evaluate the appropriateness of current inventory levels as a percentage of total assets with that of other hospitals; even if the hospital was located in a major urban area and overall operations were several times larger. As seen in Figure 5.2, the rural hospital's inventory levels seem appropriate when compared with that of other major hospitals. Vertical financial

	Rural hospital		Major hospitals	
Account title	$	%	$	%
Cash/cash equivalents	100,000	7.7	5,000,000	11.1
Accounts receivable	300,000	23.1	10,000,000	22.2
Inventory	400,000	30.8	15,000,000	33.3
Total current assets	800,000	61.6	30,000,000	66.6
Long-term assets	500,000	38.4	15,000,000	33.4
Total assets	1,300,000	100.0	45,000,000	100.0

Figure 5.2 Vertical balance sheet financial analysis.

comparison may also be completed without the dollar amounts being shown. Vertical financial analysis could also include the comparison of a company's results with industry standards, such as those published in the National Community Pharmacist Association Digest (www.ncpanet.org). Comparing and analyzing a company's financial performance with that of other companies or industry standards is known as benchmarking.

The second comparative analysis, *horizontal financial analysis*, refers to the process of comparing the financial performance and current condition of a company over several time periods. The span of time chosen for comparison depends upon the need of the individual pharmacy manager, and may be month to month, quarter to quarter, or year to year. The pharmacy manager can compare current results, via a company's financial ratios, with historical as well as future performance.

For Sample Pharmacy, the net operating income percentages (Figure 5.3) were relatively constant for 2007 and 2008 at just over 8% but dropped significantly in 2009 to only 5.4%. By showing yearly percentages horizontally, only the degree of change is apparent, with no indication of the magnitude or reasons for the changes. However, with this type of information, unfavorable (or even favorable) developments can be identified that require further investigation and analysis. Although a significant change may have been caused by a change in some accounting procedure, it is more likely the change is a result of either a decrease in total sales or operating inefficiencies.

Investigating the major deviations shown as a percentage of sales, a pharmacy manager can analyze positive or negative trends, which can help him/her take corrective action. With this type of analysis, two major components of the 3% drop in net income can be seen through review of the various expense changes. First, there is a 2% increase in payroll expense, from 13.6% to 15.6% of sales from 2008 to 2009. Perhaps there was stiffer competition in obtaining/retaining pharmacists because of location or competition. Secondly, total other operating expenses have increased from 4% to 5.2% of total sales. While the individual components have remained relatively consistent, there is flood damage expense in 2009 at 2.1%, which was not part of the previous year's expenses. By isolating the major changes in individual line items as a percent of sales, one can quickly identify the major areas affecting the reduction in net income from previous years.

The simple format of horizontal analysis can be refined to include both dollar amount changes and percentage changes through the use of comparative financial statement analysis. Comparative financial statements usually compare two successive periods, with the first period being the base period. The second period, or comparison/analysis period, is examined in relation to the base period and shown as a percentage and dollar change (Figure 5.4).

By including both the dollar amount change as well as a percentage change, a much clearer picture of the operation between the two periods is

Sample Pharmacy Income statement for the years ended December 31,	2007 %	2008 %	2009 %
Sales			
Prescription sales	72.0	74.0	74.3
All other sales	28.0	26.0	25.7
Total sales	100.0	100.0	100.0
Cost of goods sold			
Prescriptions costs	58.0	58.5	57.8
All other costs	15.8	15.7	16.0
Total cost of goods sold	73.8	74.2	73.8
Gross margin	26.2	25.8	26.2
Operating expenses-payroll			
Salaries, wages	11.6	11.9	13.3
Other payroll expenses	1.8	1.7	2.3
Total payroll expenses	13.4	13.6	15.6
Other operating expenses			
Advertising	0.5	0.5	0.4
Insurance	0.4	0.4	0.3
Store supplies, containers, labels	0.4	0.4	0.1
Prescription containers, labels	0.2	0.2	0.2
Office postage	0.1	0.1	0.1
Delivery service	0.2	0.2	0.1
Phamacy computer expense	0.4	0.3	0.3
Rent	1.2	1.2	1.0
Utilities, telephone	0.5	0.5	0.4
Pharmacy professional dues and licenses	0.1	0.1	0.1
Pharmacy continuing education	0.1	0.1	0.1
Flood damage	0.0	0.0	2.1
Total other operating expenses	4.1	4.0	5.2
Total operating expenses	17.5	17.6	20.8
Net operating income	8.7	8.2	5.4

Figure 5.3 Horizontal income statement financial analysis.

Sample Pharmacy Income statement for the years ended December 31,	2008	2009	Change	
	$	$	$	%
Sales				
Prescription sales	3,066,806	3,346,779	279,973	9.1
All other sales	1,077,526	1,157,634	80,108	7.4
Total sales	4,144,332	4,504,413	360,081	8.9
Cost of goods sold				
Prescriptions costs	2,424,434	2,603,551	179,117	7.4
All other costs	650,660	729,706	79,046	12.1
Total COGS	3,075,094	3,324,257	249,163	8.1
Gross margin	1,069,238	1,180,156	110,918	10.4
Operating expenses - payroll				
Salaries, wages	493,175	599,087	105,912	21.4
Other payroll expenses	70,454	103,601	33,147	47.0
Total payroll expenses	563,639	702,688	139,049	24.7
Other operating expenses				
Advertising	20,722	18,018	(2,704)	(13.1)
Insurance	16,577	13,513	(3,064)	(18.5)
Store supplies, containers, labels	16,577	4,504	(12,073)	(72.9)
Prescription containers, labels	8,289	9,009	720	0.2
Office postage	4,144	4,504	360	0.1
Delivery service	8,289	4,504	(3,785)	(45.7)
Pharmacy computer expense	12,433	13,513	1,080	8.7
Rent	49,732	45,044	(4,688)	(9.5)
Utilities, telephone	18,018	20,722	2,704	13.0
Pharmacy professional dues and licenses	4,144	4,504	360	0.1
Pharmacy continuing education	4,144	4,504	360	0.1
Flood damage	0	94,595	94,59 5	-
Total other operating expenses	165,773	234,230	68,457	41.3
Total operating expenses	729,402	936,918	207,516	28.4
Net operating income	339,836	243,238	(96,598)	(28.4)

Figure 5.4   Comparative income statement financial analysis.

evident. Total sales increased 8.9%, which is an indicator that the loss was not a result of competition or lost customers. Secondly, with a 21.4% increase in payroll expense, one might conclude that additional pharmacist hours were needed to handle the increased sales, since annual pay raises are not of this

	2005	2006	2007	2008	2009
Sample Pharmacy Selected operating results for the years ended December 31,					
Total sales	100.0%	105.3%	109.3%	114.8%	120.0%
Cost of goods sold	100.0%	110.5%	119.3%	127.8%	138.1%
Payroll expense	100.0%	104.2%	108.9%	111.7%	110.3%

Figure 5.5 Trend analysis.

magnitude. Finally, the magnitude of the loss from flood damage can be seen. Clearly it is in excess of a reasonable insurance deductible, and the existence of a flood insurance policy is certainly questionable.

For companies that have been operating for many periods, trend analysis may prove to be a useful tool. This form of horizontal analysis can help reveal patterns developing over several operating periods. When using trend analysis with only selected financial data, such as total sales, COGS, and total payroll expenses, the base-year concept is applied and the percentage increase from the base year is calculated. With this type of analysis, trends can provide essential information for future performance and long-range planning. As can be seen in Figure 5.5, while total sales have been trending with an annual 5% increase over the 5-year period, COGS has increased at a much more rapid pace, while total payroll has been held constant except for apparent annual cost of living increases.

Ratio analysis

As seen above, financial and comparative statements provide useful information to identify trends. However, further analysis is needed in order to understand the sources of these trends, which is where financial ratios are used. A ratio is an expression of a mathematical relationship between one quantity and another. A financial ratio is computed by dividing one financial statement item by another. This allows users to evaluate a company's performance by focusing on specific relationships between various items on the balance sheet and income statement. To be most useful, the components of the ratio need to express information that has a meaningful relationship.

While many individual ratios exist, they can be universal in nature, as well as specific to certain companies or market sectors. The three most common classifications of ratios include ratios related to liquidity, solvency, and profitability. *Liquidity* refers to the ability of a company to meet short-term cash requirements, which is significantly affected by the timing of various inflows and outflows of cash, as shown in Table 5.4. These indicators use the different assets and their relative liquidity in determining the overall efficiency of a company in relation to its short-term debt.

Table 5.4 Selected liquidity indicators

Description	Formula	Measure of company's
Current ratio	Current assets ÷ Current liabilities	Ability to pay short-term debt
Quick or acid-test ratio	(Cash + accounts receivable + short-term investments) ÷ Current liabilities	Ability to pay short-term debt without the use of less liquid inventory
Cash ratio	(Cash + cash equivalents + investments) ÷ Current liabilities	Ability to pay short-term debt with only the most liquid assets
Accounts receivable turnover	Net sales ÷ Average accounts receivable	Efficiency in collecting credit sales
Inventory turnover	Cost of goods sold ÷ Average inventory	Efficiency in managing inventory
Day's sales In accounts receivable	(Ending accounts receivable ÷ net sales) × 365	Liquidity in accounts receivable
Day's sales In inventory	(Ending inventory ÷ COGS) × 365	Liquidity in inventory

In conjunction with liquidity, the *solvency* ratios take the analysis a step further by attempting to quantify a company's ability to satisfy long-term debt obligations as well as the corresponding viability of the company to continue future operations. The selected solvency indicators shown in Table 5.5 relate the use of assets and shareholder equity to the total liabilities of a company.

Further, Table 5.6 contains the last of the universal classification of financial ratios, the *profitability* indicators. Profitability, as the name implies, relates to the company's relative ability to generate profits through the efficient use of its assets and provide a return to shareholders on their invested capital.

As can be seen in the previous three tables, there are important relationships between various balance sheet and income statement items common to all companies. Within pharmacy practice, ratio analysis can also be refined

Table 5.5 Selected solvency indicators

Description	Formula	Measure of company's
Debt ratio	Total liabilities ÷ Total assets	Liquidity and reliance on credit
Debt–equity ratio	Total liabilities ÷ Total stockholder's equity	Owner's reliance on credit
Interest coverage ratio	(Net income before interest and income tax expense) ÷ Interest expense	Ability to pay interest on total debt outstanding

Table 5.6 Selected profitability indicators

Description	Formula	Measure of company's
Net income ratio	Net income ÷ Net sales	Amount of net income per dollar of sales
Return on assets	Net Income ÷ Average total assets	General profitability of assets
Return on equity	Net income ÷ Average shareholder equity	Earnings on the investment of shareholders

in order to provide pharmacy managers with essential information. Remember, ratio analysis can reveal conditions and trends that often cannot be noted by inspection of actual dollar amounts on the financial statement or the individual components of the ratio. Appropriate use of financial ratios within various pharmacy practices will result in better understanding of your business and decision making.

Selected Sample Pharmacy liquidity ratios

To evaluate Sample Pharmacy, we begin by evaluating the business's short-term liquidity. This is the ability of Sample Pharmacy to meet its current debt obligations. Liquidity implies an ability to convert assets, such as inventory, into cash. In evaluating liquidity, a pharmacy manager examines information relating to the amounts, timing, and certainty of a company's future cash flow.

Liquidity and certain areas of operating activity are dependent upon the working capital position of a firm. Net working capital is the excess of current assets over current liabilities. The amount of and changes in net working capital from period to period are significant measures of a company's ability to pay its debts as they mature. Net working capital is generated to a great extent through events that occur during the operating cycle of a business, including transactions involving investing in inventories, converting inventories through sales to receivables, collecting the receivables, and using the cash to pay current debts and replace the inventory sold. Liquidity and activity ratios are useful in evaluating certain trends and relationships involving various aspects of the operating cycle of a business.

For Sample Pharmacy, we will calculate the liquidity ratios of net working capital, current ratio, and the quick ratio from the Sample Pharmacy balance sheet as shown in Figure 5.6.

Net working capital is defined as:

Current assets – Current liabilities = Net working capital
$1,564,200 – $462,600 = $1,101,600

	$	%
Sample Pharmacy Balance sheet as of December 31, 2009		
Current assets		
Cash and cash equivalents	439,200	24.4
Accounts receivable	358,200	19.9
Inventory	657,000	36.5
Other current assets	109,800	6.1
Total current assets	1,564,200	86.9
Net fixed assets	131,400	7.3
Other assets	104,400	5.8
Total assets	1,800,000	100
Current liabilities		
Notes payable (within one year)	45,000	2.5
Accounts payable	289,800	16.1
Other current liabilities	127,800	7.1
Total current liabilities	462,600	25.7
Long-term liabilities		
Notes payable to owner(s)	138,600	7.7
Other long-term liabilities	54,000	3
Total long-term liabilities	192,600	10.7
Total liabilities	655,200	36.4
Total owners' equity	1,144,800	63.6
Total liabilities and owners' equity	1,800,000	100

Figure 5.6 Sample Pharmacy balance sheet.

Given that current assets are defined as those assets that are expected to be converted into cash (or used up within a year) and current liabilities are those liabilities that must be paid within a year, large values of net working capital are preferred. Larger balances in net working capital provide an additional cushion for the company to purchase extra amounts of inventory and meet current obligations, the least of which is payroll. In general, increases in net working capital over time are also a positive sign of a company's operating efficiency. Since the absolute dollar amount of net working capital does not provide extensive information, further refinement is achieved with the current ratio, defined as:

Current assets ÷ Current liabilities = Current ratio
$1,564,200 ÷ $462,000 = 3.38

The current ratio of 3.38 means for each dollar of current liabilities, there are $3.38 of current assets. The general guide for most businesses is to have a current ratio of at least 2 : 1; therefore Sample Pharmacy is relatively strong as measured by the current ratio.

The final measure of short-term liquidity to examine is the quick (or acid-test) ratio, which includes the most liquid assets of the company, cash, cash equivalents, and accounts receivable to current liabilities through the formula:

(Cash+Cash equivalents+Accounts receivable)
÷ Current liabilities = Quick ratio
($439,200 + $358,200) ÷ $462,200 = 1.72

Inventory and other prepaid expenses are not considered quick assets because they may not be easily convertible into cash. This makes the quick ratio a better test of a company's short-term ability to pay debt than the current ratio, with a rule of thumb for the quick ratio at about 1 : 1. From all the measures of short-term liquidity, we see Sample Pharmacy is in reasonably good shape and has ample ability to meet its short-term debt needs.

As can be seen in the review of the three liquidity ratios, the ability of a company to meet current obligations is very important. Further analysis of the current assets may often also be necessary, to identify underlying problems that may be contributing to poor ratios. However, pharmacy practice is distinct in that third party payers constitute a significant portion of sales and, therefore, are subject to contractual payment schedules; however, the accounts receivable turnover still provides information for pharmacy managers. The accounts receivable turnover is calculated by the following formula:

Credit sales ÷ Average accounts receivable
= Accounts receivable turnover

Notice that with only one balance sheet, the appropriate information is not available to perform the calculation. Remember, comparative financial statements may need to be provided to complete most ratio analyses properly.

With the income statement shown in Figure 5.4, and assuming an average accounts receivable balance equal to the December 31, 2009 number, the accounts receivable turnover would be:

Credit sales ÷ Average accounts receivable = Accounts receivable turnover
$4,504,413 ÷ $358,200 = 12.8

A high accounts receivable turnover ratio suggests the receivables are being effectively managed, fewer resources are invested in receivables, and better credit and collection practices are in place.

The inventory turnover and cash conversion cycle are also important ratios to be monitored by pharmacy managers and are discussed in detail in Chapter 6.

Unique pharmacy ratios

When analyzing a pharmacy business, the first thing that comes to mind is prescription dispensing, whether in the community or institutional setting. Therefore, ratio analysis can be tailored to the specific practice setting and provide pharmacy managers with information necessary to develop appropriate staffing requirements and provide quality patient care. Table 5.7 contains a sample of ratios related to prescription activity. Although many of these ratios may be used in various practice areas, many more individual ratios may be developed as long as they provide meaningful information to the pharmacy manager.

Table 5.7 Ratios related to prescription activity

Description	Formula	Measure of company's
Prescriptions dispensed per day	Number of prescriptions filled per day of operations	Volume of pharmacy activity (basis for staffing requirements)
Average prescription sales price	Prescription sales ÷ Number of prescriptions dispensed	Mix of medications dispensed
Percentage of new prescriptions	Number of new prescriptions ÷ Total prescriptions dispensed	Volume of new prescriptions
Percentage of refilled prescriptions	Number of refill prescriptions ÷ Total prescriptions dispensed	Volume of refilled prescriptions
Third party percentage	Third party prescription payments ÷ Total prescription sales	Sales mix of third parties
Generic percentage	Generic medication COGS ÷ Total medication COGS	Sales mix of generic medications
Medication expense per patient day	Annual medication cost ÷ Average patient days	Medication cost as a function of patients
Technician order entry	Number of new prescriptions entered by technician ÷ Total number of new prescriptions	Percentage of new prescriptions entered to fill by the technician

One measure of analysis important to most all pharmacies is customer service. Currently, most, if not all, large chain pharmacies use customer service measures for evaluation purposes. Customers call in and go through an automated telephone survey regarding their recent pharmacy visit, typically scoring their pharmacy experience and the staff on a scale of 1 to 4 or 5. In addition to some of the more traditional ratios mentioned in Table 5.7, in particularly daily/weekly prescription volume, customer service measures have become a primary focus of community pharmacy business evaluation.

Indirectly related to customer service, large community pharmacy corporations typically measure work flow through their internal computer technology, including whether the stock bottle was scanned for label generation, percentage of new prescriptions entered by the technician (checking to make sure the pharmacist is not heavily involved in the dispensing process), and whether the prescription is filled in a timely manner.

Since the most significant payroll cost within a pharmacy practice is the pharmacist's salary, much attention can be given to the proper management of this item. Table 5.8 describes many traditional ratios used for the effective management of payroll in relation to the overall prescription activity.

For those pharmacy managers wishing to continually monitor their profitability in relation to assets, dividends or stock, Table 5.9 provides various ratios which can be used to assess these relationships. Of particular interest to independent pharmacy owner/managers would be the ratio of net

Table 5.8 Activity ratios related to payroll expense

Description	Formula	Measure of company's
FTE per prescription dispensed	Number of FTEs ÷ Number of prescriptions dispensed	Indicator of FTE staffing levels relative to prescription dispensing volume
FTE per patient day	Number of FTEs ÷ Number of patients in hospital per day	Indicator of staffing levels relative to total number of patients in the hospital
Total payroll per prescription dispensed	Total payroll ÷ Number of prescriptions dispensed	Indicator of total staffing (full- and part-time) levels relative to prescription dispensing volume
Prescription sales per store hour open	Total prescriptions dispensed ÷ Total store hours of operations	Indicator of prescription activity relative to each hour operation. Aids in determining hours of operation of the store or pharmacy department
Prescriptions filled per pharmacist per hour	Number of prescriptions dispensed by each pharmacist per hour	Indicator of the efficiency of each pharmacist on duty each day

FTE = full-time employee.

Table 5.9 Profitability ratios commonly used in pharmacy practice

Description	Formula	Measure of company's
Ratio of net sales to assets	Net sales ÷ Average total assets (excluding long-term investments)	To assess the effectiveness in the use of assets
Rate earned on total assets	(Net income + interest expense) ÷ Average total assets	To assess the profitability of the assets
Rate earned on total shareholder's equity	Net income ÷ Average shareholder's equity	To assess the profitability of the investment by shareholders
Rate earned on common shareholder's equity	(Net income − Preferred dividends) ÷ Average common shareholder's equity	To assess the profitability of the investment by common shareholders
Earnings per share on common stock	(Net income − Preferred dividends) ÷ Shares of common stock outstanding	To assess the profitability of the investment by common shareholders
Price-earnings ratio	Market price per share of common stock ÷ Earnings per share of common stock	To indicate future earnings prospects, based on the relationship between market value of common stock and earnings
Dividends per share of common stock	Dividends ÷ Shares of common stock outstanding	To indicate the extent to which earnings are being distributed to common stockholders
Dividend yield	Dividends per share of common stock ÷ Market price per share of common stock	To indicate the rate of return to common shareholders in terms of dividends

sales to assets. This allows for asset evaluation, including whether or not the owner/manager is using the assets to generate sales.

Other types of financial analysis

There are other useful forms of financial analysis that pharmacy managers should be familiar with, including cash flow analysis and cost-volume-profit analyses, discussed in Chapter 8. Along with financial ratio analysis, these are valuable tools that can be used by pharmacy managers to better understand and plan business activities.

Summary

In this chapter, the basics of finance, including time value of money and simple versus compound interest, have been examined. Further, through comparative financial statement analysis, we have shown the pharmacy manager usable metrics to assess the internal business performance. These principles and analyses can be used to determine the necessary resource allocation for staffing, inventory and investment, as well as the overall current and future business direction.

Suggested reading

Chisholm-Burns MA, Vaillancourt AM, Shepherd M. *Pharmacy Management, Leadership, Marketing, and Finance*. Sudbury, MA: Jones & Bartlett Publishers, 2011.

Carroll NV. *Financial Management for Pharmacists: a Decision-Making Approach*, 3rd edn. Baltimore, MD: Lippincott Williams & Wilkins, 2007.

Friedlob GT, Plewa FJ. *Financial and Business Statements*, 3rd edn. Hauppauge, NY: Barron's Educational Series Inc., 2006.

Warren CS, Reeve JM, Duchac JE. *Accounting*, 23rd edn. New York, NY: Random House, 2008.

Walther L. *Principles of Accounting*. Logan, UT: Utah State University. www.principlesofaccounting.com

Review questions

1 An independent community pharmacy owner, BB, has just been approached by the third party health insurance carrier for the new plant being completed in his market area. This new plant will become the town's biggest employer and wants to negotiate a contract with BB for the employees' prescription benefits. BB is currently reviewing the contract and wants to fully understand the financial impact that accepting this contract will have on his business. The basic details are as follows:

   - Estimated number of participants is 400.
   - Estimated amount of prescription sales is $1,000,000.
   - Reimbursement rates should provide an 18% gross margin.
   - Average payment time on claims filed is 40 days.

   BB currently serves approximately 800 customers and has nearly 100% third party reimbursement. Current annual sales volume is $1,500,000 with a gross margin percentage of 15%. Although his pharmacy is profitable, cash flow is extremely critical each month to allow BB to pay all his bills on time, which he currently does. His current accounts receivable are collected, on average, within 15 days of billing, which is completed on a daily basis. Assuming that no additional expenses (staff or other operating) will be needed to meet this new demand, should the contract be accepted as is, in addition to factoring in a $70,000 inventory increase. Discuss how financial analysis would help BB in considering whether or not he should accept this new contract.

2   BB, the independent community pharmacy owner discussed in the previous question, was playing golf with his local banker, HH. During the course of their round, the discussion evolved to the new plant coming to town. BB expressed his remorse for having to give up $180,000 in net income because of his cash flow problem. HH was surprised a business owner would miss such an opportunity and questioned BB further. After a brief time, HH realized BB was tremendously afraid of borrowing any money, and currently there was no debt on the balance sheet of his pharmacy other than current debts recorded in accounts payable. BB was acutely aware of solvency ratios, although he did not fully understand them as much as he did the liquidity ratios. HH offered to discuss this situation in his office after he had a chance to review the pharmacy financial statements. Later in the week at the bank office, HH offered BB a short-term loan of $100,000 for six months at an interest rate of 10%. HH discussed the cash flow concerns with BB, and assured him that this loan would meet the needs of building inventory levels and the increase in average accounts receivable outstanding if BB accepted the new contract. As predicted, BB was initially quite hesitant, but accepted the offer. Discuss some of the import aspects that HH relayed to BB in order for him to accept the financing arrangement.

3   After six months, business as a result of the new contract was booming and BB made his final payment to the bank to retire his short-term loan. With the increase in prescription volume, the amount of customers in the pharmacy was always constant and the wait time was very reasonable, at about 10 minutes. BB was anxious to begin expanding his pharmacy with new revenue streams from additional merchandise, services, or gifts, ever since he had attended the annual convention of his state pharmacy association. Having the extra space within the pharmacy posed a problem; however, the tenant next to his pharmacy had recently moved and there was space available. The pharmacy's cash flow had improved and there was much greater flexibility, which BB welcomed and enjoyed. BB was also more comfortable in borrowing and saw the advantages of prudent leveraging. To attract more customers to support this new endeavor, the idea of opening a lunch counter was also on BB's mind, since the small town offered very few lunch options. After researching the potential profitability of lunch counters, BB saw operating them was usually break-even at best; however, increased customer traffic, especially in small towns, was very well-established. From the information provided by the

state association, the gross profit percentage for selling gifts ranged from 40 to 55%, and a beginning inventory of $60,000 was adequate to provide for a variety of products. The construction estimate to layout the lunch counter and expand the pharmacy through the adjoining wall was $40,000. BB scheduled an appointment to discuss the proposition of another short-term loan with HH, his local banker. Discuss some of the possible responses HH had for BB.

4   Consider the following information: Two companies began making $100,000 contributions to their endowment funds on an annual basis 15 years ago. Each company began with an original investment of $1,000,000 and both earned 5% interest over the entire period. Company A has a final investment balance of $4,344,677, while company B only has $4,236,785. Since the original balances were equal, as were annual contributions and interest rate earned, can you explain the difference in the ending balances?

5   Living Well, Inc. is a long-term care facility that operates throughout the region. The CEO of the corporation has requested information from the Director of Pharmacy regarding the installation of new equipment throughout the 46 locations. The decision has been made to purchase electronic medication administration records and bedside barcode scanning equipment for each location at a cost of $10,000 per location. The vendor has offered the following payment options:

- option A: $460,000 due in full upon completion of installation
- option B: $230,000 at the end of the next 2 years at 6%
- option C: $92,000 at the end of the next 5 years at 5%.

The CEO has enlisted your help in determining the best option. Discuss some of your replies regarding total cost and overall cash flow.

6   In financial statement analysis, expressing all financial statement items as a percentage of base-year amounts is called:
A   Horizontal analysis
B   Ratio analysis
C   Vertical analysis
D   Trend analysis

7   In general, the more frequent (or shorter) the period of compounding, the greater the impact of compounding on the principal balance. True or false?

8 Which of the following financial statement analyses is most useful in determining whether the various expenses of a given company are higher or lower than industry averages?
   A Horizontal analysis
   B Vertical analysis
   C Activity ratio analysis
   D Trend analysis.

9 Benchmarking tells how a company's financial performance is improving or deteriorating over time. True or false?

10 Which of the following would be the most preferred minimum set of ratio analysis indicators?
   A Large net working capital; current ratio of 1 : 1; quick ratio of 2 : 1
   B Small net working capital; current ratio of 2 : 1; quick ratio of 2 : 1
   C Small net working capital; current ratio of 1 : 1; quick ratio of 1 : 1
   D Large net working capital; current ratio of 2 : 1; quick ratio of 1 : 1.

Answers

1 The importance of financial analysis can be seen in this case in several ways. When examining the impact upon profits, the expected gross margin percentage of 18% is superior to BB's current performance and, therefore, accepting the contract seems appropriate. The new gross margin percentage of 18%, when multiplied by the expected annual sales increase of $1,000,000 will yield additional gross profit (and net income before taxes) of $180,000 over the next year. Roughly, this will occur at a rate of $15,000 positive cash flow per month. However, liquidity issues are a concern as determined by the recurring cash flow problems each month. Since the new contract establishes an accounts receivable turnover nearly three times as long (40 versus 15 day turnover) as the current accounts receivable turnover, BB is very concerned. Using the predicted accounts receivable turnover of 40 days, BB calculates the average accounts receivable balance from the accounts receivable turnover formula. In this case, the average accounts receivable is estimated to be $25,000 each month [40 days = ($1,000,000 ÷ x)]. Although the net income is greater at $15,000 per month, BB knows his accounts receivable balance, a use of cash, will increase at $25,000 within one month, and BB will

have to absorb this, in addition to the $70,000 cash outlay to increase his inventory levels, relatively quickly. Therefore, based upon the results of his financial analysis, BB decides against accepting the insurance contract since the pharmacy cannot absorb the additional cash requirements of nearly $80,000 within the first month of accepting the contract.

2 HH reviewed the balance sheet of his pharmacy with BB, noting it was extremely unusual for a company not to have debt and that BB would not be a failure if he accepted the financing. HH showed his calculations for the debt ratio and debt-equity ratio for BB's pharmacy if the financing was approved. BB expressed a concern over having to pay $10,000 in interest payments during the loan period. HH reviewed the principles of the time value of money and showed BB that total interest would be just over half of that amount, since interest rates are always expressed in annual terms. Therefore, since the loan would be for only six months, only one-half of the 10% would eventually be charged to BB. When HH showed the effect on the income statement of receiving an additional $180,000 in net income, in relation to the interest expense of $5,000, BB's fears were diminished. The contract for the financing with the bank was signed the next day, and BB negotiated the contract in confidence with the third party health insurance provider for the new plant.

3 HH was very excited to learn about BB's proposals, especially after reviewing the income statement for the previous six months and the time repayment of the short-term loan. After careful consideration of the anticipated projects and the related estimates, HH rejected BB's request. Instead, he offered to finance the new projects with a 10-year long-term loan. The basis for a long-term loan lies in the life of the projects. These improvements should secure the pharmacy's viability within the community for years to come. Additionally, the new plant is also very successful and shows no signs of closing. Therefore, in order to project a healthier balance sheet for the pharmacy, the corresponding financing for these improvements should be shown in the long-term liabilities (debt) section as opposed to the current liability section. The long-term assets will reflect the improvements, while the current assets will record the newly purchased gift inventory. The bank was also able to reduce the interest rate from the 10% rate to the current rate of 5%, as a result of both the credit history of the pharmacy and the loan's term. In general, when borrowing, long-term interest rates are much better than those offered in the short term. BB was more than

thrilled to discover this fact and even more anxious to begin his pharmacy expansion and diversification.

4   The time value of money concept referred to interest rates and years of investment. However, implicit in the concept of the time value of money is the length of total time money is invested and earning interest. Company A made their $100,000 annual contribution at the beginning of each year, whereas company B contributed on the last day of the year. Therefore, company A earned additional interest for 15 years and the effect of the time value of money explains the difference of $107,892.

5   The basis for determining the best financing options lies in the concept of present value. Like future value, present value helps determine the current value of future payments at a specified interest rate, called the discount rate. The absolute amount of payments for each option is $460,000 but, given the time value of money, when each payment is due determines the ultimate present value. Option A has a present value of $460,000 as it is being paid without any effect of the time value of money. Option B, taking into consideration the time value of money for the 2-year period at 6% results in a present value of $421,680. Following the same logic as option B, option C has a present value of $398,312. In discussing with the CEO, you would need to know the ability of the company to earn interest in the current and expected market place. If the interest that the company can earn is less than 5% or 6%, taking advantage of the time value of money would lead you to conclude that option C should be taken since it has the lowest present value amount because of the length of time and interest rate. However, if the company can earn interest at rates greater than 5% or 6%, option A should be chosen to pay the debt in today's dollars. Any excess funds available to the company should be invested at the higher interest rates and yield a greater future value over time. Conversely, if cash flow is a concern to the company, either because of profitability or needs to expand, then extending payments, regardless of the interest rate that could otherwise be earned, is the greatest factor to consider, and then option C should be chosen.

6   A is correct. Expressing financial statement items as percentages of corresponding base-year figures is a horizontal form of percentage analysis that is useful for evaluating trends. The base amount is assigned the value of 100% and the amounts for other years are denominated in percentages compared with the base year.

Regarding the other options, ratio analysis is a general term; vertical percentage analysis presents figures for a single year expressed as percentages of a base amount on the balance sheet (e.g., total assets) and on the income statement (e.g., sales); and the term "trend analysis" is most often applied to the quantitative techniques used in forecasting to fit a curve to given data.

7   The statement is true. The shorter the period of compounding, monthly instead of annually, leads to a greater impact on the principal balance, especially during the final periods. A longer period of compounding, every 2 years compared with every year, would not have as great an impact on the principal balance.

8   B is correct. Vertical analysis is the expression of each item on a financial statement in a given period in relation to a base figure. On the income statement, each item is stated as a percentage of sales. Thus, the percentages for the company in question can be compared to industry norms. Horizontal analysis indicates the proportionate change over a period of time and is useful in trend analysis of an individual entity. Activity ratio analysis includes the preparation of turnover ratios such as those for receivables, inventory, and total assets. A trend analysis indicates changes in an individual entity over a period of time.

9   The statement is true. Benchmarking is comparing one company's financial results with results from other companies or with an industry average. Trend analysis indicates in which direction a company is headed.

10   D is correct. Larger values of net working capital are desired. Also, the current ratio of 2 : 1 and a quick ratio of 1 : 1 are the minimum desirable values, meaning the company has at least double the amount of assets to liabilities and the ability to pay short-term debts.

Glossary

Compound interest   Applies to interest over more than one period. To calculate compound interest we begin just as with simple interest; however, during the second and all future periods, the interest rate is applied to both the original principal plus the interest earned in the first period and each subsequent period.

Horizontal financial analysis	Refers to the process of comparing the financial performance and current condition of a company over several time periods.
Liquidity	Refers to the ability of a company to meet short-term cash requirements, which is significantly affected by the timing of various inflows and outflows of cash.
Simple interest	The interest computed on the principal amount for one period of time and calculated as such: $FV = P(1 + r)$.
Solvency	Attempts to quantify a company's ability to satisfy long-term debt obligations as well as the corresponding viability of the company to continue future operations.
Time value of money	A dollar today is worth more than a dollar at some date in the future because the dollar today can earn interest (or be invested) and the value of the dollar will grow as the future date is approached. The idea is that money available at the present time is worth more than the same amount in the future because of its potential earning capacity.
Vertical financial analysis	Refers to the process of comparing the financial performance and current condition of a company in relation to a base amount.

6

Financial aspects of inventory management

Learning objectives

- Describe the cash conversion cycle and its importance to inventory management
- Identify and understand the four main costs of inventory, including purchase, ordering, carrying, and stock-out costs
- Understand the importance of avoiding stock outs and maintaining safety stock
- Describe and develop the economic order quantity and reorder point, then understand their importance in optimizing inventory control
- List and explain inventory management considerations

Introduction

Pharmacy managers face unique challenges when it comes to the proper management of inventory, with balancing inventory levels that satisfy patients' needs while minimizing costs the primary goal. This goal is not met when inventory is managed without careful planning and analysis – for example, just ordering substantial quantities of each formulary medication in an institutional setting. While this method of controlling inventory may result in meeting the objective of appropriate patient care, it will also result in excess levels of inventory sitting on the shelves and represent a significant use of cash. The second major consideration for pharmacy managers is to decide the appropriate level of resources (cash) to be committed to inventory. Recognizing that inventory is included on the balance sheet as a current asset, it is less liquid given its little value to the pharmacy operation until it is dispensed, billed for and payment/reimbursement collected, which is known as the *cash conversion cycle*. Recently in large chain/grocery chain/mass merchandise pharmacies, inventory control has become automated using barcode technology to provide identification of inventory and track transactions in real time as they occur.

These automated systems require less effort on the part of pharmacy managers – but the underlying principles and goals of inventory management must still be understood. Efficiently balancing patient needs and the right level of inventory investment is discussed in this chapter.

Cash conversion cycle

The flow of cash is vital to all companies and maximizing inflows while minimizing outflows can increase overall operating efficiency and, ultimately, increase profitability. The elapsed time between the purchase of inventory items and the collection of cash resulting from its sale is known as the cash conversion cycle. When the decision is made to purchase inventory, cash outlays are required to pay for the requested items. Once the inventory is received, it is placed on the shelves until it is needed for prescription orders, which represents a use of cash. Obviously, an unrestrained level of inventory items in stock does not meet the goal of minimizing cash outlays. The cash conversion cycle continues with the ultimate dispensing, or use, of the medications in stock. Correspondingly, the medications dispensed must be billed to the patient or their third party payer, which in turn creates an account receivable, another current asset shown on the balance sheet. Of note is that accounts receivable is more liquid than inventory, as there has been an expressed promise to pay for the inventory received. All accounts receivable have descriptions of the terms of payment, usually expressed in days. Often, additional finance charges, or interest, are added to the original balance if the agreed upon terms are not met. The cash conversion cycle is completed when the cash payment is received by the company (Figure 6.1).

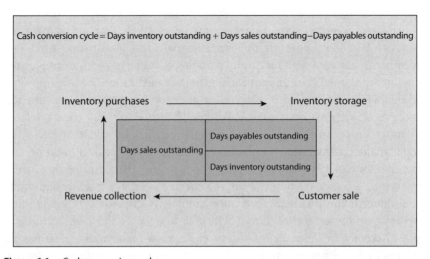

Figure 6.1 Cash conversion cycle.

The matching of inflows and outflows with regard to inventory and accounts receivable is vital to all companies, because the cash needs of the company resulting from the differences between these two processes must be funded from other sources. If additional borrowing is required by the company, the associated finance costs will reduce the profitability of the company. In addition, if payments are delayed to vendors for inventory purchases, problems can arise. Vendors may refuse to offer any type of discounts and possibly even begin to require cash payment upon delivery. Loss of discounts reduces gross profit and overall profitability. Accounts receivable must also be managed aggressively, as delayed payments may indicate severe financial difficulties from customers, which may ultimately result in non-payment. While management of accounts receivable may be beyond the traditional duties of a pharmacy manager, understanding the importance of the cash conversion cycle and its effect on the company's profitability is critical. Additionally, since the physical inventory maintained on site is a significant use of a company's cash flow, pharmacy managers in all practice environments must understand how appropriate management of inventory has its affect.

Basic inventory costs

When discussing inventory costs, most managers first think of the actual purchase cost of inventory. However, there are other basic costs attributed to the overall cost of inventory, including ordering, carrying, and stock-out costs. Purchasing costs are the most easily identifiable inventory cost. The purchase price is very objective, usually being stated outright with terms noted for prompt payment, rebates, or other incentives creating sales discounts. Discounts, such as the *prompt pay discount*, are offered by vendors to entice their customers for prompt, or even early, payment in order to help them maintain their own cash conversion cycle. Often '2% net 10', this means that a 2% cash discount of the total invoice may be taken if the entire balance is paid within 10 days instead of the traditional 30 days. Given the time value of money, sales discounts usually provide a large annual rate of return and should be taken by companies, even if short-term borrowing is required. Another common purchasing discount is known as quantity discounts, which give certain percentage discounts as the quantity purchased increases.

Case-in-point 6.1 Prompt payment discounts

Some large chain pharmacy operations, community based as well as hospital based, operate their own warehouses as their primary distribution method to individual pharmacy locations. These chains also supplement their inventory needs with other full service wholesalers and distributors, when needed. Consider such a warehousing chain servicing a broad geographic, SB Pharmacy. SB maintains direct purchasing accounts with selected name brand and generic manufacturers which it stocks in corporate warehouses. With an average monthly corporate inventory purchase of approximately $20 million, taking advantage of a 2% prompt payment discount would result in an annual inventory cost savings of $4.8 million. On this large scale, it is easy to see the benefits of taking advantage of the prompt payment discount. However, regardless of the size of the pharmacy operation, the prompt payment discount provides a significant reduction in inventory costs. For example, consider a long-term care institution which purchases $65,000 of generic medications annually to provide prescriptions to its residents, staff, and family members. Contracting with a full line generic manufacturer offering a prompt payment discount (e.g., 2% net 10) would result in a savings of $1,300 off invoice pricing.

However, purchasing in today's business environment can become quite complicated. With contract bidding, buying groups and wholesaler source programs offering special pricing and purchase terms, most corporate buying is beyond the duty of the majority of pharmacy managers and handled within the accounting department. These programs can be a significant benefit for smaller pharmacy operations because they permit them to take advantage of volume purchasing through the larger buying group or wholesaler. Manufacturers like negotiating with these groups since they can represent significant increases in market share when their products are selected for distribution among members or buyers in the group.

Case-in-point 6.2 Wholesaler source programs

Most major wholesalers offer "source" programs for multisource medications, where certain manufacturers' products are featured and given distribution preference over other manufacturers' products. In these source programs, wholesalers and distributors negotiate directly with the manufacturers, trading preferred distribution, which increases market share, for larger discounts. The savings are then passed along to the members of the buying group or wholesale customer. Other benefits of source programs may include consistency of supply and one-stop shopping for a variety of products.

Other types of buying agreements can include competitive bidding or bundling the purchase price of one product with the amount of an additional product's purchase quantity. In many institutional or large warehousing chain practices, market share contracts are offered by various manufacturers. Under a market share contract, additional discounts or rebates are awarded if the percentage market share of all purchases within a certain category exceeds a contracted level. These contracts recognize the importance of individual retailers' professional purchasing decisions on manufacturers' market share. However, in most larger chain settings, pharmacy managers are not the individuals who negotiate these more complicated purchasing contracts. Pharmacy managers may, however, be asked to contribute information to the contracting, bidding or accounting department where these kinds of negotiations occur.

The next basic inventory cost is *ordering costs*, which are those costs associated with placing an order and processing the corresponding payment. Any costs associated with receiving the goods and getting them to the shelves for dispensing can also be included. For simplicity's sake, ordering costs are usually not separately identified, as most pharmacy environments place daily orders with their wholesalers and payment is made through the accounting department. Putting the order on the shelves is also considered part of routine daily duties of the pharmacy staff; although, if significant, these costs could also be identified separately. Though, if an institution wishes to make bulk purchases of intravenous supplies and these orders require additional outlays, such as offsite storage and labor to unload and re-distribute when needed, these costs should be added to the overall purchase price when placing orders.

Not all items in inventory generate the same level of profits. Further, some items require more inventory space than others. This is where the third basic inventory cost, known as *carrying costs*, comes into focus. The *capital investment*, or the inventory's actual purchase price, is the major and most easily identifiable component of carrying costs and the primary factor in relation to the cash conversion cycle. Inventory service costs, such as handling, insurance, and taxes are another component. Thirdly, storage costs outside of the actual pharmacy contribute to carrying costs of inventory. Finally, there are the risk costs, which are made up of *obsolescence*, damage, and *shrink*. Therefore, good inventory management is often a trade-off between the costs associated with keeping inventory on hand (e.g., carrying costs) and the benefits of having the inventory in stock (ability to sell the inventory and convert it into cash). In other words, the carrying costs of maintaining higher levels of inventory must be balanced with the less easily measurable costs of stock outs, lost sales, poor patient care/satisfaction and even the business's or institution's reputation.

Case-in-point 6.3   Inventory loss

Product obsolescence, theft (shrink), and natural disasters occur in all businesses. The impact of these events is obvious. However, for most retailers, there are more subtle risks that can impact inventories. For example, medications that need to be refrigerated can be placed at risk when power outages occur. Flooding and other types of water damage, such as that from a broken pipe or water heater, can also create inventory losses. Losses can also occur as a result of poor inventory storage, such as when inventory is improperly stored, e.g., boxes stacked too high and they become unstable and there is breakage. While some level of risk is inherent, proper management can reduce these kinds of risks to a minimum.

Considering all medications have an expiration date after which the value is substantially reduced, obsolescence is a major consideration in inventory management. Proper rotation of stock is essential, as is regular monitoring of expiration dates. Many wholesalers allow for a return of inventory items based upon their expiration dates, and effective pharmacy managers will keep a close eye on individual inventory items and their expiration dates to take full advantage of any return programs, given the magnitude of potential losses. Damage to inventory is possible at any time, just by the existence of the inventory on the shelves. Although damage is usually accidental, pharmacy managers should strive for proper housekeeping of inventory to minimize such occurrences.

Case-in-point 6.4   Damages/damage reports

Throughout the work day or week, medications are spilled, IV bags are broken or pills are crushed, leading to damaged inventory. To handle these situations, managers can keep an exact report/log of all damaged products and adjust the inventory accordingly, or properly dispose of the damaged product and let it exist as shrink on the year-end inventory. Either way, the inventory was purchased but not able to be sold and, at the least, recoup the associated cost. Pharmacy managers must diligently stress to the staff the negative impact damaged inventory can have on sales and work to reduce damages and, therefore, maximize sales potential.

The final risk cost included in inventory carrying costs is shrinkage, or simply "shrink". When the final calculated inventory value in a company's accounting records is compared with the final valuation from the physical inventory, any shortage is referred to as shrink. Inventory shrink is expressed in the actual dollar amount difference, or as a percentage of the total inventory balance. Usually, theft is attributed to the existence of shrink, both by customer shoplifting and employee theft. Proper controls over access to inventory and good housekeeping by pharmacy managers can contribute greatly to keeping inventory shrink to a minimum.

Case-in-point 6.5   Employee theft

Theft of inventory, also referred to as "shrink," occurs across all industries. It may be particularly troublesome in pharmacy since medications have such significant implications when used improperly or abused. Shrink can be caused by shoppers or employees. A rule of thumb is that nearly one-half of all shrink occurs at the hands of employees. Employee theft occurs just like shoplifting, when an employee conceals merchandise and removes it from the business. Theft can also be the result of an employee allowing others to steal from the business. Regardless of how the theft occurs, the result is inventory loss. Ideally, there would be some way to identify a dishonest employee. Unfortunately, dishonest employees are found in all work settings and it is impossible to identify these individuals by some demographic or physical characteristic. Careful screening of employees (e.g., character, honesty, and integrity) and corporate policies (e.g., lockers for personal items such as coats or purses, clear policies that all theft will be prosecuted and result in termination) that reduce opportunity are the best defense against employee theft.

Not having a medication in stock, in any pharmacy arena, has expensive costs associated with it. These costs are the final basic inventory cost, stockout costs. For example, if an extreme emergency requires that the out-of-stock item be procured overnight, a non-discounted price with additional overnight shipping charges is often paid. While these costs are readily quantifiable, sometimes they are not. Consider the case of an extremely upset customer at the independent community pharmacy. The lack of availability of the item may cause them to take their entire prescription business to a competitor, or worse, customers who are close friends of the irritated customer may sympathize and change pharmacies as well. This lost opportunity may exist for only a few weeks, or forever. Therefore, prevention of stock outs is a goal of proper inventory management. Stock outs may be avoided by maintaining a safety stock, or minimum amount to always be on hand. It is determined in relation to expected usage as well as any delivery lead times. Although there are carrying costs associated with safety stock, the potential cost of damaging customer relations and future business usually exceeds them and justifies having a cushion of safety stock.

Case-in-point 6.6   Stock outs

JB is a 40 year old diabetic who uses insulin 500 units/ml. This concentration is convenient and saves JB from having to give multiple injections because of his high insulin dose requirement. Even so, his insulin dose has remained relatively constant over time. He has recently changed pharmacies because the pharmacy he had been patronizing required him to call a day ahead so the insulin he needed could be ordered, rather than stocking it routinely. The pharmacy maintained that having this concentration was not desirable since it could be accidentally sold to a patient who might inject it as if it were the 100-unit concentration. JB was accepting of this, but, on several occasions over the past year, the insulin was not available from the wholesaler on short notice and JB had to resort to multiple injections. This prompted him to switch to a pharmacy willing to keep the 500-unit concentration in stock. In fact, the new pharmacy manager decided to order JB's supply after each purchase so that a safety stock could be maintained and JB's needs would be sure to be met.

Case-in-point 6.7   Stock outs – large chain pharmacy perspective

Most large-chain pharmacy district managers continually monitor ordering levels, especially for items typically available from the store's own warehouse. As discussed above, emergency overnight purchases through a wholesaler are made at much greater costs than from the chain's warehouse. District managers want to see as low a percentage of emergency/non-warehouse purchases as possible.

Inventory record keeping methods

There are two basic ways to keep a record of inventory values and quantities, known as perpetual and periodic methods. The *perpetual inventory* system is most commonly used, and, as implied by its name, this system can provide details of the inventory quantities and values whenever they are needed. When using the perpetual inventory method, each purchase is recorded along with individual sales when they occur. Since a beginning balance for any time period is available, this period activity is recorded and an ending inventory balance is shown as illustrated in Figure 6.2. Note that both dollar and quantity details of purchases and sales are shown.

Date	Purchases		Sales		Balance on hand	
Perpetual inventory Plavix 75 mg tablets 100 count bottles						
	No.	$	No.	$	No.	$
4/1/20xx	300	500.00 per bottle			300	1,500.00
4/5/20xx			60	300.00	240	1,200.00
4/17/20xx			90	450.00	150	750.00
4/29/20xx			60	300.00	90	450.00
4/30/20xx	300	525.00 per bottle			390	2025.00

Figure 6.2 Perpetual inventory example for single item.

The perpetual recording of activity produces both the inventory recording method's name as well as inventory details. When this process is replicated many times over for each individual item (referred to as SKUs, or stock keeping units), the sum of all SKUs will produce the final inventory amount, which is shown on the balance sheet. In theory, the actual inventory quantities on the pharmacy's shelves should exactly agree with the values shown in the perpetual inventory record keeping systems. Discrepancies between recorded quantities and actual quantities are a result of various factors, such as counting or recording errors.

Case-in-point 6.8   Perpetual inventory

When a retail pharmacy operation places an inventory order, either from a full service wholesaler or a company owned warehouse, the inventory received in each order must be added to the quantity on hand, to accurately reflect new inventory levels. This is usually done by "applying" the order to the existing inventory maintained in the pharmacy computer system. Applying the order serves to increase the inventory count of the products received. Invoices are then provided to the accounting department for collating and payment, as well as inventory auditing.

Description	Balance in $
Beginning balance	0
Add: April purchases	600,000
Total available	600,000
Less: 4/30/20xx physical count	390,000
Quantity sold during April 20xx	210,000

Figure 6.3 Periodic inventory example for single item.

The second inventory record keeping method, the *periodic inventory* system, is less often used because it provides fewer details. As one can imagine from the name, the inventory value is determined on a periodic basis. Since the periodic system is less sophisticated, many details regarding prices and quantities are not maintained as shown in Figure 6.3. Under this system, at the end of various operating periods, the inventory account is updated to reflect the actual value of the ending inventory on the balance sheet and the corresponding amount to be recorded as COGS. During the period, all of the inventory purchases are recorded only in the total dollar amount of purchases. At the end of an operating period, the ending inventory value is determined by taking a physical inventory.

A physical inventory is a labor-intensive process and each inventory item is physically counted on a specific date. Owing to the nature of taking a physical inventory, there are various vendors available for hire by companies to complete a physical inventory. By employing personnel trained in counting pharmacy inventory, a physical inventory can be completed quickly and efficiently with the appropriate preparation.

Completing the actual physical count is only half of the process. After obtaining details of all SKUs and their corresponding quantities, the appropriate cost information must be assigned. The extension process begins whereby the actual quantity on hand is multiplied by the current cost, which yields an extended inventory. The extended inventory provides the final dollar value of the inventory and is shown on the balance sheet.

There are benefits, as well as drawbacks, to each of these two inventory record keeping methods. If simplicity is desired, the periodic system functions very well, although there is much less timely information available for pharmacy managers. Since only dollar amounts of purchases need to be reflected in the accounting records, summary entries can be made. In contrast, the perpetual system requires more recording effort; however, computers and automation have greatly reduced this impact with much of the information being provided electronically from wholesalers and other vendors. The periodic system has a significant limitation in being unable to provide COGS on a regular basis, thus preventing the preparation of a consistent income statement. Some pharmacy managers have operating environments that are able to function effectively in this manner, namely the independent owners of community pharmacies. They are often very skilled at understanding their pharmacy's operations and can estimate operating results through cash flow and visual inspection of inventory levels. On the other hand, the perpetual inventory system provides pharmacy managers and others with much more timely inventory details. Additionally, each accounting period may be closed and COGS be calculated along with the corresponding net income. One of the major strengths of the perpetual inventory system is the ability to perform individual item analysis and identify, assess, and correct inventory shrink.

Inventory valuation methods

As previously mentioned, the physical flow of inventory is implicit – oldest items are sold first, and then replaced with newer items. In pharmacy practice, this means medications with earlier expiration dates are dispensed first and normally replaced with medications that have much later expiration dates. When a company determines an inventory value at the end of any accounting period, there are three inventory valuation methods which may be used. It is important to emphasize that these inventory valuation methods are obtained through the accounting system information flow from detailed transactions of company activities. Therefore, the physical flow of inventory will not match the assumed flow of the accounting data. Under each inventory valuation method, assumptions must be made regarding the flow of inventory costs. As a result, COGS are different under each inventory valuation method, which in turn will yield different ending inventory balances, gross profit and net income amounts. Regardless of the inventory valuation method chosen, the flow of the actual physical inventory dispensed should always be based upon the earliest expiration date of individual inventory items. A detailed discussion of each of the three inventory valuation methods follows, using the detail of purchases for one month as shown in Figure 6.4. It is important to note that regardless of the inventory valuation method used, the inventory purchases are recorded in exactly the same manner.

Perhaps the easiest inventory valuation method to understand is the one that simulates the actual physical flow of inventory throughout a company.

Any Hospital Name Detail inventory sheet March 20XX D5W, 1 liter bags, 12 count cases			
Date	Cases received	Per case cost	Total cost
3/8/20XX	60	$15.25	$915.00
3/16/20XX	80	$14.93	$1,194.40
3/28/20XX	90	$15.37	$1,383.30
Total purchases	230	$15.19 (average case cost)	$3,492.70

Figure 6.4 Sample inventory purchases.

Therefore, the *first-in, first-out method*, known as FIFO, reduces inventory value for dispensed inventory in the same order in which shipments are received. Since the FIFO inventory valuation method results in the remaining inventory items being those most recently purchased, it is sometimes also referred to as *last-in, still here* or LISH. The advantage of the FIFO inventory valuation method is shown on the balance sheet, where the ending inventory value reflects the most recent purchase costs.

Under FIFO, the cost of goods sold (COGS) is based upon the cost of material bought earliest in the period, while the cost of inventory is based upon the cost of material bought later in the period. This usually results in inventory being valued at a higher level. During periods of inflation, the use of FIFO will result in the lowest estimate of COGS and higher net income.

As the name implies, the *last-in, first-out* (LIFO) inventory valuation method is the direct opposite of the FIFO inventory valuation method. The earliest inventory items purchased are the last inventory items sold, therefore LIFO may be referred to as *first-in, still here*, or FISH. Accordingly, since the last inventory items purchased are assumed to be the first inventory items to be sold, there is a better matching on the income statement with COGS reflecting the current cost of inventory items. Under the FIFO inventory valuation method, the income statement reflects earlier inventory acquisition costs, which may or may not reflect current inventory replacement costs. The importance of the closer matching of current inventory costs on the income statement under the LIFO inventory valuation method is critical in periods of inflation or rising costs. In essence, LIFO will produce the highest estimate of

Any Hospital Name Affects of inventory valuation methods D5W, 1 liter bags, 12 count cases			
Method	Ending quantity	Ending inventory value	COGS
FIFO	75	$1,152.75	$2,339.95
LIFO	75	$1,138.95	$2,353.75
WAC	75	$1,139.25	$2,353.45

Figure 6.5 Affects of inventory valuation methods. (See the chapter glossary for an explanation of the abbreviations.)

COGS and lowest corresponding net income estimate when compared with FIFO.

The effect of these two methods can also be seen on the balance sheet. LIFO will understate the inventory values on the balance as compared with the FIFO inventory valuation method. Some firms may use a LIFO approach for the tax benefits during periods of high inflation. When firms switch from FIFO to LIFO in valuing inventory, there is likely to be a drop in net income and a concurrent increase in cash flows (because of the tax savings). The reverse will apply when firms switch from LIFO to FIFO.

The *weighted average cost* (WAC) inventory valuation method is a compromise between FIFO and LIFO. The WAC per unit is calculated by taking the COGS available for sale and dividing this by the total number of units for the period. At the end of each accounting period, this weighted average cost per unit of inventory is determined and reflected in both the balance sheet and income statement as COGS. The WAC valuation method levels out the effects of market fluctuations in inventory prices, as seen with the FIFO and LIFO inventory valuation methods in periods where prices are rising. Therefore, in periods of fluctuating prices, the effects on both the balance sheet and income statements can be minimized through the use of the WAC inventory valuation method.

Figure 6.5 compares the various ending inventory valuations and corresponding COGS shown on the balance sheet and income statement when the three inventory valuation methods are used. This example assumes there was no beginning inventory balance and a periodic inventory system is used. A physical inventory count resulted in the ending inventory quantity remaining for March 20XX of 75 cases. Pay close attention to the variation in both the COGS and ending inventory values under each inventory valuation method. It is important to note the selection of which inventory valuation method is employed by a particular company, especially in the chain and hospital setting, is often made by upper management or the accounting department, not pharmacy managers.

The ending FIFO inventory value of $1,152.75 is determined as if all of the remaining 75 cases were part of the last purchase of 90 cases at a cost of $15.37 per case. The COGS amount is calculated by the formula:

Beginning inventory ($0) + Purchases ($3, 492.70)
– Ending inventory ($1, 152.75) = $2, 339.95

Using the LIFO inventory valuation method, the remaining 75 cases are valued at $1,138.95, the cost of the initial 75 purchased [(60 cases @ $15.25) + (15 cases @ $14.93/case)]. WAC produces an ending inventory value of $1,139.25 and uses the average cost per case for the period to value the ending 75 cases (75 cases @ $15.19/case).

Managing inventory turnover

Other than physical facilities, inventory represents one of the largest uses of cash within a pharmacy. Once purchased, inventory must be sold and the funds from the sale received before the firm's cash can be used for various aspects of the pharmacy operation. In institutional and chain settings, pharmacy managers may not be directly responsible for the cash flow of the business, but these managers are acutely aware of the impact high inventory levels can have on operating efficiency. Inventory is perhaps the most carefully controlled of all operating costs and an expected function of all pharmacists involved in dispensing in any way.

Financial ratios (discussed in Chapter 5) are routinely used to assess the effectiveness of a pharmacy operations inventory control techniques. The most common of these ratios is the inventory turnover ratio. The *inventory turnover ratio* is a benchmark used by pharmacy managers to assess inventory control and measure how many times the inventory of a company is used up during a period, usually a year. The expression "turns" or "turn days" is calculated by dividing 365 by the annual inventory turnover. This number is used to estimate the number of days of inventory available for sale.

The inventory turnover ratio is calculated by the formula:

Inventory turnover = Cost of goods sold / Average inventory

Average inventory is calculated by averaging the beginning and ending inventory balance (from the balance sheet) and given by the equation:

Average inventory = (Beginning inventory+Ending inventory) / 2

For the year ended December 31, 20XX			
Description	Actual	Budget	Last year
Average inventory			
Prescription sales	$159,848	$150,980	$140,844
Other sales	65,716	56,624	52,130
Total	225,564	207,604	192,974
Cost of goods sold			
Prescription	$1,678,407	$1,670,545	$1,575,241
Other sales	536,748	411,002	331,105
Total	2,215,155	2,081,547	1,906,346
Inventory turnover ratio			
Pharmacy	10.5	11.1	11.2
Front end	8.2	7.3	6.4
Combined	9.8	10.0	9.9

Figure 6.6   Sample inventory turnover analysis report.

In general, an inventory turnover ratio of approximately 12 turns per year is considered optimal for most pharmacy operations. This means, on average, the pharmacy will operate with about 30 days, or one month, of inventory on hand. Some items may have higher turnover rates than the overall operation. These items, usually referred to as "fast movers" in the pharmacy environment, vary by area and represent the most commonly used medications. Fast movers may be purchased in larger quantities, turnover more frequently and can have a significant impact on profitability. Thus, it is important to price these items carefully, which is discussed in Chapter 8.

Using the information shown in Figure 6.6, the pharmacy's actual prescription inventory turnover of 10.5 for the year is determined by dividing the prescription COGS by the pharmacy average inventory.

Inventory turnover (IT) = COGS / Average inventory
Inventory turnover (IT) = $1,678,407 / $159,848 = 10.5

A separate turnover can be calculated for other sales (OTC, etc.):

Other sales IT = COGS / Average inventory
Other sales IT = $536,748 / $65,716 = 8.2

Accordingly, the overall inventory turnover ratio for the entire pharmacy business would be:

Overall IT = Combined COGS / Combined average inventory
Overall IT = $2,215,155 / $225,564 = 9.8

Generally, pharmacy managers track inventory turnover year by year to assess the effectiveness of their inventory control efforts. Industry averages or benchmarks are often used to further assess pharmacy operations inventory policies. When the inventory turnover ratio is lower than the benchmark (12 turns per year), this can be an indicator that inventory is too high. Possible reasons for this might include deterioration, damage, obsolescence or over-estimation of need. When the inventory turnover ratio is higher, it usually means pharmacy managers are using inventory more efficiently. Higher inventory turnover ratios indicate the purchases of new inventory items are replacing the inventory actually being sold and fewer inventory items are sitting idle on the shelves. This means less cash is tied up in inventory and is available for other uses, including increased profitability.

Other inventory control techniques

In today's pharmacy business, inventory is often received daily and many pharmacy practice environments control inventory by ordering products to arrive just in time as it is needed for sale. This is known as a *just-in-time* (JIT) inventory control method. JIT is a quality-control process aimed at reducing inventory costs. This method can benefit a pharmacy business by reducing average inventory and even improving customer satisfaction when stock outs do not occur. JIT inventory control is generally not sensitive to rapid changes in demand, for example, during allergy season when there can be rapid increases in demand for certain allergy, cough, and cold medications.

While today's automated computer systems certainly facilitate a JIT system by maintaining a perpetual inventory, more information is needed to maintain an optimal inventory level and customer satisfaction. To assist the pharmacy manager in making purchasing decisions, the ideal inventory level is also needed. This is based on how much of a product a business uses, how fast they use the product and the costs associated with ordering and carrying the product. When a business places orders based on these variables, it can minimize total inventory costs (ordering and carrying costs). Using this information, a pharmacy manager can determine the most efficient quantity of product to order – known as the *economic order quantity* or EOQ. EOQ should be used as a tool to inform the JIT inventory process.

Inventory models for calculating optimal order quantities, such as EOQ; have been available to business managers for many years. Computerization has automated the decision making associated with these kinds of models, and is an excellent tool for pharmacy managers to use in determining when to purchase and how much to purchase. Mathematically, the quantity is given by:

$$EOQ = \sqrt{\frac{2(\text{Annual usage in units})(\text{Order cost})}{\text{Annual carrying cost per unit}}}$$

where the annual carrying cost per unit is the unit cost times the carrying cost percentage.

Based on the formula for EOQ, the total cost of inventory is given by:

Total inventory cost (TIC) = Purchase cost + Order cost + Carrying cost

or

Total inventory cost (TIC) = [(Cost per unit × Annual utilization) + (Annual utilization / EOQ) + (EOQ / 2)]

Example: Assume a pharmacy has an annual requirement of 1,000 bottles (units) of a product and the cost per order is $2. If the cost per unit is $10 and the carrying costs are 5%, the EOQ would be calculated as:

$$EOQ = \sqrt{\frac{2(\text{Annual usage} = 1000)(\text{Order cost} = \$2)}{\text{Cost/unit} = \$10 \times \text{Carrying cost } \% = 5 \text{ (or 0.05 numerically)}}}$$

$EOQ = \sqrt{4,000 / 0.5}$
$EOQ = \sqrt{8,000}$
$EOQ = 89$

The total inventory cost would then be calculated as:

TIC = Purchasing + Ordering + Carrying costs
TIC = (Cost/unit = $10 × Annual utilization = 1,000) + (Annual utilization = 1,000 / EOQ = 89) + (EOQ = 89 / 2)
TIC = 10,000 + 11 + 45
TIC = $10,056

The total cost for the year would be $10,056. This means it would be cheaper for the pharmacy to order 89 units at a time as opposed to any other quantity. All other quantities will result in higher total costs.

Once the EOQ is calculated, the number of orders per year is found by dividing the annual utilization by the EOQ, or 1,000 units / 89 = 11.2 or approximately 11 orders per year.

Along with knowing the optimal quantity of inventory to purchase, the pharmacy manager also needs to know when to place an order. This is known as the *reorder point* (RP). Calculating the RP also requires you to know the lead time from placing to receiving an order. Thus, the RP is computed as follows:

RP = Lead time × Average usage per unit of time

This tells you the inventory level at which a new order should be placed. If you need a safety stock to limit situations where there are stock outs, then increase the RP by a few days to ensure consistency of supply.

Case-in-point 6.9   EOQ example

Pharmacy operations are frequently presented with special pricing and deals associated with purchasing larger quantities of merchandise. EOQ is a useful tool for the pharmacy manager to use in determining whether or not the deal actually makes good business sense. For example, if a pharmacy purchases 1,600 bottles of cough syrup annually with a unit cost of $4, order cost of $25 and inventory carry costs of 5%, the EOQ for this product would be $\sqrt{(2 \times 1,600 \times \$25/(\$4 \times 0.05))}$ = 632 units per order. The total cost of inventory would be $4/unit × 1,600 units + $25 (1,600/632) + 0.05 (632/2) = $6,479.05. If the terms of the deal were a $3.75 purchase price if ordered in quantities of 300 bottles at a time, the total cost of inventory for the purchase deal would be: $3.75 × 1,600 + $25 (1,600/300) + 0.05 (300/2) = $6,140.50. This analysis would imply that even though smaller quantities would be purchased more frequently, the deal will lower total inventory costs.

Optimizing inventory decisions

Using modern computer systems, knowledge of EOQ and RP, and understanding the needs of one's customers enables the pharmacy manager to make inventory management decisions that result in fewer out-of-stock situations and minimal inventory costs. Given the realities of modern day pharmacy operations, including lower profit margins, it should be clear inventory management is critical to the prudent pharmacy manager.

Summary

Pharmacy managers should routinely use the financial information from their businesses, along with knowledge of the marketplace and customer needs, to appropriately control the inventory of a pharmacy operation. Proper inventory control starts with an understanding of the four basic inventory costs described in the chapter (purchase, ordering, carrying and stock out). Applying the understanding of these costs, along with indicators such as inventory turnover, EOQ and RP, should result in optimal inventory levels which keep costs to a minimum while at the same time ensuring customer satisfaction. In managing inventory, a pharmacy manager must keep these principles in mind while routinely:

- monitoring the adequacy of inventory levels, balancing this with expected demand; this is especially important for products or services that fluctuate seasonally, such as Tamiflu® for influenza

- taking full advantage of pricing discounts such as prompt payment discounts and other price incentives
- conducting a physical review of the inventory periodically, to look for slow-moving or obsolete items; this will reduce inventory carrying costs and improve cash flow
- maintaining an awareness of the average inventory level, keeping it to a minimum, since this is the source of carrying costs and can dramatically impact profitability
- keeping enough inventory on hand to ensure patients' needs are met
- using the financial information to ensure inventory levels are providing sufficient profitability, in particularly by monitoring the financial ratios associated with inventory, EOQ, RP, and inventory turnover.

Suggested reading

Chisholm-Burns MA, Vaillancourt AM, Shepherd M. *Pharmacy Management, Leadership, Marketing, and Finance*. Sudbury, MA: Jones & Bartlett Publishers, 2011.

Desselle SP, Zgarrick DP. *Pharmacy Management: Essentials for all Practice Settings*, 2nd edn. New York, NY: McGraw-Hill, 2009.

Carroll NV. *Financial Management for Pharmacists: a Decision-Making Approach*, 3rd edn. Baltimore, MD: Lippincott Williams & Wilkins, 2007.

National Community Pharmacists Association (2008). *Managing the Pharmacy Inventory*. Alexandria, VA: NCPA. www.ncpanet.org/members/pdf/ownership-managinginventory.pdf

Blackburn J (2010). *Fundamentals of Purchasing and Inventory Control for Certified Pharmacy Technicians*. The Woodlands, TX: J&D Educational Services. https://secure.jdeducation.com/JDCourseMaterial/FundPurch.pdf

McKesson Corporation. *Home Page*. San Francisco, CA: McKesson Corp. http://www.mckesson.com

AmerisourceBergen Corporation. *Home Page*. Valley Forge, PA: AmerisourceBergen Corp. www.amerisourcebergen.com

Cardinal Health, Inc. *Home Page*. Dublin, OH: Cardinal Health, Inc. http://www.cardinal-health.com

Review questions

1 The carrying costs associated with inventory management include:

   A Insurance costs, shipping costs, storage costs, and obsolescence

   B Storage costs, handling costs, capital invested, and obsolescence

   C Purchasing costs, shipping costs, set-up costs, and quantity discounts lost

   D Obsolescence, set-up costs, capital invested, and purchasing costs

2   The ordering costs associated with inventory management include:
    A   Insurance costs, purchasing costs, shipping costs, and spoilage
    B   Obsolescence, set-up costs, quantity discounts lost, and storage costs
    C   Purchasing costs, shipping costs, set-up costs, and quantity discounts lost
    D   Shipping costs, obsolescence, set-up costs, and capital invested

3   Shrink related to employees is not an issue to be concerned with in a pharmacy business. True or false?

4   The result of the economic order quantity formula indicates the:
    A   Annual quantity of inventory to be carried
    B   Annual usage of materials during the year
    C   Safety stock plus estimated inventory for the year
    D   Quantity of each individual order during the year

5   In inventory management, the safety stock will tend to increase if the:
    A   Carrying cost increases
    B   Cost of running out of stock decreases
    C   Variability of the lead time increases
    D   Variability of the usage rate decreases

6   Calculate the EOQ for a chain pharmacy using 15,000 bottles of Lipitor 10 mg per year at a cost of $100 per bottle. Assume carrying costs are 5% and it costs the pharmacy $50 to place a direct order from the manufacturer.

7   A JIT inventory can be used in conjunction with EOQ to optimize inventory control. True or false?

8   When the inventory turnover ratio is lower than the benchmark (12 turns per year), this can indicate:
    A   Inventory levels are too low
    B   Overestimation of the inventory needs
    C   Efficient use of inventory
    D   Increasing sales

9   Which inventory system provides the pharmacy manager with much more timely inventory details – periodic or perpetual inventory?

10   Discuss the impact of inventory management on customer service and store performance.

Answers

1   B is correct: Storage costs, handling costs, capital invested, and obsolescence.

2   C is correct: Purchasing costs, shipping costs, set-up costs, and quantity discounts lost.

3   The statement is false.

4   D is correct: The quantity of each individual order during the year.

5   C is correct: The variability of the lead time increases.

6   $$EOQ = \sqrt{[2 \times (15,000)(50)]/[(100)(0.05)]}$$
$$= \sqrt{[1,500,000/5]}$$
$$= \sqrt{[300,000]} = 548.$$

7   The statement is true.

8   B is correct: Overestimation of the inventory needs.

9   Perpetual inventory gives more timely details.

10   As discussed in the text, inventory management, customer service and store performance are all interconnected. In a primarily product-driven business, a pharmacy manager must have adequate inventory on hand to meet customers' needs. The main area where this becomes a problem and negatively impacts service levels and store performance is with partial fills and stock outs, especially with maintenance medications. A customer who has received a prescription for a new treatment just on the market, or one rarely used, can understand the product not being stocked and needing ordered. However, the same customer who comes to the pharmacy every month and gets the same three prescriptions will not appreciate having to make multiple trips to the pharmacy because you do not have enough or any of those medications. This decreases customer service and possibly negatively impacts store performance if that customer, and possibly many others, decides to patron another pharmacy.

Glossary

Capital investment	Actual purchase price of the inventory, major and most easily identifiable component of carrying costs and the primary factor in relation to the cash conversion cycle.
Carrying costs	Expenses associated with having inventory, including the capital investment or actual purchase price of the inventory, inventory service costs, such as handling, insurance, and taxes, and storage costs outside of the actual pharmacy.
Cash conversion cycle (or cash cycle)	The length of time, usually expressed in days, needed to return cash outlays for purchases of inventory (a use of cash) back into collected cash (a source of cash) after the sale of the inventory and the corresponding collection of the accounts receivable from the customer or third party payer.
Economic order quantity (EOQ)	Most efficient quantity of product to order and should be used as a tool to inform the JIT inventory process.
First-in, first-out (FIFO) method	Inventory valuation method which reduces inventory value for dispensed inventory in the same order in which shipments are received and results in the remaining inventory items being those most recently purchased. The advantage of the FIFO inventory valuation method is shown on the balance sheet, where the ending inventory value reflects the most recent purchase costs.
Inventory turnover ratio	A benchmark used by pharmacy managers to assess inventory control and measure how many times the company's inventory is used up during a period, usually a year. "Turns" or "turn days" are calculated by dividing 365 by the annual inventory turnover, which is then used to estimate the number of days of inventory available for sale.
Just-in-time (JIT) method	A quality control process aimed at reducing inventory costs control inventory by ordering products to arrive just before it is needed for sale.

This method can benefit a pharmacy business by reducing average inventory and even improving customer satisfaction when stock outs do not occur.

Last-in, first-out (LIFO) method	Inventory valuation method which is the direct opposite of the FIFO method. With LIFO, the earliest inventory items purchased are the last inventory items sold. Accordingly, since the last inventory items purchased are assumed to be the first inventory items to be sold, there is a better matching on the Income Statement with COGS reflecting the current cost of inventory items.
Ordering costs	Those costs associated with placing an order and processing the corresponding payment. Any costs associated with receiving the goods and getting them to the shelves for dispensing are also included, for example, putting the order on the shelves is also considered part of routine daily duties of the pharmacy staff. If significant, these costs could also be identified separately. If an institution wishes to make bulk purchases of intravenous supplies and these orders require additional outlays, such as offsite storage and labor to unload and redistribute when needed, these costs should be added to the overall purchase price when placing orders.
Periodic inventory	Inventory maintenance method where a physical count of the inventory is performed at specific intervals. This method only keeps track of the inventory at the beginning of a period, the purchases made and the sales during the same period.
Perpetual inventory	Keeping book inventory continuously in agreement with stock on hand within specified time periods. In some cases, book inventory and stock on hand may be reconciled as often as after each transaction. This is useful in keeping track of actual product availability and determining the correct time to reorder.
Product obsolescence	Product condition that occurs when an existing product becomes out of date or obsolete.

Prompt pay discount

Discount offered by vendors to entice prompt, or even early, payment in order to help them maintain their own cash conversion cycle. Often quoted as, for example, "2% net 10", meaning a 2% cash discount of the total invoice is taken if the entire balance is paid within 10 days instead of the traditional 30 days.

Shrink

Any shortage after the final calculated inventory value in a company's accounting records is compared with the final valuation from the physical inventory.

Weighted average cost (WAC) method

Inventory valuation method which is a compromise between FIFO and LIFO. The WAC per unit is calculated by taking the inventory purchases and dividing this by the total number of units for the period. At the end of each accounting period, WAC per unit of inventory is determined and reflected in both the balance sheet and income statement as COGS.

7

Budgeting

Learning objectives

- Explain the benefits and limitations of business planning and developing budgets, including budgeting for pharmacy cognitive services
- Understand the importance of sales forecasting as a starting point for budget development
- Describe the similarities and differences between different types of budgets, e.g., operating budget, sales budget, operating expense and cash budget
- Understand the behavior of costs within a relevant range
- Discuss the importance of controllable and non-controllable costs
- Examine performance evaluation based on budget performance and the motivational impacts of budgets

Introduction

There is an old saying that "planning makes perfect." Obviously, planning for the future cannot in itself be perfect, but one can obtain a measurable degree of success if proper attention is devoted to the planning process. All companies must plan for the future, and a plan is simply the formal objectives to be achieved by a company over a defined time period. Most companies plan for profit maximization in the long term, referred to as strategic planning. Strategic planning often involves time horizons of 5 to 10 years, usually involves senior management and uses information external to the organization. Long-term goals can be defined as those objectives that cannot be achieved in only one operating cycle, and consist of an examination of a company's future market potential, new and existing services to be provided, and the company's ability to meet these goals. These strategies involve using the company's entire capital, financial, and human resources to establish long-term objectives. While strategic planning is beyond the specific duties of most pharmacy managers, essential elements of a strategic plan involve stating overall objectives, strategies to achieve each essential objective, ultimate goals, and evaluation of the accomplishment of these goals. It is the implementation of the strategic plan and its effects on employees' current and futures duties which is relevant.

However, often shorter time segments are used, such as the operating cycle or fiscal year. The *operational plan*, an integral part of the company's strategic plan, is a more detailed plan focusing on the coming year's overall profitability. Operational plans include major corporate initiatives and those responsible in obtaining them, along with the specific resources needed and anticipated time frames.

It is this operational plan that serves as the basis for an annual budget, the management tool most often used to project financial events for future periods and an essential component of the planning process. While some budget reports may often look very similar to management's operating reports and financial statements, it is important to point out that budgetary accounting focuses on an examination of the future, especially in relation to the anticipated cost of planned acquisitions and the use of various economic resources. Also known as profit planning, the operating budget is a formal statement of management's expectations of the company's overall operating performance for the future period. Figure 7.1 demonstrates these relationships.

Budget types

While the entire budgeting process for a company involves many different levels of interaction from various managers and departments, it is important to understand the basic overall structure to preparing a budget and importance of a pharmacy manager's specific role within the process. The following discussion focuses on four primary budget types:

- operating budget
- sales budget
- operating expense budget
- cash budget.

The operating budget, also known as the master budget, is prepared first and consists of many smaller budgets, which, when summarized, reflect the overall anticipated activities of a company over the next fiscal year. The operating

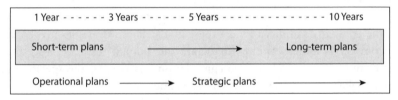

Figure 7.1 Time span of operational and strategic plans.

budget is defined by the nature of the company and its size, anticipated market conditions, and executive management's response to them. Based upon numerous estimates, projections, and assumptions, the operating budget is expressed in terms of expected sales and related operating expenses for the forthcoming year. The format of the operating budget is therefore a pro forma (planned or projected) income statement. Often, a pro forma balance sheet is also developed, which projects ending balance sheet accounts based upon the forthcoming period's budgeted operational activity. Underlying budgets that support the operating budget include, but are not limited to, the sales and collections budget, the cost of goods sold budget, inventory and purchases budget, and the operating expense budget.

In the chain community practice environment, sales budgets are often prepared by the home office based upon historical experience, include projected sales volume increases or decreases expected by management and are simply provided to pharmacy managers as a goal to achieve, without major input from them. It is usually expressed in the number of prescriptions expected to be dispensed for the budget period, often detailed to weekly projections (e.g., a pharmacy filling an average of 250 prescriptions per day translates into a weekly projection of 1,750 prescriptions). The corresponding dollar sales amount is derived by multiplying this expected prescription activity by the historical or revised average prescription price, which is calculated by dividing the total prescription sales amount in dollars by the actual number of prescriptions dispensed:

Dollar sales = Expected prescriptions count × Average prescription price

As always, meeting these revenue projections, which in a chain pharmacy environment are continually monitored by the district pharmacy supervisor, may best be achieved by providing exceptional customer service and optimal patient care.

The COGS budget and inventory and purchases budgets are usually not produced for pharmacy managers. The efficient management of inventory levels is expected in relation to actual sales volumes. This inventory efficiency is measured by the inventory turnover, discussed in Chapter 6.

Next, the operating expense budget is most familiar to pharmacy managers in almost all practice settings, as it is the most relevant and under the pharmacy manager's ability to control. The operating expense budget identifies all operating expenses such as payroll, rent, supplies, advertising, insurance, and taxes. Costs can be classified into two categories, controllable and non-controllable. *Controllable costs* are able to be contained based upon actions taken by pharmacy managers, whereas non-controllable expenses are not. For example, payroll expenses are under a pharmacy manager's direct control as a result of scheduling. Rents, utilities, and corporate overhead are examples of *non-controllable costs*.

Lastly, a cash budget plans for a company's projected cash inflows and outflows for the period and is derived from important information contained in the operating budget. Annual sales revenues represent inflows for the period, and are usually provided as monthly or quarterly estimates based upon the cash cycle of the company. The *cash cycle* is the length of time, usually expressed in days, needed to return cash outlays for purchases of inventory (a use of cash) back into collected cash (a source of cash) after the sale of inventory and the corresponding collection of the accounts receivable from the customer or third party payer. The cash budget is critical in that payment for inventory purchases, payroll, and other operating expense must be made on a regular basis in order for operations to run smoothly. In addition, an owner pharmacist must have cash to run his/her business on a day-to-day basis and give change back to the patient who pays for their $20 prescription with a $100 bill. Again, the main responsibility for this budget remains with upper-level management in a traditional chain or institutional setting.

Larger companies will also typically prepare a capital budget, which shows the estimated amounts planned for long-term projects or other future capital assets planned. Capital budgets may span several years based upon the strategic plan of upper management; however, only the estimated cash outflows for the current budget period are included in the cash budget.

Budget development

Regardless of the budget type being prepared, a series of steps is necessary to complete the process in an orderly and efficient manner. The process begins with the company setting the overall financial and operating objectives for the budget period. Essential to this step is the thorough analysis of the corporate resources available to obtain the established goals. Given these first steps are usually the responsibility of upper-level managers, negotiations will ensue between various divisions or departments within the entire organization in the establishment and final approval of the operating budget. Finally, the approved operating budget must be distributed in a timely manner to the appropriate managers, along with other necessary supporting budgets and reports.

Developing the budget may employ several methods, depending upon the company's level of sophistication. One of the easier methods to prepare the operating or operating expense budget is to use the prior year historical performance as a base with which to begin the budget period. Barring any known or anticipated market shifts in the economy, the actual performance of the prior year serves many companies well in guiding the budgets for future periods. Taking this approach a step further, the use of several prior years' performance may be analyzed to provide an average that can also be used for the budget period under development. This method is especially useful in chain pharmacies, which can use historical information in planning for expansion of new outlets. Another method employs the use of base performance from the prior year as a base from which to begin. Pharmacy managers can apply a predetermined percentage increase, decrease, or even no change to each individual line item of prior year actual performance to derive the budget amounts for the planning period. Further refinement of this percentage method could be adjustment of each individual line item independently, in the direction that is deemed most appropriate, given current estimates and goals.

A more difficult method, requiring further analysis and decision making, is the *zero-based budget method*. Even though more time intensive, this work often yields a more realistic budget perceived as being more obtainable by pharmacy managers. When developing a budget using the zero-based method, individual line items within the budget are "zeroed out" and any amount assigned must be justified based upon attaining previously set goals or future expected operating conditions. The resulting final balances are then deemed to be justifiable and obtainable.

Given the uncertainty in making estimates regarding the future performance of the company's operations, a flexible operating expense budget may be prepared. A flexible budget is more dynamic and anticipates the variability in company operations, for example, a new pharmacy competitor moving in across the street, especially within narrow ranges of operations. To begin this type of budget, management must determine a relevant range of anticipated activity in terms of sales volume and the corresponding expenses incurred in meeting these different sales volumes. The *relevant range* is defined as the range of activity (i.e., volume of prescriptions dispensed) over which the company expects the behaviors of expenses to be consistent (or linear). Then, the expenses for the budget period must be characterized as either fixed, variable, or semi-variable (mixed). *Fixed expenses* are those that do not change within a certain range, or level of activity, whereas *variable expenses* change in direct relation to the level of activity. *Semi-variable expenses* contain an element of both fixed and variable expenses for the given level of activity, for example, rent that includes both a fixed portion and a percentage of sales. For the variable and semi-variable expenses, a methodology is developed to project how they will vary within the projected range of sales volume. The result is a flexible budget, which reflects different operating expense amounts according to different sales volumes. The resulting scenarios can project expenses to be incurred within various levels of sales activity; a "best case" (optimistic), a "no-growth case" (continue as usual), or "worst case" (conservative). This is further depicted in Figure 7.2.

Expense ($ '000)

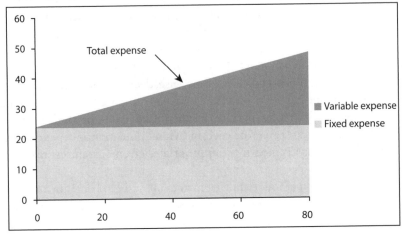

Figure 7.2   Total expense components – flexible budget.

> ## Case-in-point 7.1   Flexible budget
>
> A flexible budget may prove instrumental in determining future hiring needs. If the best case scenario is deemed attainable and the market conditions for hiring additional pharmacists is very tight, the pharmacy manager may want to initiate a search to hire a new pharmacist relatively soon. Alternatively, if the market supply for pharmacists is abundant, the pharmacy manager could closely monitor actual performance on a monthly basis and make the hiring decision if warranted.

In many operating expense budgets, there are expenses that are allocated directly from upper management to the pharmacy, which is operating as a profit center, or department, within the overall operating structure of the company. Profit centers have a revenue generation component in addition to the operating expenses and are expected to produce an overall profit. Allocated costs include the equitable assignment of general and administrative (i.e., non-revenue-generating) departments within a company to the various profit centers, which include the pharmacy department. Given the nature of allocated costs, they are considered non-controllable by most pharmacist managers since they are not directly involved in the operations of the department's cost (e.g., distribution warehouses, corporate advertising, executive management salaries, etc.) being allocating to their operating budget. Costs incurred by the general and administrative departments are a vital part of the operation of the company and must be allocated to the revenue-generating departments within the company on an equitable basis.

Case-in-point 7.2   Chain pharmacy operating expense budget allocation of warehousing expenses

Consider a major chain pharmacy serving a large geographic region and maintaining its own warehouse facilities used to provide weekly inventory deliveries to all of its individual stores. These facilities act as a central depository for over 95% of the inventory requirements of the company. With the large capacity of the warehouses, large quantities of inventory may be housed, allowing for the bulk purchase of many items with corresponding quantity discounts from the manufacturers, owing to the chain's buying power. Assuming that the operating costs (e.g., warehouse labor, depreciation, utilities) for the various warehouse locations are $5 million annually (not including COGS) and the chain pharmacy operation has 500 store locations, each individual pharmacy would receive a warehousing allocation of $10,000 ($5,000,000 ÷ 500) in their annual operating expense budget. The use of the warehouse allows the company as a whole to better meet customer needs, successfully negotiating contract pricing for inventory and to maintain competitive pricing. Consequently, the costs associated with that economic benefit are allocated to individual stores as the users of the warehousing services.

Business performance evaluation

As discussed previously, the overall purpose of the budget is to provide guidance in meeting the company's operational goals, including the company's profitability projections. To document the efficiency of the pharmacy manager's operations and the potential to meet objectives, a performance evaluation must be performed on a regular basis. One commonly used tool to evaluate financial performance is *variance analysis*, which can help appraise the overall productivity, identify successful operations and areas which need attention and possibly corrective measures. Simply stated, variance analysis identifies differences in actual performance with that of the budget through a line item comparison. Understanding both negative and positive variances can aid pharmacy managers to take corrective action, if needed. For example, while an overspending variance in pharmacist payroll costs may initially be perceived to be unfavorable, further analysis might reveal a significantly positive variance in prescription dispensing activity requiring additional pharmacist staff. Effective use of variance analysis can greatly increase the pharmacy manager's ability to fully understand their operating environment.

Employees, budgets, and motivation

Budgets can also be used to affect employee attitudes and performance. Budgets should be participative and include input from both managers and those whose work is reflected in the budget application. When frontline employees are included in the budgeting process, their knowledge of the day-to-day operations can increase the accuracy of budgets, as information is exchanged between managers and staff. When employees are included in the budget development process, motivation is increased because participants will internalize the budget goals as their own. Conversely, when a budget is simply imposed on the staff, this can have a negative effect on employee motivation. This means budgets, in addition to being an important strategic planning and control tool, should also be a motivational tool.

In the end, in order for budgets to be most useful, they should represent challenging but attainable business goals. Further, budgets must also be realistic. Consider the staffing or personnel expense line item in an operating expense budget. If the staffing budget amount is not realistic and does not provide for sufficient technician support for a specified level of prescription volume, motivation may be lower because employees will believe that no matter how hard they work they will not be able to meet customer expectations because of insufficient staff. On the other hand, if budgeted sales volume goals are set too low, complacency will arise and employees' work ethic may suffer as little effort is required to attain the budgeted activities. Therefore, an appropriate middle ground is needed. As a rule of thumb, setting budget target goals at levels that can be attained by most managers 80–90% of the time has proven effective. If performance levels exceed this level, then employees should be rewarded with incentives including bonus compensation, promotions, or additional responsibility. By doing this, pharmacy managers provide the greatest likelihood that planning will be followed and business goals met.

Budgeting for pharmacy services

Budgeting may seem to make more sense for areas of business that require certain levels of inventory (e.g., prescription dispensing, sales of OTC medications or durable medical equipment) or production (e.g., compounding medications or home infusion intravenous solutions). However, budgeting concepts can be applied to pharmacy services, which are not associated with maintaining large amounts of inventory. For example, pharmacy businesses, including institutions and community pharmacies, may be interested in offering cognitive services such as medication therapy management, lifestyle counselling, or anticoagulation management. Businesses interested in these types of service offerings (Table 7.1) can benefit from properly designed budgeting.

Table 7.1 Types of cognitive pharmacy services

Service	Description
Medication therapy reviews	An organized process of gathering patient information, reviewing medication therapies from a global perspective, discerning the most relevant medication therapy issues and crafting a plan to optimize therapy and minimize problems
Pharmacotherapy consults	Consultant services provided by pharmacists through a referral system from other health care providers or pharmacists. More often than not these services are provided to complex patients who are experiencing medication therapy problems or have a high risk of developing problems. Typically, pharmacists providing these services have advanced training in the condition and may be Board Certified in their specialty by the Board of Pharmaceutical Specialties
Disease management	Pharmacists providing disease management services address health and wellness from a global perspective. They incorporate medication therapy, non-drug therapy and lifestyle changes needed to change a patient's behavior and enable overall disease management while decreasing cost and positively affecting quality of life
Pharmacogenomics applications	Pharmacists providing these services incorporate a patient's genetic information into their drug therapy in an effort to ensure the highest level of care while minimizing risk
Anticoagulation management	Pharmacists providing these services work with patients on anticoagulants, in particularly warfarin. These therapies must be continually monitored in order to ensure optimal anticoagulation and minimize bleeding risks. Pharmacists monitor an individual's INR levels, adjust dosing if necessary and educate on the interactions and precautions associated with anticoagulant use
Medication safety surveillance	Pharmacists providing these services are focused in an emerging field. This encompasses the entire medication use process and system. They work to prevent medication errors and adverse events by analyzing every step throughout the process. This works to ensure patient and healthcare worker safety
Health, wellness, public health	Pharmacists providing these services work to benefit the overall health and wellness of their community, state and country. These services include screening programs, nutritional planning, weight loss, smoking cessation counseling, and community brown bag sessions
Immunizations	Pharmacists providing these services administer immunizations under the laws of their given state. In addition to identifying candidates for vaccination, pharmacists directly immunize patients, including vaccinations for seasonal flu, H1N1, herpes zoster, and many others
Other clinical services	Other clinical services provided by pharmacists include employee health services & screening, specialized compounding, veterinary, gestational diabetes and many others

Adapted from http://www.pharmacist.com/AM/Template.cfm?Section=MTM&Template=/TaggedPage/
TaggedPageDisplay.cfm&TPLID=87&ContentID=22413#nogo

Division	Units	Price	Expected sales
Prescription	60,000	$70	4.2 million
Over the counter	120,000	$10	1.2 million
Cognitive services	2,000 (1-Hour patient sessions)	$60-$120	$120,000-240,000

Figure 7.3   Sample Pharmacy divisional sales budget forecast.

The importance of budgeting to pharmacy managers increases as competition for services increases. The operating environment in healthcare is pointing to just such competition. In particular, demand for cognitive pharmacy services is increasing due to changes in healthcare worldwide, more advanced training for pharmacists, patient preferences for pharmacists and the cost effectiveness of pharmacy-based interventions. Yet, the practice of budgeting is not as common or well developed in the area of cognitive services. This is probably because most cognitive pharmacy services do not have associated inventory considerations. The key point to remember is that the same budgeting techniques used with other divisions of pharmacy businesses can and should be applied to service provision.

Pharmacy managers interested in developing, implementing, and growing pharmaceutical care/cognitive services should first develop an overall budget or profit plan for the year. Moreover, they must provide a way to monitor and adjust the plans based on operating results. The major difference in budgeting for services relates to the types of costs incurred. For services, the primary cost is the employee's time. This cost is reflected in salaries and benefits, as well as any commissions or bonuses that may be provided. This means budgeting techniques for cognitive services will be concerned primarily with planning the use and effectiveness of personnel. The pricing of cognitive services is discussed in Chapter 8 but, generally, prices are budgeted based on an hourly rate or a fixed price for a given service, such as $15 for the administration of an immunization.

A pharmacy business providing cognitive services could develop a divisional sales budget and allow management to compare revenue expectations between divisions such as the prescription business, cognitive services, and OTC sales, as described in Figure 7.3.

Case-in-point 7.3   Medication therapy management (MTM) services

Determining sales volume for non-traditional services is more difficult for pharmacy managers than manufacturing businesses, because demand is less predictable. For example, even though obtaining an annual flu vaccination (this service is part product and part service) is recommended for a large portion of the population (e.g., children, older adults, those with chronic diseases, etc.), many patients may choose not to be immunized because they do not see themselves at risk for the seasonal flu, may fear injections, are concerned with various side effects, or face economic barriers to being immunized. News of seasonal flu vaccine shortages could work to increase demand, while a recall of a contaminated batch of vaccine or break-out of a new strain, e.g., H1N1, could devastate patient trust and decrease demand. This kind of thinking can be applied to a wide range of cognitive services such as those described in Table 7.1. However, with the belief that demand for these services will exist and, over time, increase, a pharmacy manager can and should create a budget for this type of service.

Another consideration when budgeting cognitive pharmacy services is that they may be scheduled to provide for more efficient use of the pharmacist's time. As a result, owing to cancellations and missed appointments, some providers might overbook appointments. While this can ensure maintaining sales goals, it can result in longer waiting times for patients and even turning business away when schedules are full. Budgeting can assist with determining appropriate service provision levels, monitoring of decisions made with respect to volume of services offered, and adjustment of plans according to the results obtained.

In general, the revenue to be obtained from the provision of cognitive services is simply the price of the service multiplied by the number of service offerings possible:

Number of services offered × Price = Revenue

These estimates can be made for each type of clinical service offered (Figure 7.4). Projected sales revenues can then be estimated on a daily, monthly, or annual basis. Using various periods for estimating the volume of services may be the most useful when performing services with seasonal variations, such as immunizations or lifestyle services. It is not uncommon for consumer demand of lifestyle services to increase around the New Year. Other disease management services may be relatively constant throughout the year.

The expected revenues shown in Figure 7.4 seem small in relation to the revenues obtained for prescription dispensing and sales of OTC medications (see Figure 7.3). However, in some practice environments not operating at full capacity, pharmacy practitioners may be able to provide some portion of these services without increasing personnel costs. This would provide

Service	Units	Average price	Relevant periods	Expected revenues
Immunizations	2,000	$25	Fall	$50,000
Diabetes education	250	$120	Entire year	$30,000
Weight loss	100	$600	Winter/entire year	$60,000
Smoking cessation	100	$500	Winter/entire year	$50,000
Hypertension	100 patients x4 visits/year = 400	$120	Entire year	$48,000
Bone density screening	520	$60	Entire year	$31,200

Figure 7.4 Projected revenue for selected cognitive services.

incremental profits without increasing fixed costs, especially for those services not requiring inventory (i.e., educational services). Further, analysis can be made of the cost–volume–profit relationship of these services in a given practice setting. This is fully discussed in Chapter 8.

Pharmacy managers should also note the payer mix (i.e., where is the reimbursement coming from) for services and include this analysis in estimating the timing of payments for cognitive services, and how this will impact the cash budget. It should be obvious that a company could be short on cash to pay bills or invest in new services if payments are delayed or reduced. For most pharmacy goods and services, payment from patients is expected at time of service. This will be different for patients with health and prescription insurance where payment may be delayed from weeks to months. Pharmacy managers should consider cash, credit card, insurance payments, and level of bad debt. For pharmacies operating at full capacity with the need to hire additional personnel for service provision, a labor budget should be created.

Advantages and disadvantages of budgeting

Although it seems intuitive that budgeting is a necessary part of any business, there are some negative aspects of budgets. As with any management function, budgeting requires a commitment and the time of the appropriate personnel. Therefore, the costs of budgeting should be considered in relation to the benefits of creating, monitoring and adjusting plans based on budgets. Table 7.2 lists some of the more common advantages and disadvantages of budgets.

Table 7.2 Advantages and disadvantages of budgeting

Advantages	Disadvantages
Budgets provide a plan to be followed by managers linking objectives, resources and expectations	Some managers may artificially inflate budget requests draining resources from other business areas
Improve management decision making through detailed planning for the future	May promote setting goals that are easy to reach, but, do not challenge the organization to operate maximally
Provide benchmarks or goals for individual employees (e.g. prescription volume expectations)	Budgets are based on a certain level of judgment. Different managers may make different judgments and the environmental circumstances surrounding these judgments can change
Provides for thorough business analysis through the budget development process	Takes time from other business activities
Provides internal benchmarks from which performance can be measured so that deviations from plans can be identified early, allowing the business to adjust	Budgets don't account for business concerns such as quality of service, customer satisfaction or motivated employees
Help individuals at all levels of the business understand overall goals and how their individual responsibilities may impact overall success	Budgets can be seen as restrictive and limiting business opportunities

Summary

The environment in which pharmacy businesses operate necessitates careful budgeting. Worldwide economic trends and changes in technology and services demanded by patients will require pharmacy professionals to engage the budgetary planning process. Budgets, as a planning and control tool, however, are only as good as the information put into them. If forecasts and cost projections are inaccurate, the resulting budgets will be less useful and lead to poor management decision making. Budgets are useful in planning the delivery of new services.

Suggested reading

Carroll NV. *Financial Management for Pharmacists: a Decision-Making Approach*, 3rd edn. Baltimore, MD: Lippincott Williams & Wilkins, 2007.

Desselle SP, Zgarrick DP. *Pharmacy Management: Essentials for all Practice Settings*, 2nd edn. New York, NY: McGraw-Hill, 2009.

Review questions

1 In general, many smaller, underlying budgets are developed and support the operating budget. True or false?

2 Which of the following is a controllable expense?
A Rent
B Payroll
C Corporate overhead
D Utilities

3 Which of the following is the more difficult method of budgeting?
A Usage of prior year's historical information
B Predetermined percentage increase from prior year base
C Average of several prior years' historical information
D Zero-based method of budgeting

4 It is best to include only input from upper-level management when determining the operating budget. True or false?

5 When budgeting for providing cognitive pharmacy services, the following must be considered:
A Inventory if needed
B Consumer demand
C Cost of pharmacist's time
D Scheduling of appointments

6 Which of the following is a tool used to evaluate financial performance and help appraise the overall productivity, identify successful operations and areas that need attention and possibly corrective measures?
A Cost-effectiveness analysis
B Variance analysis
C Zero-based method
D Budget analysis

7 As the pharmacist in charge for a national community chain pharmacy, you have just completed the first year of operations after opening a new store. You are surprised to get notice from the corporate home office that you and your staff are not eligible for any performance bonus from the result of the first year's operations. The news is especially surprising since the $4,212,000 prescription sales amount of the pharmacy was 32% higher than the original budgeted amount of $3,120,000 and the net profit was

$250,000 more than the original amount projected. During your first year, your pharmacy staff developed a specialty in HIV/AIDS disease management, and, as a result, over 70% of your business has been within this area. Given the high cost of the pharmacotherapy, you realize inventory levels have been higher than budget, but the inventory turnover has remained steady at 12 turns per year, which meets the budgeted level. Upon further investigation, you discover that budgeted prescription count was 1,000 per week, while actual performance was 500 per week. The average prescription price for your pharmacy was $162, much higher than the budgeted average prescription price of $60. You know the prescription count is lower than budgeted, but feel the increased sales and net income should be taken into account and the bonus should be awarded. You decide to contact the corporate budgeting analyst and district manager who sent the notice and obtain further explanations. The budget analyst informs you that all new stores receive the same operating budget, based upon the average historical performance of new stores. The performance bonus calculation is based entirely upon prescription count, as management feels that best represents the overall efficiency of new pharmacy performance. It is noted that your store's weekly prescription count of 500 is only 50% of the projected 1,000 per week. Based upon this performance factor, your store and staff are not eligible for a bonus. Discuss some of the weaknesses in this performance evaluation.

8   From a traditional chain pharmacy environment perspective, discuss the budget issues most likely to be your focus as a pharmacy manager.

9   Describe a pharmacy practice setting in which budgeting may do more harm than good.

10   A health system that includes a 300-bed hospital, 15 additional facilities and 1,100 employees is examining whether or not to implement a bar-coded medication administration system. The vendor who approached the administration states that its system can prevent more medication, blood, and specimen errors in addition to improving nursing workflow. Discuss the financial factors involved in evaluating the vendor's proposal in addition to the impact on the system's budget.

Answers

1 The statement is true.

2 B is correct: Payroll.

3 D is correct: Zero-based method of budgeting.

4 The statement is false.

5 All of the above are correct.

6 B is correct: Variance analysis.

7 Budgeting is always an estimating process, and it is important to properly evaluate many aspects of operating performance. In this case, the prescription count per week clearly did not meet expectations; however, the average prescription price was significantly higher, resulting in both gross sales and net profit exceeding budget. Additionally, the inventory turnover met budgeted projections, even though the dollar amounts were significantly higher. Since the main goal of operations is generating net income, the net operating results should override the single evaluating factor of prescription count.

8 Other than prescription volume, as described in the previous question, in this practice environment the two most controllable areas that demand strict adherence to the budget are payroll and inventory. As discussed in Chapter 6, pharmacy district managers in a chain environment focus on these expenses compared with the budgeted allotment, not only for the purpose of examining overall store success or failure, but also as an evaluative measure for the pharmacy manager. If payroll or the amount of inventory ordered from the secondary wholesaler (as opposed to the chain's own warehouse) is over budget, expect a call or message from your district manager.

9 Even though there are many, the primary situation in which this comes into play is in the case of an owner pharmacist. Those pharmacists who own their store, particularly those involved in the lion's share of prescription filling, may not have the time to analyze their income and expenses and still provide the necessary service to their customers. An outside accountant could be considered if the owner pharmacist was in need of the analysis and could pay for the service.

10 There are many factors to be considered in this case, especially ones that can impact the budget years into the future. The primary factor is the vendor's capital cost for the bar-coding system, which could be anywhere from $500,000 to $2 million, depending upon the system. Digging deeper into the capital costs is whether or not training and maintenance of the system is included. These ancillary costs might greatly impact future budgets if they are paid annually. Other costs to consider include whether or not separate equipment must be purchased to bar code all patients and individual medications. Though the vendor may explain all the associated costs, every detail in terms of dollars paid out must be known. From a budgeting perspective, the capital cost must be weighed against the long-term return through a decrease in medication errors. Depending on the size and scope of a hospital, medication errors and the adverse drug events associated can cost millions of dollars per year, not only through additional direct costs, but also through an increased length of stay. A decrease in medication errors could result in a positive cash flow to the budget and, over time, easily pay for the initial capital costs. However, a hospital or health system must have the financial stability to incur the initial capital costs, while hoping that the vendor's system does all the great things it reports to do. A thorough budget analysis based on the health system's financial information must be conducted to fully assess the impact of such a system.

Glossary

Cash cycle	The length of time, usually expressed in days, needed to return cash outlays for purchases of inventory (a use of cash) back into collected cash (a source of cash) after the sale of the inventory and the corresponding collection of the accounts receivable from the customer or third party payer.
Controllable cost	A cost able to be contained based upon actions taken by pharmacy managers (e.g., payroll).
Fixed expense	Those expenses that do not change within a certain range or level of activity.

Non-controllable cost

A cost not able to be contained based upon actions taken by pharmacy managers (e.g., rent).

Operational plan

A more detailed strategic plan focusing on the coming year's overall profitability. Operational plans include major corporate initiatives and those responsible in obtaining them, along with the specific resources needed and anticipated time frames.

Relevant range

The range of activity (i.e., volume of prescriptions dispensed) over which the company expects the behaviors of expenses to be consistent (or linear).

Semi-variable expense

Expenses that contain fixed and variable elements for the given level of activity, for example, rent that includes both a fixed portion and a percentage of sales.

Variable expense

Those expenses that change in direct relation to the level of activity.

Zero-based budget method

A budget method requiring more analysis and decision making, which yields a more realistic and obtainable budget. Individual line items within the budget are "zeroed out," and any amount assigned must be justified based upon attaining previously set goals or future expected operating conditions.

8

Pricing goods and services

Learning objectives

- Understand the critical nature of making pricing decisions for a pharmacy business
- Recognize how to strategically price products to maintain and grow the business
- Identify and describe all costs involved with dispensing a prescription
- Apply pricing principles and financial data to a sample pharmacy
- Understand the factors to consider when pricing cognitive services

Introduction

Understanding how and why pricing decisions are made can make the difference between a successful pharmacy operation and one that is only marginally profitable; or that fails completely. Pharmacists working in the community or hospital setting may believe pricing is less important because it, more often than not, represents business decisions made at the administrative or corporate level and calculated by the computer system with little or no pharmacist input. Pharmacists may also see pricing as less important because prescription insurance programs remove competitive pricing issues, as reimbursement is established by contract and prices for patients are fixed by co-payments or co-insurance, over which the pharmacy has little or no control. Pharmacies that sell over-the-counter (OTC), non-prescription items, while offering added convenience to the shopping experience, must also be competitive to attract and maintain sales.

Institutional pharmacy operations are characterized by less direct ownership than community pharmacy businesses, and pricing is set within the institution, sometimes based on costs, diagnosis codes, or profit goals. However, even though institutional pharmacy managers may not bring the same ownership perspective to pricing decisions, these managers must still strive to meet the profit objectives of the institution, board of directors, owners, etc.

This chapter examines how financial information can be used in formulating pricing decisions. Pharmacists and pharmacy managers need to understand the process of making pricing decisions because it is critical to, among other things:

- the evaluation (participate or not) of third party prescription programs
- ensure that there is consistency between pricing and other customer service activities
- the making of competitive pricing decisions, including cash business, at the pharmacist level
- being evaluated favorably by superiors because, even though pharmacists may not have direct input into pricing, they are evaluated on the profitability of their operations.

Recognizing that some costs are controllable, a better understanding of the cost of operations can assist pharmacists in making pricing decisions. Understanding costs of operation in relation to pricing decisions can result in more consistent decision making, supporting the pharmacy business's goals.

Prescription pricing

A price for any product or service will be based on the following components:

- the product cost (COGS)
- the cost of dispensing (COD)
- the product
- the profit.

The relationship is expressed as:

Total price = COGS + COD + Profit

where COGS represents the cost of the product being sold, and COD is the average cost of dispensing a prescription (this is sometimes referred to as cost to dispense or CTD), determined from the income statement.

COD includes costs such as prescription department salaries and benefits, other prescription department costs, other facility costs such as rent, utilities, and operating supplies.

The final component in establishing prices is the profit objective of the business. This is the desired profit level for the owners or shareholders. While it may seem inappropriate to discuss profitability when it comes to healthcare, omission of this component of pricing will result in insufficient net business income to meet the needs and expectations of owners, stockholders, and investors.

In a recent study of over 230,000 community pharmacies representing 832 million prescriptions, the accounting firm Grant Thornton determined a national COD equal to $10.50, ranging from a low of $8.50 per prescription in Rhode Island to $13.08 in California.[1] This chapter reviews how to determine COD and use it on the cost structure of the business to make a variety of pricing and business decisions.

Pricing information sources

The income statement contains most of the information necessary to establish prices for future periods. The income statement contains historical information that will be meaningful within certain time periods and sales levels. This is known as the *relevant range*. When examining the future, where sales and costs may be different, adjustments must be made to the financial information to account for future changes in order to have relevant information.

> **Case-in-point 8.1   *Future business based on local external environment***
>
> A pharmacy business in a high residential growth area could experience significant increases in volume over relatively short periods of time. Further, a new manufacturing facility, corporate headquarters or other larger employer moving into an area could also quickly increase business volume levels. This could also be true at the opposite end of the spectrum when a particular manufacturing plant closes and sales shrink.

When planning for future periods, costs must be adjusted to reflect expected levels and ensure meaningful cost information. Estimates about the volume of business, namely the numbers of prescriptions dispensed, are also needed for developing a pricing strategy. Customers, the media, and competitors are valuable sources of information related to a pharmacy's pricing. In fact, competitors' customers can be a prime source of cash prescription prices, perceptions of pricing and even the service level accompanying the competitor's pricing strategy.

Product pricing strategies

Coordination of goals and objectives associated with accounting and marketing principles is essential to developing a complete pricing strategy, especially given product prices can be viewed from both an economic and a marketing perspective.[1–5] Economically, prices can be expressed as follows, with the information needed to calculate these prices being readily available from the financial statements and operating characteristics of the business:

Product price = Product cost + Operating cost + Profit

When determining prices for prescriptions, this formula is expressed as:

Prescription price = Product cost (COGS) + Cost of dispensing (COD) + Profit

However, examining pricing from a marketing perspective requires pricing decision makers to consider, in addition to concern over costs, factors such as:

- consumer needs and wants
- marketplace dynamics, such as supply and other competitive factors
- the profit objectives of the business
- the pricing strategy goals, such as to attract new customers, sell more to existing customers, or to introduce new products or services.

Once the costs of operations and business objectives are understood, a firm can develop a pricing strategy or strategies that work toward meeting its goals. There are many basic pricing strategies that can be adopted by a pharmacy business (Box 8.1) including, for example, cost-plus, marginal cost, penetration and value pricing. For most pharmacy operations a combination

---

Box 8.1 *Basic pricing strategies*

Penetration pricing

The price charged for products and services is set artificially low in order to gain market share. Once this is achieved, the price is increased.

Cost-plus pricing

The firm calculates the cost of producing (dispensing) the product and adds a percentage (profit) to that price to give the selling price. This method, although simple, does not consider demand, and there is no way of determining if potential customers will purchase the product at the calculated price.

Price = Cost + Desired profit

Price skimming

A firm may employ this strategy and set a high product price when it has a substantial competitive advantage in the marketplace. However, in most cases, this advantage is not sustainable. The high price tends to attract new competitors into the market but price usually falls because of increased competition.

Loss leader pricing

Selling a product below cost to attract customers is likely to be deemed illegal under EU and US competition rules. Also called predatory pricing, this strategy, if used only for a short period, can be seen as being in the interest of customers. Problems have arisen when loss leader pricing puts the competition out of business and the originator then raises prices.

Contribution margin-based pricing

Once a level of sales is reached where fixed costs are covered, this method can maximize the profit generated from a product, based on the difference between the product's price and variable costs. The product's contribution to total firm profit (i.e., to operating income) is maximized when a price is chosen that maximizes contribution margin per unit × number of units sold.

Target profit pricing

Pricing method whereby the selling price of a product is calculated to produce a particular rate of return on investment for a specific volume of production. The target pricing method is used most often by public utilities, such as electric and gas companies, and companies whose capital investment is high, like automobile manufacturers.

Marginal cost pricing

This is the practice of setting the price of a product to equal the extra cost of producing an extra unit of output. With marginal cost pricing, a firm charges, for each product unit sold, only the addition to total cost resulting from materials and direct labor. Businesses often set prices close to marginal cost during periods of poor sales thinking that a small increase in revenue is better than no sale at all.

Psychological pricing

This approach is effective with consumer goods and creates a price image in the mind of the consumer, such as $3.99 rather than $4.00. Big box retailers, such as Wal-Mart, use a psychological pricing strategy when it sets prices at $1.97, 3 cents off the dollar.

Promotional pricing

Promotional approaches such as frequent shopper discounts, buy-one-get-one-free can generate excitement for products and stimulate sales. This might include coupons for transferred prescriptions.

Value pricing

This approach is used where external factors, such as recession or increased competition, force companies to provide 'value' products and services to retain sales, e.g. the CVS Extra Care® Customer Rewards Program, which provides rebates on other merchandise for prescription purchases.

of these strategies is needed. In this chapter, we focus on the development of a cost-plus pricing strategy.

Even though businesses frequently employ strategies that price products at or below cost for periods of time, in the long run, a viable business must operate at a level where, on average, the total costs of operation (and some profit level) are covered by revenues generated from sales. Understanding the cost structure of a business is critical to ensuring both customers' needs and business objectives are met.

Case-in-point 8.2   Pricing decisions – third party reimbursement

Reimbursement programs for third party prescriptions are a prime example of an area where management will need a thorough understanding of the firm's cost structure in order to make appropriate decisions. Third party reimbursement is based on a benchmark price that is reflective of actual acquisition cost plus a dispensing fee. Acquisition costs may include average wholesale price (AWP), wholesale acquisition cost, or other benchmark. In the United States, there is growing concern over which cost most accurately reflects actual acquisition cost, and many programs are moving away from AWP as the reimbursement basis.

As reimbursement rates have declined over the years, thus yielding lower payments to pharmacies, there has been great pressure placed on pharmacy managers in deciding whether or not to participate in various programs. While many factors must be considered in the overall decision about accepting a third party contract, such as the impact of a particular contract on sales volume, this understanding of pricing and COD is also required to make sound financial decisions.

Case-in-point 8.3   Pricing decisions – Wal-Mart's $4.00 program

Recently, Wal-Mart was the first major retailer to introduce $4.00 pricing for a specified list of generic medications. Although many of the major retailers have since followed suit with their own version of this program, independent pharmacy owners and pharmacists have had to strategize regarding their response to this price competition. To keep any and all business, would they match the pricing for patients or stick to a premium pricing and service strategy, and risk losing business based on these prices? Each pharmacy manager/owner must then consider their global pricing strategy and the issues and analyses described below.

Cost identification

The starting point for developing a pricing strategy is to identify costs. This process is done by examining all costs and determining their purpose or nature. When talking about the cost structure of a business as relates to pricing, the initial focus will be on fixed and variable costs:

- *Fixed costs* are those costs that are independent of output. They remain constant throughout the relevant range and are usually not considered relevant to output decisions. Examples include rent and liability insurance.
- *Variable costs* are those costs that vary with output. Generally, variable costs increase at a constant rate relative to labor and capital. Examples include prescription labels and vials.

Understanding, categorizing, and allocating these costs to the various aspects of the business operation is essential in developing a pricing strategy. In addition to fixed and variable costs, we also consider total costs as part of a pricing strategy. *Total costs* (TC), from the pricing perspective, are the sum of all costs being considered for the purpose of the analysis. Remember, however, these costs are relevant for the periods from which they were derived and must be adjusted for future periods. The total cost is the sum of total variable cost (TVC) and total fixed cost (TFC) of operation:

$$TC = TVC + TFC$$

For example, total fixed costs (TFC) will be represented by the sum of the identified fixed costs of operation. Total variable costs (TVC) are the sum of the variable costs of operations. TVC are costs that vary in direct proportion to changes in activity such as prescription vials, gasoline for delivery vehicles, or prescription label supplies, each of which increases as prescription volume increases. TFCs, on the other hand, remain constant regardless of changes in activity. This could include rent for the physical facility, liability insurance, or the pharmacy business license.

It is helpful to note that, while fixed costs can never be zero, the TVC is zero when output is zero because no variable inputs need be employed to produce products or services. However, as output expands and the business begins to sell more products and services, the greater the usage of variable inputs and the greater TVC.

One additional type of cost to address in the discussion of product pricing is the concept of *marginal cost*. This is the cost of producing an additional unit of output. For example, the marginal cost of the 250th prescription dispensed can be calculated by finding the difference in total cost at 249 prescriptions (units of output) and total cost at 250 prescriptions. Marginal cost is thus the additional cost of one more unit of output, or, in this example, one more prescription. Marginal cost is simply the change in TVC associated with a unit change in output. When the relevant range of sales activity is exceeded, marginal costs may eventually become fixed as the pharmacy requires additional facilities, etc. to be able to support the new sales volume.

In a pharmacy business, the marginal cost of operations (e.g., dispensing prescriptions) is assumed to be increasing in most cases. Therefore, generally, marginal cost is the same thing as the incremental cost between levels of output, such as prescription volume. Marginal cost is important from a pricing perspective, in that a business can develop a marginal cost pricing strategy for certain products or groups of customers that represent significant opportunities. For example, a pharmacy that understands its cost structure and knows the marginal cost of dispensing could decide to accept a prescription insurance plan that pays less than others, but still covers the marginal cost of dispensing. This is discussed below, in relation to break-even analysis.

Cost-volume profit and break-even analysis

Cost-volume-profit (CVP) analysis allows managers to perform many useful analyses of how profit and costs change with changes in sales volume. CVP analysis looks at the effects on profits caused by changes in such factors as variable costs, fixed costs, selling prices, volume, and mix of products sold. This makes CVP analysis quite useful to a pharmacy manager interested in developing a pricing strategy based on the costs of operations and desired profit levels.

Break-even analysis, a branch of CVP analysis, determines the break-even sales. The break-even point is where total revenue (TR) received equals the total costs associated with the sale of the product (TR = TC). A break-even point is typically calculated to determine if it would be profitable to sell a proposed product, as opposed to attempting to modify an existing product so that it can be made lucrative. Break-even analysis can also be used to analyze the potential profitability of an expenditure in a sales-based business. Although the break-even point is not a figure that shows up on financial statements, it is based on the information gleaned from these statements and is an important analytic tool for managers.

The break-even point represents the level of sales volume equaling the total of the variable and fixed costs for a given volume of output and particular capacity use rate. For example, you might want to know the break-even point in a particular pharmacy operation. Generally, given a fixed level of sales and all other variables, a lower break-even point would increase the profit potential and decrease the operating risk. The break-even point also provides managers with insights into profit planning. The *equation approach* is based on the CVP equation, which shows the relationships among sales, variable and fixed costs, and net income.

$$TR = TVC + TFC + \text{Net income}$$

At the break-even volume,

$$TR = TVC + TFC + 0$$

Using this break-even analysis, a pharmacy manager can determine the volume of prescriptions needed to cover all costs of operation, excluding profit. Besides determining the break-even point, CVP analysis determines the sales required to attain a particular income level or target net income. The formula is:

Target income sales volume =
(Total fixed costs + Target income) ÷ Unit contribution margin

Unit contribution margin (Unit CM) is defined as the difference between the unit selling price and the unit variable cost. For example, if the sales price is $25 and the unit variable cost is $15, then the unit CM is $10 ($25 − $15). This means each unit sold contributes $10 toward the fixed cost or profit. It must be remembered that this analysis becomes more complex as we examine unit CM from the perspective of multiple products and product lines. A unit CM can be calculated for a specific prescription product as described above; alternatively, unit CM may be calculated for a product line (such as prescription or non-prescription items) that assumes a relatively constant mix of products within the product line.

Relevant costs of dispensing

From a managerial standpoint, perhaps the most important way to classify costs is by how they change with respect to increases or decreases in activity, such as prescription volume or number of immunizations provided and previously defined as the relevant range. Within each relevant range, costs can be classified as either fixed or variable. Identifying and understanding fixed and variable cost data (described above) are important in many business decisions because they are the basis for profit calculations. However, not all costs are of equal importance in decision making, and managers must identify the costs applicable to a decision, defined as relevant costs. With regard to prescription pricing, we must determine these relevant costs and how they need to be incorporated into the prescription pricing model presented above.

For prescription dispensing, costs are broken down even further to include: direct, indirect, and labor costs. *Direct costs* are those solely associated with the dispensing process. This would include, for example, the cost of an online subscription to a prescription information reference. *Indirect costs* are those at least partially associated with the dispensing function, but, the portion needs to be allocated on a basis other than the space-to-sales ratio. Indirect costs can also be considered semi-variable costs, or costs that change in relation to volume but not in direct proportion. *Labor costs* are the costs of labor related directly to the dispensing function. This further delineation of costs will allow us to make the most accurate estimates of the cost of dispensing.

Cost of dispensing

To begin calculating the cost of dispensing (COD), we must develop two ratios used to allocate fixed and variable costs to the dispensing process. First, the sales ratio is the percent of sales accounted for by prescription business. Next, we must calculate the space ratio, which allocates floor space between the pharmacy and other departments within the store. The sales ratio is used to allocate variable costs and the space ratio is applied to fixed costs. Labor costs are allocated by identifying each store employee and estimating the percent time spent in prescription related duties.

"Sample Pharmacy" example

Consider a small-to-medium sized pharmacy operation occupying space within a medical office-type retail location of $350\,\mathrm{m}^2$ (3,800 square feet). Because of the location and size, this pharmacy has a large portion of its sales coming from prescriptions. Sample Pharmacy's income statement is provided

Income Statement Item Description	Amount in $
Sales	
Prescription sales	3,344,571
All other sales	1,159,842
Total sales	4,504,413
Cost of goods sold	
Prescriptions costs	2,605,742
All other costs	719,110
Total cost of goods sold	3,324,852
Gross profit	1,179,561
Operating expenses – payroll	
Salaries, wages	599,136
Payroll taxes, workers' comp., employee benefits	104,374
Total payroll expenses	703,510
Other operating expenses	
Advertising	17,034
Insurance	12,570
Store supplies containers, labels	5,695
Prescription containers and labels	10,400
Office postage	3,265
Delivery service	6,065
Pharmacy computer expense	13,317
Rent	44,719
Utilities, telephone	16,356
Pharmacy professional dues and licenses	4,010
Pharmacy continuing education	3,000
All other operating expenses	98,157
Total other operating expenses	234,588
Total operating expenses	938,098
Net operating income	241,463

Figure 8.1 Sample Pharmacy income statement.

in Figure 8.1. If the pharmacy department accounts for 120 m² (1,300 square feet) of space, including inventory and storage areas, the space ratio can be calculated:

Space ratio = Total department area ÷ Total facility area
= 120 ÷ 350 = 0.342 or 34.2%

Likewise, the sales ratio can be calculated:

Sales ratio = Department sales ÷ Total store sales
= $3,344,571 ÷ $4,504,413 = 0.742 or 74.2%

To allocate labor, the pharmacy manager needs to estimate how each employee spends their time with respect to the pharmacy department and the overall business. For example, a pharmacy technician that spends all of his or her time in prescription-related duties would be allocated 100% to the pharmacy operation. On the other hand, a pharmacist who owns their store would also spend part of their time doing managerial functions, such as accounting or scheduling, and would be allocated based on the best estimates of the time breakdown between prescription and other duties. The salaries and benefits for each of these employees need allocated to the prescription department. Figure 8.2 provides a table summarizing Sample Pharmacy's estimated labor allocation.

Employee type	Salary and benefits in $	% Time in prescription related duties	Prescription dept allocated salaries in $
Owner	200,000	60	120,000
Staff pharmacist	106,000	90	95,400
Staff pharmacist	92,000	75	69,000
Pharmacy technician	40,000	100	40,000
Cashiers	2 @ 15,000	50	15,000
Intern	12,010	100	12,010
Delivery personnel	4,500	50	2,250
Non-pharmacy related employees	7 @ 3,000	0	0
Other (part-time students, other personnel)	6,000	10	600
Total	493,510		354,260

Figure 8.2 Sample Pharmacy personnel cost allocations.

Next, the pharmacy manager needs to allocate the direct pharmacy costs. Direct pharmacy costs are the income statement costs associated only with the prescription department operations. For Sample Pharmacy, this would include:

- pharmacy continuing education expenses
- professional dues and licenses
- pharmacy computer expenses
- prescription labels and containers.

Referring to Figure 8.1, direct costs for Sample Pharmacy would be $30,727 (by summing the four categories above). Prescription vials and labels can be viewed as variable costs, since more of them would be used as prescription volume increases, but these costs can be allocated directly to the prescription department since they are not used outside of the dispensing function.

Fixed costs, the short-run costs that do not change with changes in output and sometimes referred to as facilities costs, are allocated to prescription department based on area. For Sample Pharmacy, this would include:

- rent
- utilities
- telephone
- insurance.

We can total these costs from the income statement (Figure 8.1) for a total of $73,645. When allocated by the space ratio, the amount assigned to the pharmacy operation for fixed costs is:

$$\text{Total fixed costs} \times \text{Space ratio} = \text{Fixed costs allocation to COD}$$
$$= \$73,645 \times 0.342 = \$25,187$$

Therefore, $25,187 is the amount of fixed costs attributed to the cost of dispensing.

Variable costs, those that change proportionally with increases in output, are allocated by sales dollars. For Sample Pharmacy, this would include:

- advertising
- store supplies
- office postage
- delivery service
- all other operating expenses.

When totaled from the income statement (Figure 8.1), these variable costs account for $130,216. When subsequently allocated by the sales ratio, the amount of variable costs attributed to the cost of dispensing is:

$$\text{Total variable costs} \times \text{Sales ratio} = \text{Variable costs allocation to COD}$$
$$= \$130,216 \times 0.742 = \$96,620$$

For chain pharmacy or franchise operations, there may also be a cost item for corporate overhead. In some cases, this is included in advertising expenses. If not, and there is a separate cost identified as corporate overhead, this cost can be included in one of three ways. First, allocated corporate overhead could be included in the COD as a fixed cost, and allocated based on the space ratio. Secondly, if pharmacy sales and space allocations are disproportionate, as in the case of Sample Pharmacy, it is also acceptable to include allocated corporate overhead as a variable cost and allocate based on the sales ratio. Finally, in some cases it may be appropriate to include allocated corporate overhead as a direct expense, particularly if this cost is primarily related to the dispensing function. This would be the case for many large chains where the pharmacy operation is not directly accountable for OTC items. The principle of conservatism, described in Chapter 2, would dictate the method selected should be the one most accurately reflecting the relevant cost to the dispensing process. It should be clear that the method selected to allocate corporate overhead will variably impact COD. Based on a manager's subjective view, the allocation most closely representing the true cost of operating the pharmacy should be selected, not the method that provides the highest or lowest COD, which could bias cost estimates.

Total costs

Now that labor, direct, allocated fixed and variable costs have all been identified, we can calculate the total COD. This is represented by the formula:

Total COD = Labor cost + Direct cost + Allocated FC + Allocated VC

For Sample Pharmacy (from Figure 8.2):

Total COD = \$354,260 + \$30,727 + \$25,187 + \$96,620 = \$506,794

A unit or average COD can be determined once prescription volume for the period is identified. For Sample Pharmacy, assuming the total prescriptions dispensed were 55,743, the average COD can now be calculated as:

Average COD = Total COD ÷ Number of prescriptions
= \$506,794 ÷ 55,743 = \$9.09

Thus, for Sample Pharmacy, based on the assumptions made in this calculation, the average COD would be \$9.09 per prescription. This amount is used going forward to examine pricing and pricing strategy in more detail.

Profits

The next consideration for the pharmacy owner/manager is to determine the desired profit level. This can be done both in terms of total desired profit and average profit per prescription. To estimate total desired profit, or total net income, the owner/manager can estimate profit figures based on average store operations. For example, a pharmacy such as Sample Pharmacy can expect to earn a net income of approximately 3–6% with gross profit margins of about 25% (Lilly Digest 2007).

For the current year, Sample Pharmacy's net operating income was $241,463 (Figure 8.1). Allocating these profits to prescription and non-prescription sales can be done using the sales ratio:

$$\text{Total profit} = \text{Net income} \times \text{Sales ratio}$$
$$= \$241,463 \times 0.742 = \$179,166$$

This would equate to a net profit per prescription of ($179,166 ÷ 55,743 prescriptions) = $3.21 per prescription.

Profit, from the perspective of the owner, may be seen to include the owner's compensation before taxes. This may be the preferred method for determining profit in a sole proprietorship. For larger operations, a better approach to target profit is to determine a target profit per prescription. Whichever method is used, the goal of the pharmacy operation is to remain viable in the marketplace and meet the return on investment objectives of the owner/shareholders, while balancing marketplace dynamics.

Inventory

Effective management of pharmacy inventory levels is essential to profitability, cash flow, customer service, and accurate estimations of future needs. Too much inventory can cause inadequate cash flow and profitability, while not enough inventory damages customer service levels. For a full review of pharmacy inventory issues, refer to Chapter 6.

Prices

A pharmacy owner who has conducted a COD analysis now has the information necessary to develop a competitive pricing strategy. For any prescription, a total price can now be calculated as:

$$\text{Price} = \text{COGS} + \text{COD} + \text{Profit}$$

Thus, for a prescription product with COGS at $17.50, the total prescription price would be:

$$\text{Price} = \$17.50 + \$9.09 + \$3.41 = \$30.00$$

For a product with an acquisition cost (COGS) of $92, the total prescription price would be:

Price = $92 + $9.09 + $3.41 = $104.50

However, this simple calculation is limited in its usefulness to the pharmacy owner because it is insensitive to competitive pricing in the marketplace and does not account for payment limitations, such as reimbursement by third party prescription programs. With third party programs, payments to pharmacies are established by contract and reimbursement is set at levels other than those that meet the pharmacy's pricing objectives.

Comprehensive price strategy

A price strategy sensitive to marketplace dynamics and profitability goals is necessary to ensure the success of a pharmacy business. This importance is reinforced when you consider that more than 85% of the prescription business at most pharmacies is paid by third party insurance programs.

Through the information gained in determining the cost of dispensing, a pharmacist can then evaluate profits and losses that will incur by participating in various third party programs using the full cost price formula as a benchmark. Third party program analysis also gives the pharmacist insight regarding how various third party reimbursements will affect strategy on other prices, such as cash payment prescriptions, which are estimated to be about 15% of the average pharmacy's prescription sales. For Sample Pharmacy, assuming a constant COGS between various payment systems (cash versus Medicaid) the target full cost recovery would be: COD + Profit.

To evaluate the impact of profitability, the pharmacy manager can now calculate a profit or loss for each prescription payment program. If a particular third party payer offered a reimbursement contract based on actual acquisition cost plus a $5.15 dispensing fee, Sample Pharmacy can now determine the impact on profitability for this third party reimbursement plan. Full cost coverage at Sample Pharmacy was calculated to be:

COD + Profit = $9.09 + $3.41 = $12.50

Holding product cost (COGS) constant, and with a third party dispensing fee of $5.15, Sample Pharmacy would lose $7.35 on each prescription reimbursed under this plan. If the third party payer offered the pharmacy a reimbursement rate that included some amount of profit based on product cost, then this loss per prescription would be offset by any profits attainable through prudent purchasing (e.g., if a third party program offers reimbursement at AWP – 10% and the pharmacy can purchase from the wholesaler at AWP – 15%, this gain can be considered to offset the lower dispensing fee).

Thus, profit or loss for third party programs can be calculated with the following formula:

$$\text{Gain (loss) per prescription} = (\text{COD} + \text{Profit}) - [\text{Dispensing fee} + \text{AWP gain (loss)}]$$

This information can then be used to determine the impact of the program considering the volume of prescription business possibly generated by accepting a particular third party plan.

In the above example, if accepting the third party plan were to result in an increase in prescription volume of 5%, expected cost of dispensing should be recalculated given the increased prescription volume. For Sample Pharmacy, an increase in prescription volume of 5% would result in 58,530 total prescriptions ($55,743 \times 1.05 = 58,530$ prescriptions), or an increase of 2,787 prescriptions. This would reduce the average COD from $9.09 to $8.66 per prescription (total COD $\div$ number prescriptions $= \$506,794 \div 58,530 = \$8.66$). With no change in profit expectations, full cost for this prescription reimbursement program would be $8.66 + $3.41 or $12.07.

As illustrated, third party prescription reimbursement is a conundrum for pharmacy managers since dispensing fees may be set at levels that reflect full cost coverage. Pharmacy managers must balance total reimbursement (dispensing fees and any profits that can be obtained from prudent purchasing) with volume of sales possible through bringing new third party prescription programs on board.

Cash prescription pricing

Although cash prescriptions represent only a small percentage of the average pharmacy business's sales, pharmacy managers must still have a pricing strategy in place for this segment. For a pricing strategy to be competitive, it should reflect marketplace dynamics and price pressures and include, for example, prices for competitive, staple, and premium products. It should also be based on a thorough understanding of the marketplace and sound financial information. A competitive pricing strategy will enable pharmacy managers to make informed decisions about pricing. A sound pricing strategy, combined with well informed pricing decisions, ensure a competitive position in the marketplace.

Pricing categories

For cash customers, there are three basic price categories: competitive, staple, and premium prices. The competitive product category would include products for which there is intense price competition. Competitive products may be sold at or near cost, to attract customers and remain competitive. Staple products are generally defined as products sold at full cost, while premium products are those sold at a premium, returning greater than full cost coverage.

However, there are unlimited possibilities for expansion of these basic categories. For example, the competitive category could include both *loss leader* products (sold below full cost) and *competitive products* (sold at or near full cost). If products are sold at acquisition cost (COGS), then the COD and profit are not earned on each sale of a competitive product. Therefore, this loss will need to be recovered in another product category less sensitive to price competition, such as *staple* and *premium* products. The goals in the competitive product category are to sell products at the lowest possible price, project a favorable price image in the marketplace and, at the same time, ensure pharmacy profitability objectives are met.

To calculate the loss to be recovered, the pharmacy manager needs to know the volume of products in each of the price categories (competitive, staple, and premium in our example). In this example, we will allocate:

- competitive products 10% of prescription volume
- staple products 55% of prescription volume
- premium products 35% of prescription volume.

This means Sample Pharmacy will sell approximately 10% of its products at or below cost. The loss to be recovered (LTBR) on competitive prescriptions would be:

$$
\begin{aligned}
\text{LTBR} &= (\% \text{ Competitive prescriptions}) \\
&\quad \times (\text{COD} + \text{Profit}) \div (\% \text{ Premium prescriptions}) \\
&= 10\% \times (\$9.09 + \$3.41) \div 35\% \\
&= \$3.57
\end{aligned}
$$

The pharmacy manager would then need to recover \$3.57 on each premium prescription to make up for revenue not earned on each competitive prescription and attain profitability goals. For staple products, the pharmacy manager can price at or near to full cost in order to remain competitive in the marketplace.

Pricing pharmaceutical care/cognitive services

In addition to the issues discussed related to budgeting for provision of pharmaceutical care/cognitive services, there are two major factors to consider when pricing these services:

- price per unit of service
- opportunity cost associated with using the pharmacist's time.

Typical pharmacist salaries range from \$40–60 per hour and up for pharmacy owners, which does not take into account the opportunity cost of the pharmacist's time. For example, while providing a cognitive service or administering a vaccine, the pharmacist would not be performing the functions related to dispensing and generating revenue. Typically, pharmacy managers have set the hourly rate for pharmacist's time at between \$60 and \$120 per hour.

Thus, to set a price for administration of a flu shot, the pharmacy manager can establish an hourly rate of \$120 for the pharmacist's time. Assuming it takes 7 minutes to collect the information necessary, provide the immunization and counsel the patient, this would represent a service cost of \$2.00 per minute or \$14.00 for the flu shot. The ingredient and supply costs used to provide the immunization must then be added to determine the total cash price for the vaccine.

Over-the-counter pricing

Since third party prescription insurance programs with a flat co-pay structure reduce the impact of a pharmacy's prices on prescriptions – by making the price the same to an individual no matter where they get the prescription filled – OTC pricing of products can be critical for pharmacy businesses in achieving target profit goals. Many pharmacy practice environments merchandise and sell OTC products in addition to prescription products. The cost-plus markup method described above for prescriptions provides a method for better understanding costs and provided information useful in making pricing decisions. Although OTC products have different demand characteristics, similar analyses can be conducted to assist pharmacy managers with OTC pricing decisions. Generally, OTC products are priced using a percent markup approach. For example, in a pharmacy where the OTC markup is 40%, a product with a \$10.00 cost would be priced at \$14.00:

$$
\begin{aligned}
\text{Price} &= \text{Product cost} \times (1 + \% \text{Markup}) \\
&= \$10.00 \times (1.4) = \$10.00 \times 1.4 \\
&= \$14.00
\end{aligned}
$$

For Sample Pharmacy, the total COD was determined to be \$506,794. Assuming all other sales are OTC sales, the balance of the operating costs is allocated to the total OTC cost allocation. Therefore, the costs allocated to selling an OTC item can be determined by subtracting the COD from the total operating costs (Figure 8.1).

$$
\begin{aligned}
\text{OTC cost allocation} &= \text{Total operating cost} - \text{COD} \\
&= \$938,098 - \$506,794 = \$431,304
\end{aligned}
$$

Using this number, we can determine the average markup on OTC cost:

$$\text{Average OTC markup} = \text{OTC cost allocation} \div \text{Total OTC sales}$$
$$= \$431,304 \div \$1,159,842 = 0.372 \text{ or } 37.2\%$$

A pharmacy manager could then apply a 37.2% markup to OTC products as a fixed pricing strategy. This figure does not include a premium for desired profit levels, but rather, reflects the profit obtained during the prior period as shown in the income statement. If greater profits are desired in the future, then a premium can be added to the average OTC markup.

However, OTC products must be sensitive to competitive market pressures, much more so than prescription prices. This is true because of the number of non-pharmacy business competitors also selling OTC products, creating a much more competitive market.

An effective pricing strategy for OTCs would create a competitive strategy based on marketplace dynamics and spreading cost recovery unequally across competitive, staple, and premium OTC product sales. Losses on competitive OTC prices, similar to the losses on competitive cash prescriptions, can be recovered on premium OTC product sales.

For Sample Pharmacy, the pharmacy manager has determined that competitive, staple, and premium products should account for 15%, 50%, and 35% of the OTC product sales. This means: $173,976 of sales would be derived from competitive OTC products; $579,921 of sales would be derived from staple OTC products; and, $405,945 would be derived from premium OTC sales.

Given 15% of the OTC products need to be sold within the competitive category, this would imply that, on average, these products are sold at or near cost (slightly above or below cost). The LTBR (comp. OTC) can be calculated to be:

$$\text{LTBR (comp. OTC)} = (\% \text{ Comp. OTC}) \times \text{Total OTC cost allocation}$$
$$= 15\% \times \$431,304 = \$64,696$$

This LTBR (comp. OTC) can now be added to the premium product category:

$$\text{Premium OTC cost allocation} = (\text{Total OTC cost allocation}$$
$$\times \% \text{ Premium products}) + \text{LTBR (comp. OTC)}$$
$$= (\$431,304 \times 0.35) + \$64,696 = \$215,652$$

Based on total sales expected in the premium OTC category, the percent markup for premium OTC products can now be determined:

$$\text{Premium OTC markup} \% = \text{Premium OTC cost allocation}$$
$$\div \text{Premium OTC sales}$$
$$= \$215,652 \div 405,945 = 0.531 \text{ or } 53.1\%$$

In summary, Sample Pharmacy's OTC pricing strategy would sell competitive OTC products at or near the products acquisition cost. Staple products would be sold at about a 37% markup and premium products would sell at about a 53% markup. However, as with cash prescriptions and the numerous third party plans associated with prescription pricing, there can be an unlimited number of product categories reflecting various competitive OTC price requirements. To be more sensitive to market prices, many pharmacy operations have used the services of wholesalers to assist them in determining market prices.

The method described above can be expanded to include as many or few categories as the pharmacy manager desires. For example, a pharmacy manager could choose to include loss leaders (sold below average acquisition cost), competitive (sold at or near acquisition cost), competitive staple (sold near full cost coverage), staple (sold at full cost coverage), premium staple (sold slightly above full cost coverage) and premium (sold above full cost coverage). The percent markup for each of these categories can be determined using the methodology described above.

Summary

This chapter developed and discussed the impact of pricing strategies for prescriptions, cognitive services, and OTC products. The importance of knowing and calculating the cost of dispensing (COD) was also illustrated. Although pricing decisions in many pharmacy practice areas have been removed from the individual pharmacist's control, understanding the components and importance of a given price only adds to managers' abilities to better serve their patients and customers.

References

1 Coalition for Community Pharmacy Action. *Cost of Dispensing Study.* Alexandria, VA: CCPA. www.rxaction.org/publications/COD_Study.cfm (accessed September 24, 2009).
2 Nelson AA Jr (1980). Prescription pricing I: Concepts and systems. *Pharm Manage* 152: 17.
3 Zelnio RN, Nelson AA Jr (1980). Prescription pricing II: Computational methods. *Pharm Manage* 152: 57.
4 Perri M (1991). The basics of a competitive pricing strategy. *Consult Pharm* 6: 142–147.
5 Perri M (1991). Pricing policies under a competitive pricing strategy. *Consult Pharm* 6: 262–263.

Suggested reading

Carroll NV. *Financial Management for Pharmacists: a Decision-Making Approach*, 3rd edn. Baltimore, MD: Lippincott Williams & Wilkins, 2007.

Review questions

1   Describe why a higher volume pharmacy could be viewed as more efficient than a smaller pharmacy.

2   What is cost-volume-profit (CVP) analysis? How is it useful to managers?

3   List some assumptions underlying break-even analysis.

4   Given the income statement for Sample Pharmacy, assume that the pharmacy manager has decided that a markup of 54% for products is too high and customers will balk at prices set at this level. To remedy this, the pharmacy manager decides to include multiple levels of staple prices: competitive staple (1/3 of the staple category), staple (1/3 of the staple category) and premium staple (1/3 of the staple category). The pharmacy manager wants to sell the competitive staple products at a 25% discount compared with the staple category and the premium staple products at a 25% premium. What will be the impact of this expansion of the staple category on the average percent markup in the staple (competitive staple + staple + premium staple) category?

5   What would be the actual percent markup for the premium staple category?

6   Explain the advantages and disadvantages of establishing a pricing strategy for OTC products that includes a straight markup on product cost.

7   If a third party prescription insurance plan offered a pharmacy manager a plan that included a $4.65 dispensing fee and the COD for the pharmacy in question was $7.25, under what circumstances could the pharmacy manager consider accepting that plan?

8   Discuss how psychological price points, such as $1.97 as opposed to $2.00 can be used to attract the interest of customers.

9   One of the most important factors to consider when pricing cognitive services is the opportunity cost associated with the pharmacist's time. True or false?

10   Which of the following statements about break-even analysis is false?

A   The break-even point is where total revenue (TR) received equals the total cost (TC) associated with the sale of the product.

B   A lower break-even point is associated with higher operating risk.

C   Break-even analysis can determine the volume of prescriptions needed to cover all costs of operation, excluding profit.

D   Break-even analysis can be used to analyze the potential profitability of an expenditure in a sales-based business.

11   With respect to OTC products, there is a much smaller competitive marketplace compared with the prescription marketplace. True or false?

Answers

1   Efficiency and volume are not necessarily related. Smaller operations can and do operate efficiently when well managed. However, from a cost perspective, a higher volume pharmacy could be seen as more efficient than a smaller pharmacy owing to economies of scale resulting from a larger business operation. This would include a lower average cost to dispense since the fixed, variable, labor, direct and indirect costs are spread over a larger volume of prescriptions.

2   CVP analysis examines how profits and costs change with a change in volume. CVP gives pharmacy managers the ability to analyze their profit based on changes in such factors as variable costs, fixed costs, selling prices, volume, and mix of products sold. An independent pharmacy owner/manager, for example, may want to know what volume of a cognitive service is needed to break-even or to achieve a desired level of profit. Therefore, the importance lies in how a manager would use these analyses in developing or changing the overall, or a specific, pricing strategy.

3   Break-even analysis is an important tool for pharmacy managers when developing budgets for the next operating period, expanding existing operations, or when deciding to open a new venture entirely. Since the main purpose of break-even analysis is to determine the effect varying levels of sales affect operating costs and ultimately profits, it is often called cost-volume-profit analysis. The main assumptions that form the basis of any break-even

analysis are type of costs, either fixed or variable, and a relevant range of production or sales volume. Fixed costs remain constant within the established relevant range, regardless of the level of sales activity. For example, rent for the building not only must be paid whether or not the business was open, but also remains the same given various levels of sales volumes. Variable costs are those costs that are incurred in direct relationship to the sales volume or level of operations. A common variable cost in a community pharmacy would be dispensing supplies; these increase as prescription sales volumes increase. The point at which total costs (fixed and variable costs added together) match the sales receipts of a given prescription dispensing volume is known as the break-even point. The relevant range becomes important when prescription dispensing volume increases to a point where additional space will be needed to be leased; a new break-even analysis will have to be completed to account for the increase in the fixed costs anticipated with the higher levels of business activity.

4   Given the manager is deciding to decrease competitive staple pricing by 25% (i.e., not making as much profit on these products) and also increasing premium staple by 25% (i.e., making more profit on these products), the resulting impact on the average percentage margin is zero. This pricing strategy can be greatly effective given the nature of different prescription and OTC products. Some products are highly competitive and price sensitive, whereas others are not price sensitive and consumers/patients would be willing to pay the premium pricing.

5   The actual percentage markup for the premium staple products would be 79% (original 54% + 25%).

6   Advantages of using a straight pricing markup for OTC items are the removal of uncertainty and increased efficiency. Those involved with putting the prices on the shelves have a clearly defined number with which to work for all products. By knowing a defined markup percentage, any price changes could be quickly executed without much deliberation. Disadvantages of this method could include decreased efficiency and leaving profit on the table. As just described, using a tiered pricing strategy (e.g., staple, premium, premium staple) ensures that price changes be done with much more detail and care to adhere to the given strategy. In addition, if a straight markup strategy is used, specific product prices could be lower than consumers/patients are willing to pay, possibly leaving attainable profit on the table.

7   The pharmacy manager would have to take into consideration the volume increase associated with accepting the third party plan. If the COD is reduced to near break-even (or below), the pharmacy manager could accept the plan based on the increased OTC sales offsetting the slight loss on the prescriptions. Other external factors come into play when deciding to possibly accept a third party plan, such as the demographics of the location/area. Is this the primary employer in a small town, which consists of a large percentage of the customer base? Or is this new employer entering the area, looking to further expand its employee base and, therefore, hopefully greatly increase the pharmacy's customer base?

8   Psychological price points are used in all areas of business, including pharmacy. In the question, $1.97 is compared with $2.00. Even though the cents are seen and not totally ignored, consumers may subconsciously partially ignore and see the item as not as expensive as it actually is. Research has shown that fractional prices suggest to consumers that goods are marked at the lowest possible price. Further, judgments of numerical differences often focus on the left-hand digits, a behavioral phenomenon referred to as the left-digit anchoring effect. This suggests that people perceive price and price differences based on the left-most digit so, for example, the difference between 7.99 and 9.00 is seen to be to be closer to 2.01 than to 1.01 because of this effect.

9   The statement is true.

10   B is false: A lower break-even point decreases the operating risk.

11   The statement is false.

Glossary

Break-even analysis	Determines the break-even sales point, where total revenue (TR) received equals the total cost (TC) associated with the sale of the product (TR = TC). This point is typically calculated to determine if it would be profitable to sell a proposed product, as opposed to attempting to modify an existing product instead so it can be made lucrative.
Competitive pricing	Products sold at or near acquisition cost.

Competitive staple pricing	Products sold near full cost coverage.
Cost-volume-profit (CVP) analysis	Useful analyses of how profit and costs change with changes in sales volume. CVP analysis looks at the effects on profits caused by changes in such factors as variable costs, fixed costs, selling prices, volume, and mix of products sold.
Direct prescription costs	Those costs solely associated with the dispensing process. This would include, for example, the cost of an online subscription to a prescription information reference.
Indirect prescription costs	Those at least partially associated with the dispensing function, but the portion needs to be allocated on a basis other than the space-to-sales ratio. Indirect costs can also be considered semi-variable costs, or costs that change in relation to volume but not in direct proportion.
Loss leader pricing	Products sold below average acquisition cost.
Marginal costs	The cost of producing an additional unit of output. For example, the marginal cost of the 250th prescription dispensed can be calculated by finding the difference in total cost at 249 prescriptions (units of output) and total cost at 250 prescriptions.
Premium pricing	Products sold above full cost coverage.
Premium staple pricing	Products sold slightly above full cost coverage.
Relevant range	The range of activity (i.e., volume of prescriptions dispensed) over which the company expects the behaviors of expenses to be consistent (or linear).
Staple pricing	Products sold at full cost coverage.
Total costs	From a pricing perspective, the sum of all costs being considered for analysis purposes.
Unit contribution margin (unit CM)	The excess of the unit selling price over the unit variable cost. For example, if the sales price is $25 and the unit variable cost is $15, then the Unit CM is $10.

9

Personal financial management

Learning objectives

- Identify and explain the importance of setting personal financial goals
- Understand how credit scores (FICO) are used and their impact on one's personal financial management
- Understand the risks and benefits of various investment choices, including cash, stocks and bonds, and how to develop a diversified portfolio
- Evaluate the effects of taxation on wages and interest income
- Recognize the importance of well planned retirement savings through employer-sponsored or self-employment programs

Introduction

Pharmacy practitioners have ample opportunity to work with and use financial information within their practice environment as part of their daily responsibilities. However, it is important to recognize that many of the principles developed in this text can also be applied to one's personal life. Younger pharmacy students, for example, may fully understand the concepts of inventory management and financial analysis, but then have no concept of what to do with their new six-figure salary. Students must realize that personal financial management should begin as early as possible and continue through retirement, as life's challenges present opportunities to make important decisions regarding spending, investing, and deciding how to best allocate personal resources. Being prepared for life's changes and taking charge of our personal finance will enable better financial decision making. In this chapter, the focus is on the importance of developing financial discipline, including minimizing personal debt, understanding tax implications and optimizing wealth.

Setting personal financial goals

Perhaps the most important point to remember is that building wealth is a lifelong process. Unless you inherit wealth, win the lottery or marry well, each of us must take responsibility for future planning and accumulating enough wealth to enjoy life and have a comfortable retirement. Regardless of your financial goals, you need to begin planning as early in your life and career as possible.

The first step in financial goal setting is to critically assess your current financial situation, as well as where you think you could realistically be at some point in the future. Just like when a pharmacy manager works on budgeting (see Chapter 7), it is critical to know your starting point and where you are headed in order to develop a sound plan. Although some goals require greater sacrifice than others, your plan should be realistic and attainable. Most of us set building wealth as a primary long-term goal and make accommodations within our budgets to achieve this goal. For example, living frugally as a means to this goal may prove too restrictive and, therefore, our plans are more likely to fail. Assume the following four basic aims are set:

- establish your emergency fund
- pay off your student loans ahead of schedule
- set aside for a down payment on a home
- save for retirement.

Attacking these goals too aggressively could result in a lower standard of living and general dissatisfaction with your financial plan. When this happens, plans fail.

It is important to note that your financial goals will change at various points in your life, when events such as marriage, taking a new job, or the birth of a child occur. However, regardless of whether you are preparing for the birth of your first child or saving for a down payment on a new home, what is critical to financial success is to be disciplined when it comes to implementing and adhering to your plan.

Many financial planners recommend that one of the best ways to ensure reaching your financial goals is to pay yourself first. By making an investment in yourself first, even when other choices such as monthly living expenses exert pressure on your budget, you develop the discipline necessary to be successful in meeting your financial goals. A personal budget is always a mixture of both required and discretionary costs, necessitating the need for prudent choices. However, by treating yourself as your own creditor and making payments to yourself first, you will be more likely to stay on track with savings goals. One strategy that works extremely well is to set up an automatic transfer (e.g., weekly or monthly) from your checking account into a savings, investment, or retirement account. When this savings method is used, budgeting with the remainder of your paycheck becomes easier and helps to define the amount of discretionary funds available each month.[1]

One of the most important priorities of your initial payments to yourself is to establish an emergency fund – a reserve fund to be used in case of unexpected events such as the loss of a job, an illness or accident. Most financial experts recommend an emergency fund of between 6 and 9 months of your living expenses (e.g., mortgage or rent, utilities, and food). The future can be very volatile and finding employment quickly may not be as easy as it was finding your first professional position after graduation. Medical emergencies also constitute a major reason many families claim bankruptcy because often an emergency fund was not available. Once your emergency fund reaches a sufficient level, continuing this newly developed saving behavior becomes routine, building confidence that future unexpected expenses can be handled without significant interruption to your overall financial health.

Building this important savings behavior will also have a positive impact on an essential element for all individuals in today's world – the establishment of credit and developing and maintaining a high credit rating or score. Credit scores, discussed later in the chapter, impact your financial life in a multitude of ways. High credit scores can contribute to negotiating lower interest rates when purchasing high-cost items such as a home, appliances, or an automobile. Conversely, lower credit scores will have a detrimental effect in higher interest rates or being denied credit altogether. Developing and adhering to a budget results in making timely payments on all your obligations and, ultimately, helps to increase your credit score.

Creating a home budget

Worldwide financial events such as the US recession, the Greek debt crisis, a housing bubble in China, and a high rate of personal bankruptcy should emphasize to each of us that we need to pay close attention to our personal financial decisions. Living beyond one's means (i.e., spending more than can be covered through current income levels) places one at significant financial risk. Emotions often run high and cause many of us to make purchases without a thorough analysis of our needs. By forgetting to analyze the cost and benefits of purchases, and how these decisions fit into our personal financial plan, one can quickly develop a pattern of spending behavior leading to devastating consequences if left unchecked.

Although there are many reasons why individuals get into financial trouble, not controlling the amount of one's debt is definitely a major contributor.

The act of creating a budget, just as a pharmacy owner would for his/her store, involves making detailed plans for future income and your related expenses. Budgets are most useful when they are prepared with your financial goals and priorities in mind, whether your focus is to limit spending or to build wealth. Budgets are useful tools in two ways, for which the importance of developing and adhering to cannot be overemphasized:

- A budget enables you to plan how to spend your money in exactly the way you wish to meet your goals.
- After a budget period has elapsed, it provides a detailed record enabling you to see where you actually have spent your money and how well you did in meeting your plan.

Although most think of a budget as a spending limit, a well-designed budget does not have to be restrictive. Instead, the planning that goes into developing a budget can actually provide financial freedom when you realize that it represents a comprehensive plan for how you will spend your limited resources. Budgets allow us to track spending, optimize our financial outcomes, and achieve goals. Although no two individuals share exactly the same financial goals or expenses, the principle that expenses should not exceed income is shared by all budgets.

To assist in budget development, an individual can begin with a generic personal budget worksheet. Recognizing that there will be a great deal of variability in a financial worksheet such as this, Figure 9.1 provides a sample with general categories and a reasonable starting point for creating a personal budget. Note savings and investments are listed first under expenses, consistent with the assertion of paying yourself first. It is also important to recognize that the level of detail within income and expense categories may be tailored to each individual's liking, to make the entire budget more relevant and therefore easier to implement.

Once you have identified and personalized your budget line items for the desired period (weekly, monthly or annually), you are ready to begin living on your established budget. Remember, successful implementation of your budget depends upon a good attitude, accurate recording, and little bit of discipline. There are several strategies that can help you stay on budget:

- Remember that the budget is a plan and, as a result, there can and will be deviations from the plan. While the budget should provide clear direction about your priorities and help you avoid the temptation of spending on unplanned items, remember too, that it is permissible to deviate from time to time when your financial priorities change. Still, each purchase decision should begin with, is this on budget? Is this item essential or not?
- Simply avoid places (e.g., an expensive restaurant, hobby store, or designer clothing store) where you know you might be tempted to make an impulse purchase of an item not in the budget.
- Use a debit card, cash, or checks rather than a credit card for purchases. The good news is that debit cards offer the same kind of purchase

Item	Amount
Income	
Job	
Spouse's job	
Other employment	
Other income (tax refunds, dividends, child support, etc.)	
Total income	
Expenses	
Savings	
Investing	
Rent/mortgage	
Gas/electric	
Water and sewerage	
Homeowners/renters insurance	
Homeowners association/condominium fees	
Telephone	
Food	
Entertainment (e.g. dining out)	
Medical expenses	
Car payment(s)	
Gasoline	
Repairs and maintenance	
Public transportation	
Child care	
Tuition/books/school uniforms	
Taxes (e.g. Estimated tax payments)	
Credit card payment	
Other loan payment	
Personal (e.g. hair styling)	
Clothing	
Cable television, internet access, other media	
Charitable contributions	
Cellular phone service	
Other expenses	
Total expenses	
Net monthly excess (deficit)	

Figure 9.1   Budget worksheet.

protection and detailed transaction reports as a credit card, but a debit card avoids the temptation to spend more than you can afford to pay off at month's end.

The ultimate goal of personal budgeting is achievement of your financial goals and financial success. Financial success results from behaviors, such as the discipline to stay on budget, knowledge of your goals, good decision making skills and, perhaps most of all, determination to achieve your goals.

Case-in-point 9.1   First-generation millionaires

First-generation millionaires have been found to share some common characteristics. Perhaps the most important of these is a financial focus on accumulating wealth rather than spending money. However, first-generation, self-made millionaires, also demonstrate a propensity to borrow money only when necessary, frequently pursue opportunities to advance their education, have a good balance between their career and personal life and recognize that discipline and hard work increases the probability of success. In addition, over 50% of millionaires never received any inheritance or support for college tuition from their families. Used cars are the transportation of choice for 37% of millionaires, while less than 25% ever received personal gifts of more than $10,000. Although we won't all become millionaires, possessing these characteristics can increase your chances of achieving any level of financial success. Likewise, without setting financial goals, establishing a personal budget and exercising discipline, you will be less likely to make sound financial decisions and accumulate wealth.[2]

Borrowing and credit

As noted in Chapter 5, many companies often require assistance with cash flow needs during their operating cycle and turn to credit as an effective tool in efficient operations. Therefore, the prudent use of credit in one's personal life is also an effective way to achieve financial goals. For example, when making a purchase on a credit card, the borrower receives the goods or services and agrees to repay the lender at a future date, plus interest. The *interest rate* is based on prevailing market interest rates, which can fluctuate based upon various factors such as market competition for the borrower's business and the assessment of risk that the lender assigns to the borrower. In general, lower interest rates are extended to borrowers with a better credit history, higher incomes, and greater ability to repay the credit; in other words, those borrowers who are associated with less risk. An individual's level of risk is sometimes referred to as their credit worthiness. To evaluate an individual's

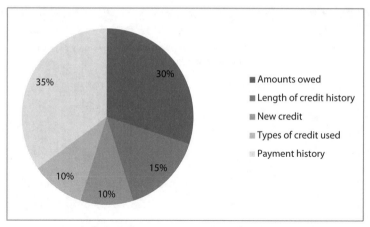

Figure 9.2 Components of a FICO score.

overall credit worthiness, many lenders rely upon the *Fair Isaac Corporation (FICO) score*.

Currently, the FICO score is the most standard indicator used by lenders to rate a borrower's potential risk, with scores typically ranging from 300 to 850.[3] Higher FICO scores are given to those persons having a lower credit risk, which results in lower interest rates and an increased likelihood of obtaining credit. Your FICO score is based upon five distinct areas of credit history as shown in Figure 9.2:

- Payment history – the number of accounts that are paid as agreed and past due, as well as the associated amounts and how long items are past due.
- Amounts owed – current account balances owed as well as the proportion of the credit limits of various types of account (i.e., credit lines, installment loans, etc.)
- Length of credit history – when accounts were established and levels of activity.
- New credit – recent credit inquiries, opened accounts, and any re-established accounts following a prior payment problem.
- Types of credit used – the details of number and types of various credit instruments currently in place.

It is important to note that all the above factors are considered in determining the final credit score. By establishing only necessary credit accounts and making regular, on-time payments, a higher FICO score can be achieved and maintained. To illustrate the effects of one's FICO score on an important purchase, a home, Table 9.1 shows the score's effect on your interest rate or monthly payment for a 30-year, fixed-rate mortgage.

In addition to a FICO score, a credit report is maintained on all borrowers and usually investigated by prospective lenders. An individual's credit report contains:

Table 9.1 Effect of consumer credit based upon FICO scores – mortgage

FICO score range	National average 30-year fixed mortgage APR (%)	Monthly payment ($)
760–850	4.520	1,524
700–759	4.742	1,563
680–699	4.919	1,596
660–679	5.133	1,635
640–659	5.563	1,715
620–639	6.109	1,820

Sample credit scores and interest rates subject to change based on economic conditions.
http://www.myfico.com/LoanCenter/Mortgage/ (accessed April 21, 2010).

- identifying information
- history of employment
- addresses
- all consumer credit for the past 7 years
- payment history
- other public records, such as bankruptcy.

In the United States, there are three credit reporting agencies: Equifax, Experian, and TransUnion. The federal government allows everyone to receive at no charge one copy of their credit report annually (obtained at https://www.annualcreditreport.com). It is recommended that individuals monitor their own credit periodically as identity theft is a threat to every credit consumer, regardless of credit score.

Case-in-point 9.2   Credit cards

Credit cards can be an integral part of a personal financial plan. Credit cards offer the same convenience as cash, but provide purchase protection and a detailed record of your financial transactions. The danger, of course, lies in using credit cards and making more "impulse" purchases not a part of your financial plan/budget. There are many types of credit cards available and strategies for their safe use. First, choose cards with the lowest interest rate and fees. Although this may seem to be a simple task, with the multitude of credit card choices available, one must make a thorough analysis of the various offers. Secondly, since carrying large balances is not a goal of using credit cards, cashback bonuses should be closely examined. Read the fine print very carefully, as you may not be regularly making the types of purchases necessary to earn rewards on many credit cards. Reward cards, such as those offered by airlines, hotels chains, or banks, offer attractive benefits, but these benefits are usually accompanied by higher annual fees. Therefore, select cards offering rewards most suitable to your personal interests. For example, if you don't travel by air much, a credit card offering frequent flyer miles may be of no interest. Perhaps you have young children, and are planning an eventual trip to Disney? A Disney Rewards® Visa® Card from Chase allows the accumulation of rewards that can be used for purchases on a Disney theme park visit or vacation. Shop around and find the one that best suits your needs.

The convenience of credit cards stems from the fact that they can be used for daily purchases, avoiding the need to carry large sums of cash. However, it is important to make sure that charges incurred are part of the personal budget and can be paid off by the due date. Using credit cards as more of a "convenience" will earn the card's unique rewards offered as well as improving your credit report and FICO score. In the event that you are unable to pay your balance in full each month, paying your minimum balance on time is critical. Failure to do so will typically result in a late fee, and perhaps a higher interest rate and a lower FICO score, and may ultimately affect the interest rates on your other credit cards.

Carrying balances and incurring monthly interest charges can be costly. For example, $1,000 borrowed at 12% on a credit card will take 70 months (slightly less than 6 years) to pay off when making the $20 minimum monthly payment. Additionally, the total interest over this period is $394.26.[4]

Major investment classes

All investment choices carry inherent risks, with the variation in potential rates of return helping to compensate for these risks. Other key factors closely tied with the rate of return include the degree of *liquidity* (the ability of an investment to be easily converted to cash) and the maturity date associated with every investment. The next discussion provides basic information examining the different investment types and the unique relationships between the aforementioned key factors.

The major categories of investment options include:

- cash (e.g., checking accounts and money market funds)
- bonds
- stocks.

(The above list ranks each investment class in terms of maturity, risk, and liquidity, beginning with the most current and liquid investments. These options are first subdivided into either short or long-term investments, with short-term investments defined as maturing within 12 months or less; while long-term investments are those maturing in excess of 12 months.)

The choice of investment vehicle depends on the preferences of the individual investor. For example, a *money market fund* offers a higher level of safety and greater liquidity, but, in most cases, significantly lower returns than stocks. In order to choose between the available options, an individual must consider the investment objectives developed as a part of their financial plan. The goal of investing is to create a diversified portfolio of investment choices that not only provides the investor's desired *rate of return*, but also is within the investor's risk tolerance zone.

Case-in-point 9.3 Liquidity

Liquidity is a primary consideration for every investor when developing an investment portfolio. A liquid asset is one that can be converted into cash with relative ease and without significant loss in value. An investor must balance investment goals and the need for cash in the future, both near and far. For example, an investor 30 years from retirement will have short-term cash needs for various living expenses, but within their retirement investments, liquidity is not a major concern. The personal budget should adequately reflect cash for current needs and have allowances for investing in the long term.

Although liquidity is a relative term, more liquid investments include cash, checking, savings, and money market accounts. Fewer liquid assets include, for example, real estate or long-term bonds. The value of these asset types may fluctuate over time and often take long periods to sell and convert to cash. For example, owning your home is a good investment choice, but does not represent a highly liquid asset because a home usually takes several weeks or months to sell, much longer than other assets such as shares in a money market fund, which can be redeemed in a day. Given the nature of the emergency fund discussed above, this savings fund should consist of only the most liquid asset classes.

Cash

Most investors keep some portion of their investment portfolio in the form of cash because it is the most liquid of all investment options and is a necessary part of everyday life. Even so, remembering the "time value of money concept", maximizing the earning potential of cash investments is important. Many financial institutions offer both interest and non-interest bearing cash accounts, depending upon the contracted availability of one's cash. Many checking accounts offer some type of interest payments or fixed fees for check writing in lieu of offering interest. Money market accounts usually pay a slightly higher rate of interest than checking accounts, although at a rate comparatively low to other classes, and the amount of monthly withdrawals may be very limited. As a general rule, since there is little risk associated with cash accounts, the interest rates paid on them are at the low end of the spectrum.

Within the category of cash investments are also cash equivalents, which are assets readily convertible to cash without any loss in value. The major difference between cash and cash equivalents is the fact that cash equivalents are generally expected to mature within 3 months and be converted back into cash. This would include, for example, investments such as money market holdings and short-term government bonds or treasury bills. Given the closeness of their maturity dates, cash equivalent investments bear little interest rate risk and any loss in value. The potential for loss of value of an investment when it is necessary to be converted back into cash is an important concept. It is precisely this market volatility which mandates that stocks, which can usually be easily converted to cash, are not considered as cash equivalents.

> ### Case-in-point 9.4   Market volatility
>
> Market volatility must be recognized by any investor who wishes to invest in stocks. For example, in response to the fears regarding the Greek debt crisis on May 6, 2010, the Dow Jones Industrial Average (DJIA) dropped nearly 7% in a single day. Although this drop was not permanent, it does illustrate the volatility of investment values on a daily basis. If an investor had to liquidate their entire portfolio on this day, a significant loss would have been sustained.

Bonds

Bonds are a form of securities (like stocks, discussed next); however, they do not provide an equity stake in a company, as do stocks. Bonds are sold in the marketplace by companies, credit institutions, and governments interested in raising capital for the cash requirements of their business's operations. Bonds are long-term debt instruments, defined as the issuer's promise to pay a specified amount with interest at a specified date. Bonds are considered less liquid given their long-term nature and can play an important role in an individual's investment portfolio.

Bonds are classified and described as follows:

- The specified amount of a bond is known as the par, face, or principal value (in the United States, bonds are issued in $1,000 increments, whereas the United Kingdom issues bonds in £100 units).

- Every bond will have a contracted interest rate associated with it and interest payments are most often due every 6 months. The amount of interest due is simply the stated interest rate multiplied by the par value of the bond. It is important to note the amount of interest paid on bonds remains constant, regardless of the bond's selling price.
- The issue price of a bond is the amount at which the investor purchases the bond, usually approximately the principal amount of the bond.
- The maturity date for a bond is the specified date on which the issuer is obligated to repay the principal amount. Most bonds have a term of up to 30 years, but there are short-term bonds with maturities of up to 1 year, medium-term bonds with maturities between 1 and 10 years, and long-term bonds with maturities greater than 10 years.
- Issuers of bonds can "call" the bond in advance of its maturity. In this case, interest is only paid through the call date.
- When the issuer provides assets as collateral for bonds, they are known as secured bonds. Alternatively, unsecured bonds are backed only by the credit risk of the issuing company.

Bonds are traded on the bond market with their value being based on investor perceptions of the company's ability to pay the debt and current interest rates. Given the contractual nature of bonds, they are generally considered less risky than stocks and therefore experience less fluctuation in market prices. Table 9.2 presents some common bond types and their characteristics.

Table 9.2 Common bond types	
Types of bonds	**Characteristics**
Fixed-rate bond	A fixed rate bond is a bond with a fixed interest rate. The rate is known as coupon rate and interest is payable at specified dates before bond maturity and may be taxed as income
Zero-coupon bond	Zero coupon bonds pay no regular interest but are issued at a significant discount. The bond holder receives the full principal amount on the redemption date. US savings bonds are an example of a zero coupon bond. The income from the bond is then taxed at redemption of the bond
Municipal bond	A municipal bond or muni is issued by a state, US territory, city, or local government. Interest income is often exempt from federal income taxes, and the state taxes in the issuing state
Asset-backed securities	Asset-backed securities are a type of bond for which interest and principal payments are backed by underlying assets such as mortgages. The safety of the bond is only as good as the underlying asset
Serial bond	The maturity dates of these bonds occur over time in equal installments. For example, a $50,000 10-year serial bond would have $5,000 maturing every year for 10 years

Table 9.3 Model portfolio allocations and returns from 1926 through 2009

Portfolio description	% Average annual return	% Best yearly return (year)	% Worst yearly return (year)	Years with loss
100% Bonds	5.5	32.6 (1982)	(8.1) (1969)	13
Balanced 50% bonds/stocks	8.2	32.3 (1933)	(22.5) (1931)	17
100% Stocks	9.9	54.2 (1933)	(43.1) (1931)	25

Adapted from: https://personal.vanguard.com/us/insights/saving-investing/model-portfolio-allocations (accessed June 18, 2010).

The contracted interest rate for bonds varies, depending upon various factors such as interest rates in the market place at the time of issuance, the credit worthiness of the issuing company, and the bond's maturity date. Over time, changing market conditions will make the interest rate of a particular bond either more or less attractive to investors. To trade in bonds, investors must compare the market rate, or current rate of interest available within the market place, to the contractual rates of bonds. When a bond's contracted interest rate is higher than the market, the bond will be sold at a premium, or a higher value than the par value. A bond is sold at a discount when the bond contracted interest rate is lower than the market rates for bonds. The amount of the premium or discount from the par value is an adjustment for the time value of money and reflects current interest rates in relation to the bond's contracted interest rate.

Because of the associated maturity dates, bonds are generally considered less liquid investments than cash or cash equivalents. Investing in bonds is generally expected to be a longer term investment. Table 9.3 shows a comparison of return rates from 1926 through 2009 by class (100% bonds, 50/50 bonds/stocks and 100% stocks).[5] From the table, it can be seen that when comparing total returns over time, 100 percent stocks provided the highest rate of return, while 100 percent bonds returned the least. Stocks also represent the class with the highest risk, as evidenced with stocks having the single worst yearly return, with bonds performing more consistently.

Stocks

Worldwide, corporations sell portions of ownership of their businesses in the form of corporate stock shares. In some cases, a stock certificate is provided, which represents the shareholder's ownership in a particular corporation and gives the owner the right to vote in corporate operations matters. However, with the advent of electronic trading, most investors no longer hold stock certificates. Instead, shareholders are assigned an electronic account, which represents their shares, including any fractional shares. Brokerage firms, which facilitate the purchase or sale of stock, such as Charles Schwab (www.schwab.com), TD Ameritrade (www.tdameritrade.com), Scottrade (www.scottrade.com), and others, have grown in popularity and made entry into investing in stocks simple and efficient. These firms typically charge very low fees (usually between $4 and $12) for the purchase or sale of a stock when compared with full service ($25 to $50 or more) brokerage firms.

A key feature of stocks is that their value is determined by the marketplace and may be significantly higher or lower than the actual book value of the company. Market value is ultimately determined by the various individuals or institutions who wish to buy or sell a particular stock. Bid and ask prices are offered, and actual trade values are determined when a trade between investors is executed. These various values fluctuate based on many aspects of the business, including the company's actual business earnings or sales growth. However, many other factors, including those outside the firm's control, impact the value of the stock, such as marketplace trends changing demand for a company's product or service, inflation, global economic trends, buyer and seller preferences, competition dynamics, and many others. The key point is that stock values constantly change, and not always in relation to a company's business results. Market fluctuations impart to stock ownership more, and sometimes significantly more, risk than liquid investments.

Case-in-point 9.5   Market versus book value

The term market value must not be confused with book value. Market value represents the current value of an individual share of stock and represents an actual price to be paid or received if it is traded. Book value is an accounting terms that refers to a business's historical cost of all assets, less all liabilities. Dividing the book value amount by the number of outstanding common shares yields the book value of a single share of stock. The two values usually bear no significant relationship to each other.

Market volatility provides investors with either a gain or loss when they sell their stock, depending upon the difference between a stock's original purchase price to an investor and the ultimate selling price received. Given stocks do not pay interest during the time they are held (owned), investors must seek investment returns, or gains, in appreciated market values of their stocks at the time of sale. Market volatility can also result in losses, and therein lays the riskiness of this class of investments. However, some stocks do pay dividends on a regular basis to shareholders. *Dividends* represent the portion of a corporation's earnings paid to shareholders (investors). Upper-level management has the ability to determine, or declare, dividend payments, although they are not legally required to do so. In general, stocks are primarily classified in two ways:

- Common – these stocks provide the shareholder certain voting rights, which are usually exercised at the annual corporate meeting.
- Preferred – these stocks do not carry voting rights; however, there is usually a guaranteed regular dividend payment in return. Since a stated dividend payment may be compared with current interest rates, often a preferred stock's value will fluctuate with interest rates. Preferred stock prices usually decline when interest rates rise, and vice versa.

However, depending upon the expected operations of a company, there are further sub-classifications of a company's stocks.

- Growth stocks – these offer the promise of significant returns and generate returns based on the anticipated increases in a stock's market value. Emerging companies in established market sectors, as well as companies developing new markets for their goods and services, often experience significant increases in market value based upon their expected growth over time. As a general rule, growth stocks keep all their earnings and re-invest in themselves and do not pay dividends.
- Income stocks – larger, more established companies often provide a history of solid earnings and pay dividends on a regular basis.
- Growth and income stocks – represent those companies that provide the investor with a combination of both increased stock values and income from dividends and are of interest to many investors as part of a balance portfolio.
- Value stocks – include companies that may be undervalued in the marketplace based upon current operating performance. Sometimes considered as riskier investments, value stocks may provide significant returns in the form of higher market values should conditions improve over time and continued improved corporate performance. Value stocks can also include companies whose stock values are reduced due to economic factors outside the control of the company and may not carry higher risk.

Case-in-point 9.6   Dot.com bubble

In the late 1990s, there was significant growth in the internet sector on a global basis. There was much excitement about potential profits from start-up companies establishing new e-services, as well as with more established companies also expanding into this growing arena. Known as the dot.com bubble, market values soared in reaction to anticipated corporate earnings and the resultant rising stock market values. Fueling this movement was the availability of venture capital, which stimulated innovation. Traditional market evaluations and prudent decision making were not adhered to and ultimately the dot.com bubble burst and market values tumbled. For a fortunate few, this provided huge returns. However, for many traditional investors, there were only losses.

Finally, stocks are also classified by the total market capitalization of the company, which is the number of outstanding company shares multiplied by the current market share price. Therefore, a company with a market share price of $100 and 20 million shares outstanding would have a market capitalization of $2 billion. Based on market capitalization, companies are generally divided into micro-, small-, mid-, or large-cap segments. Although there is no absolute standard for these segments, they are generally divided as such and help investors to determine the associated potential risk and return:

- Micro-cap – a capitalization of less than $250 million.
- Small-cap – capitalizations ranging from $250 million to $1 billion. Although they have a greater potential for organic growth than large-cap companies, they tend to be more risky because of the possibility of business failure and provide for no regular dividends. They may also be more highly leveraged, or have a greater proportion of debt than large-cap companies. These higher levels of debt are often associated with increased risk.
- Mid-cap – capitalizations ranging from $1 to $5 billion.
- Large-cap – capitalizations in excess of $5 billion. They tend to have less risk, given that they typically distribute dividends and have a strong history of earnings.

Investment strategies

Risk tolerance varies between investors, and is intimately connected with time. An individual's time horizon is important in developing portfolio goals. Greater risk may be assumed for those investors who have many years before retirement, because any investment losses may be recouped over future periods. However, when one's investment horizon is short, perhaps fewer than 10 years, risk tolerance is usually reduced since there is little time to recover potential losses from riskier investment. Although the optimal allocation of assets between, e.g., cash, stock, and bonds, is up to the individual investor, generally speaking, portfolios with a greater proportion of stock holdings are subjected to greater risk. More aggressive investors will welcome this risk in anticipation of increased rewards, while less aggressive investors tend to seek a higher bond and cash allocation. Even though there are many different investment strategies, three strategies have proven effective at reducing the overall risk of securities investing over time:

- *Dollar cost averaging* – attempts to minimize the effects of market fluctuations over time on the acquisition cost of assets.
- *Portfolio diversification* – spreads investment risk over various market sectors in the hope that declines in one sector would be offset by increases in another.
- *Portfolio balancing* – adjusts investment holdings to reflect the investor's degree of risk tolerance at various points in time.

First, dollar cost averaging, known as pound cost averaging in the United Kingdom, dictates a very systematic approach to investing with equal dollar amounts being invested at predetermined regular intervals. Therefore, investments are purchased without regard to day-to-day market value fluctuations. Although this can lead to stock purchases at higher than desired prices, it also leads to purchases lower than desired. Over time, the net effect of this strategy is expected to be a lower average share price.

Secondly, portfolio diversification is simply investing in a variety of options and classes (cash, stocks, or bonds, etc.) in order to spread the risk inherent in any one investment item, or "not putting all your eggs in one basket." It is important to recognize that portfolio diversification must also occur within investment classes as well as between them. Some investments are inherently diversified, such as *mutual funds*, which spread risk out across a wide array of securities. Further diversification can occur between mutual funds by choosing mutual funds within different market sectors as well as national and international funds.

To diversify a portfolio, one chooses investments whose market values or returns do not move together in response to a certain market event, such as an increase in interest rates, inflation, economic growth, or recession. For example, "big-box" retailers such as Wal-Mart tend to increase in value when the economy slows, whereas manufacturing companies may experience decreases in value under this same circumstance. Although a portfolio containing a mix of these investment types may not raise as much as certain individual investments during upswings in the market, the potential for significant losses when the market falls is also lessened.

Portfolio diversification through allocation of assets can be achieved by selecting an appropriate balance of liquid and non-liquid investments and multiple categories of investments within individual classes, such as a mix of stocks, bonds, or mutual funds. Although some mutual funds are dedicated to various business sectors, many mutual funds purchase shares across business sectors and offer immediate portfolio diversity. Diversification can also be obtained by dividing companies into their market sector, or core business activity, and investing in a variety of companies (small-cap, mid-cap, or large-cap).

Case-in-point 9.7 Effects of portfolio diversification

Consider an individual's investment portfolio, 70% of which is invested equally in the stock of two healthcare companies (e.g., GlaxoSmithKline and CVS), with the remaining 30% invested in corporate bonds (e.g., Apple). This portfolio could be diversified by changing the stocks owned to include companies in the financial, manufacturing, energy, or any sector other than healthcare. The concentration of stocks of healthcare companies implies a greater risk than may occur with a greater variety of stocks, especially given the volatility of national healthcare issues. The liquidity of this portfolio could also be increased by reducing the levels of stocks or bonds and establishing a cash element within this portfolio. With an increase in liquidity, there would also be a corresponding reduction in overall risk within the portfolio.

Portfolio balancing is a third strategy for protecting assets while addressing an investor's degree of risk tolerance. To determine your optimal portfolio allocation between the various asset classes, the traditional starting point is to subtract your age from 100 with the result being the percentage of your portfolio that you should keep in stocks. For example, if you're 30, you should keep 70% of your portfolio in stocks. If you're 70, you should keep 30% of your portfolio in stocks. However, many financial planners are now recommending the rule should be closer to 110 or 120 minus your age. Using this more aggressive rule to determine your optimal portfolio allocation will make retirement funds last longer, based on the higher returns that investing more in stocks can provide. Many investor websites, such as TD Ameritrade (www.tdameritrade.com), provide tools to assist you in developing your optimal asset allocation. For example, a 50 year old who would like to retire in 10 years and has an average risk tolerance, a portfolio allocation of 55% stocks, 45% bonds and cash might be suggested as shown in Figure 9.3. Since stocks tend to be a riskier investment, diversification of the stock portion of the portfolio is critical. A combination of various mutual funds is prudent and reduces risk much more than if individual stocks were included, especially given the 10-year investment horizon.

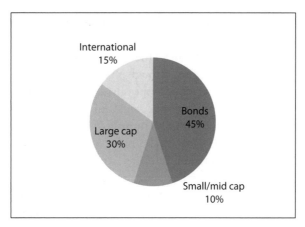

Figure 9.3   Portfolio allocation.

Case-in-point 9.8   Rebalancing a portfolio

When major sectors of the worldwide economy reduced stock values in 2007–2008, many investors found themselves with higher than desired cash-to-stock ratios in their portfolios. This was not due to changes in their investment strategy but rather changes in the values of the stocks owned. The principle of rebalancing would dictate that investors in this situation shift cash back into stocks to achieve their predetermined stock to cash ratio. The effect of this rebalancing would be to increase the percentage of stocks to cash. Rebalancing when stock values were low also meant stocks were purchased on sale. As stock values rebounded with the economic recovery, investors who rebalanced found themselves with greater gains owing to the purchase of stocks at lower prices. Rebalancing again after the recovery serves to mini-mize risk by reducing stocks, which would now be a greater portion of the portfolio, and shifting more money to cash.

Income and investing

For the typical investor, today's market place offers a vast array of investment vehicles with easy access. However, some options do require that minimum investment amounts be established. For example, it is not uncommon for a mutual fund to establish a minimum of $1,000–$2,500 in order to open a new account. If the account is opened as part of a retirement plan, these minimum levels are frequently reduced or eliminated entirely. Individual stocks may be of interest to the more aggressive investors, and online brokerage accounts have similar requirements but offer the opportunity to invest with relatively small balances.

When discussing personal finance, the issue most likely to limit investing activity is an individual's income. Although pharmacy professionals generally earn respectable salaries, investment options are somewhat limited by the amount of take-home pay, the amount remaining after all taxes and deductions. For a pharmacist earning $8,000 monthly, the net take-home pay after taxes, benefits and retirement would be reduced to approximately $5,000. Net monthly income and personal budget priorities significantly impact the amount available for investing. The effect of personal income taxes is a very complex issue and beyond the scope of this text. However, there are basic issues common to both the United States and United Kingdom, which do warrant discussion.

Taxation of an individual's income is critical to the operation of industrialized countries. Although individual systems vary, common elements do exist. Most countries begin the process with an individual's gross, or total, income from all sources and provide for various deductions or allowances (usually defined by law) in arriving at the final taxable income amount. The tax rates imposed often depends upon the income level, and different rates are usually applied to stratified layers of income. Regardless of the system employed, the impact of personal income taxes is significant. As a rule, when investing is concerned, taking advantage of investing opportunities that eliminate taxation on that portion of income (know as pre-tax) is of extreme benefit and is discussed later in this chapter. Table 9.4 illustrates the basic design of the United States federal income tax rates for individuals. Pre-tax investing not only serves to reduce total taxes paid, but can also dramatically

Table 9.4 US income tax rates for individuals in 2010

Tax rate (%)	Single ($)	Married filing jointly ($)
10	Up to 8,375	Up to 16,750
15	8,375–34,000	16,750–68,000
25	34,000–82,400	68,000–137,300
28	82,400–171,850	137,300–209,250
33	171,850–373,650	209,250–373,650
35	Over 373,650	Over 373,650

An individual (single) with a taxable income of $110,000 has a tax due as follows: The first $8,375 is taxed at 10% = $837.50; the next $25,625 ($34,000 − $8,375) is taxed at 15% = $3,843.75; the next $48,400 ($82,400 − $34,000) is taxed at 25% = $12,100.00; the next $ $27,600 ($110,000 − $82,400) is taxed at 28% = $7,728.00 for a total federal income tax of $24,509.25.

increase the return on individual investments when the tax savings are considered.

> ### Case-in-point 9.9   Student loans
>
> Many pharmacy professionals will have student loans upon graduation that they would like to pay off as soon as possible. This is an example of a personal budget priority that competes with savings and investment decisions. The concepts presented should help individuals decide how to make the decision regarding the competing goals of eliminating student loan payments and investing. Decisions will need to be made as to how aggressively to pay off the student loan versus increasing retirement savings.

Retirement

Most pharmacy professionals have the opportunity to participate in an employer's, or their own, private retirement plan. In certain cases, new employees are asked to make irrevocable choices regarding plan participation upon hire, which for some is the first time considering retirement options. Therefore, a good understanding of the types of retirement plans available and how these plans work is beneficial. Without a doubt, saving for retirement is one of the most important financial decisions an individual can make. Starting early and establishing a pattern of consistent contributions will yield great rewards in later years.

When saving for retirement, an investment made with pre-tax or deductible contributions is generally preferred because the investor receives the immediate return on their investment resulting from a net tax savings, which adds to the total rate of return. Further, because these investments grow tax-deferred, they allow more principal and interest to accumulate, while the tax savings provide additional income to a personal budget.

> ### Case-in-point 9.10   Start saving for retirement now
>
> Recalling the power of compounding discussion from Chapter 5, it can be seen that the sooner one starts saving for retirement, the greater the benefit. If you delay starting to make a monthly payment of $500 to a retirement account for 10 years, in order to catch up, you would need to invest nearly $1,200 monthly for the next 30 years. Clearly, when developing and implementing a financial plan, starting as soon as possible is very beneficial.

In the past, companies often provided retirement benefits for their employees through pension plans. These pension plans provided retirement income to reward employees for their years of service to the company. Retirement plan benefits varied, but essentially offered retirees a percentage of their working years' annual earnings, usually based on length of employment with the company. There are two major types of pension plans, defined benefit and defined contribution plans. Defined benefit plans calculated retirement income based upon a formula involving years of service and annual earnings. Defined contribution plans provided for the employer to make an annual contribution to an employee's account, which grew over time through additional contributions and investment returns. Upon retirement, the fund was usually used to purchase an individual annuity, which in turn provided annual income for the employee during retirement. As society has evolved over the years, employees became much more mobile, and lengthy employment with a single employer became rare. As a result, individual retirement accounts (IRAs) and 401(k) plans became the norm.

IRAs are a form of defined contribution plan, and contributions are provided by the employee and often, but not necessarily, the employer. The balance in the IRA is based on the annual contributions and investment earnings during an employee's service. The account is owned by the employee and may be transferred to another account if employers are changed. In the US, there are two types or IRAs: traditional and Roth.

Traditional IRAs generally allow for both pre-tax and after-tax contributions. Contributions and the accumulated earnings grow tax-free until they are withdrawn at retirement, when they are taxed as income, usually at a lower tax bracket. However, the more popular type of IRA is the Roth IRA. Differing from a traditional IRA, annual Roth contributions are not tax deductible. However, the Roth IRA is similar to a traditional IRA in that it also offers tax-free accumulation of contributions and earnings until withdrawal. Unique to the Roth IRA, and the reason for its popularity, is withdrawals are not subject to taxation. Therefore, if a retiree had $1 million dollars in a traditional IRA and wanted to take out $5,000 on a monthly basis, this would be reported as income and taxed accordingly. With a Roth IRA, however, the same $5,000 would not be taxed as income and go entirely to the retiree.

The second popular retirement choice, and most common employer-offered retirement plan, is the 401(k) plan. These plans allow employees to make pre-tax contributions to various investment options offered by the plan. These options could include company stock, mutual funds, stocks, bonds, or other investments such as a real estate investment trust (REIT). When deciding upon investment options for your contributions, remember to address diversification. A 401(k) heavily invested in company stock has little diversification in itself, and this effect is amplified when one considers that your salary is also dependent upon your employer. Employees need to be certain to diversify their investment portfolio to the extent possible, given retirement plan options.

The biggest benefit for 401(k) plans is that some employers offer a match for employees using this option to save for retirement. The contributions to 401(k) plans are made pre-tax, resulting in tax savings for the employee while building retirement wealth. Similar to a traditional IRA, the earnings on both employee and employer 401(k) contributions accumulate tax-free until withdrawal, when they are treated as taxable income.

Case-in-point 9.11   Taking advantage of the employer's match

Individually, an employee should always try to contribute the full portion of their earnings eligible for the employer match to maximize their 401(k) benefit. For example, an institution offers a 401(k) plan, which has an employer match of up to 3% of an employee's annual wages. Assuming annual wages of $100,000, the total maximum employer contribution would be $3,000. Let's assume that the employee contributes $6,000. The $3,000 match in contributions from the employer represents an immediate 50% rate of return on the employee contribution of $6,000, before investing in the plan. This represents a significant opportunity and should not be passed up. Few, if any, investment options can offer this kind of return.

There are other tax advantaged plans, such as 403(b) and 457, which may be offered by your employer (such as governmental or higher education entities). These plans operate in a similar manner to that of the 401(k), allowing for added contributions to retirement savings in addition to those previously discussed. Contributing to these additional plans must be determined on a case by case basis and consistent with an individual's retirement savings objectives.

Case-in-point 9.12   Retirement portfolio planning and actions

In 1985, JD accepted his first pharmacy position with a large chain pharmacy operation. After being hired, he elected to participate in the company's retirement program, which allowed him to contribute up to 5% of his salary with a 100% match by his employer. Based on the advice of a human resources advisor within the company, and based on his relatively young age and 30-year time frame before retirement, JD selected a portfolio of investments that was initially 80% equities and 20% bonds, cash, and other fixed investments. Over time, and by doing a bit of homework on the subject of investing, JD came to understand that portfolio allocation between stocks, bonds, and other investments, as well as diversification to various industries and even countries, to be the keys to investing success. With these objectives in mind, each year on his employment anniversary, JD rebalanced his portfolio to reflect his current risk tolerance and preferred investment sectors. By about 2007, his portfolio of retirement investments had shifted from the original 80/20 allocation to about 60% equities and 40% bonds and other investments. The total value of his retirement portfolio in 2007 was approximately $450,000. By now, at age 50, JD had a fairly conservative portfolio allocation. His allocation was somewhat conservative and risk averse, something JD felt reasonably comfortable with, given the general rule of thumb to determine your percent allocation to equities: 110 minus your age.

In 2007–2008, much to the dismay of investors' worldwide, the global equity markets began a decline that culminated in a nearly 50% decrease in value in many markets. JD's portfolio, which was allocated at about 60/40 (equities/bonds), lost almost one third of its value during this period. Although disappointed with the decrease in value, JD stayed focused on his objectives: allocation and diversification. His analysis of retirement holdings revealed that because equities had lost so much value in relation to bonds and other investments, his portfolio no longer reflected the balance he desired. In fact, the portfolio had shifted to approximately 40/60 (equities/bonds and other).

To remedy this situation, JD decided, as he had done annually up to this point in time, to again rebalance his portfolio. This meant shifting value from the bond and other investment side over to equities. To accomplish this, he shifted cash and bonds to equities, to once again be at approximately 60/40 (equities/bonds and other). This decision, as it had over the years, proved again that portfolio allocation is essential to investing success. After rebalancing, and as the global equity markets began to recover and once again gain value, JD saw his equity holdings grow more rapidly than if he had not rebalanced at the end of 2008 – because he owned more equities. In fact, because he rebalanced when the equity markets were at their low points, JD's portfolio grew back to its original $450,000 while the equity markets had only recovered about one half of their losses. His account value continued to grow as the equity markets continued to increase in value. JD also rebalanced again at the end of 2009 when the markets had increased in value by more than 50% and once again his holdings were outside his desired portfolio allocation. This time, he sold equities and moved more into bonds and other investments. This again proved to be a wise strategy as 2010 saw a retracement in equity values of about 10–15%. This strategy of selecting a desired portfolio allocation and rebalancing on at least an annual basis has dramatically increased the value of JD's retirement portfolio.

Insurance

Once a financial plan has been developed and implemented, most individuals begin to see the results of their efforts very quickly. Watching wealth grow due to good planning and discipline is very rewarding. However, personal assets can also be at risk through illness, liability, or theft. Thus, insurance is the final step in a sound financial plan.

Insurance offers the right to compensation for a possible future loss in exchange for a premium (periodic payment). Most employers provide health insurance as an employee benefit and share in the cost of this insurance with employees. Other forms of insurance that should be considered are life, professional liability, property, or long-term care insurance. For example, when considering purchasing life insurance, an assessment should be made as to the level of insurance needed, considering factors such as other assets, working spouses, numbers of dependants, and other personal needs. Although most employers offer some level of life insurance, they do not generally provide disability insurance. In the rare event that you are disabled or sick for an extended period of time and unable to work, disability insurance can provide for some portion (usually about 60%) of your wages. Disability insurance can be obtained for both short (less than 6 months) and long term (greater than 6 months) coverage. Purchase of a long-term disability policy would be a reasonable decision for an individual with a sizable emergency fund, but for those with little or no emergency fund, short-term disability insurance would provide additional security and almost be a necessity. All financial plans should include consideration of insurance to protect financial and personal assets.

Professional advice

If the words "do not attempt this at home" apply to some of the complex physical stunts seen on television, the words "seek the advice of a professional financial planner" should have just as much meaning associated with financial plans. Given the wide array of retirement, insurance, and other savings and investment options, individuals should seek the advice of a certified financial planner to assist with developing comprehensive financial plans. These professionals include financial planners, stock brokers, insurance agents, bankers and others who can offer sound advice matching your individual circumstances. To avoid bias in investment selection, seek financial planners who charge a flat hourly rate for consultations, rather than commissions for investment products sold, and have the Certified Financial Planner (CFP) credential. Additionally, some basic questions should be asked of all financial planners to ensure a high level of trust and avoid any confusion, for example[6]:

- What services do you offer?
- What experience, qualifications, and certifications do you have?

- What is your approach to financial planning?
- Will I be working with you or others at your firm?
- How much do you charge and how will I pay for your services?
- Could anyone besides me benefit from your recommendations?
- Have you ever been publicly disciplined for any unlawful or unethical actions in your professional career?
- Can I have it in writing?

Clarity on these issues will go a long way toward ensuring a positive, beneficial, and trusting relationship with a financial planner.

Summary

This chapter presents some important concepts related to personal finance including budgeting, setting financial goals, and the importance of your FICO credit score. When developing a strategy to achieve your personal financial goals and objectives, remember to consider both the short and long-term implications of your decisions, as well as their effect on your budget, credit, taxes, retirement, and, most importantly, quality of life.

Disclaimer

The information contained in this chapter is intended for educational purposes only and is believed to be accurate as of the publication date. It is not intended as professional advice to any individual. Specific advice from trained professionals should be sought before making any investment decisions.

References

1 Bach D. *Automatic Millionaire*. New York, NY: Random House, 2003. www.finishrich. com
2 Stanley TJ, Danko WD. *The Millionaire Next Door*. Atlanta, GA: Longstreet Press, 1996.
3 Fair Isaac Corporation (2010). *myFICO home page*. Minneapolis, MN: Fair Isaac Corp. www.myfico.com (accessed May 19, 2010).
4 TimeValue Software. *Credit Card Payoff Calculator*. Irvine, CA: TimeValue Software. www.timevalue.com/calculators/credit-card-calculator.aspx (accessed May 19, 2010).
5 Vanguard Personal Investors. *For Long-Term Investing, Don't Bank on Cash*. Malvern, PA: Vanguard Group Inc. https://personal.vanguard.com/us/VanguardViewsArticlePublic? ArticleJSP=/freshness/News_and_Views/news_ALL_longterm_12262007_ALL.jsp (accessed January 10, 2009).
6 Certified Financial Planners Board of Standards. *10 Questions to Ask When Choosing a Financial Planner* (brochure). Washington, DC: CFP Board of Standards, Inc. http://www. cfp.net/learn/resources.asp (accessed May 20, 2010).

Suggested reading

Bach D. *Automatic Millionaire*. New York, NY: Random House, 2003. www.finishrich.com
Stanley TJ, Danko WD. *The Millionaire Next Door*. Atlanta, GA: Longstreet Press, 1996.

Review questions

1   JB is a 54-year-old pharmacist who is currently planning on retiring early, at age 62, when his mortgage is fully paid off. Additionally, JB will also then be eligible for early Social Security benefits, although at a reduced benefit. He currently is at the end of the seventh year of a 15-year mortgage with a principal balance of $113,662.95 and a monthly principal payment of $1,445.74. JB currently makes adequate contributions to a Roth IRA, 401(a), and 403(b), although additional contributions to the latter plan could be made on a pre-tax basis. Recently, JB received a pay raise, which provided him with an additional $1,000.00 per month after taxes. JB is considering paying the extra $1,000.00 per month on his current mortgage, or investing it in his 403(b). Ignore all income tax affects. Discuss the effect of both strategies in terms of JB's financial picture.

2   However, the main benefit of a 403(b) retirement plan is the pre-tax contributions. Assuming a tax rate for any contributions made to the 403(b), show the effect of the two options identified above.

3   Assume the same scenarios as above, except the earnings rate on investments is 5.125%. Would your choice of options change?

4   Once set, financial goals are not subject to change. True or false?

5   Which of the following are reasons that individuals get into financial trouble?
A   Lack of an emergency fund
B   Excessive borrowing
C   Ignoring the warning signs associated with late payments
D   Delaying retirement savings

6   As your FICO score decreases, so does the interest rate you would be on a home mortgage loan. True or false?

7   Which of the following investment options offers the highest level of safety and liquidity?
A   Stocks
B   Bonds
C   Real estate
D   Money market funds

8   A company with a stock price of $50 per share and 1 million outstanding shares would be best classified as which of the following?
A   Large-cap
B   Mid-cap

C Small-cap
D Micro-cap

9 Bonds are generally considered less risky when compared with stocks. True or false?

10 Which of the following is not an investment strategy proven effective at reducing risk over time?
A Dollar cost averaging
B Portfolio diversification
C Automatic investment
D Portfolio balancing

Answers

1 If JB continues to pay his mortgage without any changes, the total interest paid for the remaining 96 months (8 years) is $25,128.09, and total interest and principal payments would total $138,791.04. If the additional $1,000.00 per month was added to JB's monthly payment, the time until payoff is shortened by 44 months (4.3 years) and the total interest paid for the remaining 52 months is $13,307.01; and the total interest and principal payments would total $126,969.96. Note the length of the mortgage decreases from 96 months to 52 months and total interest paid was reduced by $11,821.08. Once the mortgage is paid off completely, JB could continue to make $2,445.74 worth of contributions into his 403(b) account for the 44 months until he is eligible to retire. At a 3% interest rate, this monthly contribution would grow to $113,604.47. If JB contributes the $1,000.00 to his 403(b) account for the entire 96 months at 3%, his final balance would be $108,347.39. Therefore, JB should concentrate his efforts at paying off his mortgage early and then continuing to save the same amount for his retirement, and this option yields an additional $5,257.08.

2 JB can take advantage of the 40% tax rate and increase either of his contribution options by that amount. Therefore, the $2,445.75 equates to $3,424.05 ($2,445.75 × 1.4), which yields $159,046.91 at 3% for 44 months. The $1,000.00 monthly contribution, after tax, equates to $1,400.00, which yields to $151,686.34 at 3% after 96 months. Again, the higher total savings balance is generated when the mortgage is eliminated first, with residual amounts invested thereafter when interest rates in investments are less than the mortgage interest rate.

3   Ignoring income taxes, the option of early payment of the mortgage yields an investment balance of $118,111.45, while the option of 96 months of $1,000.00 investing yields $118,361.64. Notice the closeness of the ending balances, a direct effect of the interest rate being paid on the mortgage equaling the interest rate that is being earned on the additional investments. After taking the effect of income taxes into account, the early mortgage payment yields a final balance of $165,356.71, while the option of 96 months of $1,000.00 investing yields $165,706.30. Again, the ending investment balances are quite similar. In this case, the tax benefit on the lower payment of $1,400.00 for 96 months is overpowered by the effect of the much higher $3,424.05 amount for only 44 months. Therefore, when making investment decisions, the time value of money, interest rate earned, time invested, and amount invested on a regular basis all play significant roles in determining the final balances. Decision making will often require the investor to "crunch the numbers" to obtain a more objective decision rather than relying on their "gut" feeling. (See Table 9.5.)

Table 9.5 Effect of additional $1,000.00 monthly principal mortgage payments

Original balance	Number of monthly payments	Monthly payment amount ($)	Total interest paid ($)	Total amount repaid ($)
$113,662.95	96	1,445.74	25,128.09	138,791.04
$113,662.95	52	2,445.74	13,307.01	126,969.96

Option 1 – Additional principal mortgage payment plus 403(b) contributions

Description	Monthly investment ($)	Interest rate (%)	Number of months	Final balance ($)
(Ignore taxes)	2,445.74	3.0	44	113,604.47
(After taxes)	3,424.05	3.0	44	159,046.91
(Ignore taxes)	2,445.74	5.125	44	118,111.45
(After taxes)	3,424.05	5.125	44	165,356.71

Option 2 – Additional 403(b) contributions

Description	Monthly investment ($)	Interest rate (%)	Number of months	Final balance ($)
(Ignore taxes)	1,000.00	3.0	96	108,347.39
(After taxes)	1,400.00	3.0	96	151,686.34
(Ignore taxes)	1,000.00	5.125	96	118,361.64
(After taxes)	1,400.00	5.125	96	165,706.30

4 The statement is false.

5 All of the answers are correct.

6 The statement is false.

7 D is correct: Money market funds.

8 D is correct: Micro-cap.

9 The statement is true.

10 C is correct: Automatic investment.

Glossary

After-tax	Amount (usually income) after taxes has been subtracted.
Bond	Long-term debt instrument expressed at par, or face, value often issued in $1,000 increments at a fixed interest rate; the purpose is to raise capital by the issuer, with a guarantee to repay principal and interest.
Certificate of deposit (CD)	Evidence of a deposit, written by a bank or other financial institution, with the issuer's guarantee to repay the deposit, plus earnings, for a specified period of time at a specified interest rate.
Discount rate	Interest rate used in determining the present value for future cash flows.
Dividends	Corporate payments to shareholders representing a return of corporate earnings.
Dollar cost averaging	Systematic investing of regular amounts at time intervals without regard to the current purchase price in order to minimize the effects of market fluctuations over time.
Federal Insurance Contributions Act (FICA)	The US law requiring US employers to match the amount of Social Security tax deducted from an employee's paycheck.

Inflation rate	The rate of increase in the general price level of goods and services resulting in a decrease in the purchasing power of common currency.
Interest expense	The cost of borrowing funds in the current period. It is shown as a financial expense item within the income statement.
Interest rate	Rate charged for the use of money (as in a loan), and usually expressed as an annual percentage of the principal amount.
Itemized deductions	Various personal expenses defined by the IRS as being deductible in calculating taxable income. The most common included are medical expenses, mortgage interest, charitable contributions, and state income taxes.
Liquidity	Ability of an asset to be quickly converted to cash.
Marginal tax rate	The highest rate of income tax applied to an individual's earnings.
Maturity value	The amount to be received at the time a security is redeemed at its maturity. Often, maturity value equals par value (as in bonds).
Money market fund	A fund investing in short-term investments such as commercial paper, certificates of deposit, and Treasury Bills.
Mutual fund	A fund using the collective investments of many investors investing in stocks, bonds, and other investments designed to reduce overall risk. Individual investors in the fund own shares, which represent ownership of the entire fund. The fund is managed by a professional money manager.
Opportunity cost	The cost to a company or individual of the path not taken, calculated by measuring the projected return of the chosen option compared with the anticipated return of the highest yielding alternative investment.

Prepaid tuition plan	A college tuition savings account that allows parents/guardians the opportunity to pay the cost of their child's college tuition in today's dollars, even though their child might not attend college for several years. This type of plan allows parents/guardians to "lock-in" the cost of college tuition for their child by buying tuition units at an institution now, and therefore pay no additional tuition when their child attends that institution even if tuition rates have increased in the intervening years.
Present value	The value of a payment or stream of payments to be received in the future, discounted at specific interest or discount rate, in order to recognize the time value of money.
Pre-tax	Before taxes have been deducted.
Prime rate	The interest rate that banks charge to their most creditworthy customers. The prime rate affects other rates such as the federal funds rate, credit card, and home mortgage interest rates.
Rate of return	The gain (or loss) of an investment over a specific time period, including all interest income and capital gains, quoted as a percentage. The rate of return, adjusted for the effects of inflation, results in the real rate of return.
Risk tolerance	The amount of risk, or potential loss, an individual investor will allow in an investment.
Standard deduction	Amount determined by federal law that reduces the income of taxpayers who do not itemize allowable deductions on their tax returns.
Stock	Document indicating a shareholder's ownership in a corporation.
Tax deduction	An item or expense subtracted from adjusted gross income to decrease the amount of income subject to tax, thereby reducing tax reliability.

Trade Cost	Expenses associated with the purchase and sale of shares of stocks and other investments.
Withholding tax	Amounts withheld from an individual's wages on their behalf and remitted directly to the government to account for that individual's tax liability on their compensation.

Index